# Lighting by Design

# Lighting by Design

2nd edition

Christopher Cuttle

AMSTERDAM • BOSTON • HEIDELBERG • LONDON • NEW YORK • OXFORD • PARIS
SAN DIEGO • SAN FRANCISCO • SINGAPORE • SYDNEY • TOKYO

Butterworth-Heinemann is an imprint of Elsevier

Architectural Press is an imprint of Elsevier
Linacre House, Jordan Hill, Oxford OX2 8DP, UK
The Boulevard, Lanford Lane, Kidlington, Oxford OX5 1GB, UK
84 Theobald's Road, London WC1X 8RR, UK
Radarweg 29, PO Box 211, 1000 AE Amsterdam, The Netherlands
30 Corporate Drive, Suite 400, Burlington, MA 01803, USA
525 B Street, Suite 1900, San Diego, CA 92101-4495, USA

First edition 2003
Second edition 2008

**British Library Cataloguing in Publication Data**
Cuttle, Christopher
    Lighting by design. – 2nd ed.
    1. Lighting, Architectural and decorative  2.  Lighting, Architectural and decorative – Design I. Title
    729.2'8

**Library of Congress Cataloguing in Publication Data**
A catalogue record for this book is available from the Library of Congress

**Library of Congress Catalog Number:** 2008931250

ISBN: 978-0-7506-8768-3

For information on all Architectural Press publications
visit our web site at http://elsevierdirect.com

Typeset by Charon Tec Ltd., A Macmillan Company. (www.macmillansolutions.com)

Printed and bound in Slovenia

08 09 10 11 12   10 9 8 7 6 5 4 3 2 1

Working together to grow
libraries in developing countries

www.elsevier.com | www.bookaid.org | www.sabre.org

ELSEVIER     BOOK AID
             International     Sabre Foundation

# Contents

## Part Three: Realization                                                         169

# Preface to first edition

The need for this book arises from the fact that many architects and interior designers do not envision electric lighting as part of their design philosophies. Generally, architects recognize Le Corbusier's dictum that 'Architecture is the masterly, correct and magnificent play of masses brought together in light'. As they create space, architects position apertures with care, admitting daylight to reveal forms and their textures, and so define the space, and as Corbusier had observed, this involvement with light lies at the heart of architecture. But then a strange thing can happen. The design is handed over to a building services engineer, whose range of responsibilities includes ventilation, heating and air conditioning; sound systems; sprinklers; and electric lighting. For all of these services, the engineer's overriding concern is to achieve uniform distributions, and in the case of lighting, this typically means that a prescribed illuminance is provided uniformly over a horizontal work plane 700 mm above floor level. The result brings untold dismay to architects. By day, their building has light and shade, with forms and textures interacting with the flow of light induced by the thoughtfully located fenestration. By night, all of this recedes into the dull blandness of consistent, invariant illumination.

The first group that this book is intended for is architects and interior designers who seek to achieve their design objectives both by day and by night. However, that does not mean providing a daylit appearance around the clock. Electric lighting has its own aesthetic, and a prime aim of the book is to get designers to appreciate the different ways in which daylight and electric lighting interact with buildings. This consideration may bring the designer into contact with specialist lighting designers, which may include building services engineers who have developed a passion for lighting, and these people are the second group for whom the book is intended. Overall, the book is intended for designers seeking to bring in-depth understanding of electric lighting into the architectural design process.

## The Artist

One evening there came into his soul the desire to fashion an image of *The Pleasure that abideth for a Moment*. And he went forth into the world to look for bronze. For he could only think in bronze.

But all the bronze in the whole world had disappeared, nor anywhere in the whole world was there any bronze to be found, save only the bronze of the image of *The Sorrow that endureth for Ever*.

Now this image he had himself, and with his own hands, fashioned, and had set it on the tomb of the one thing he had loved in his life. On the tomb of the dead thing he had most loved had he set this image of his own fashioning, that it might serve as a sign of the love of man that dieth not, and a symbol of the sorrow of man that endureth for ever. And in the whole world there was no other bronze save the bronze of this image.

And he took the image he had fashioned, and set it in a great furnace, and he gave it to the fire.

And out of the bronze of the image of *The Sorrow that endureth for Ever* he fashioned an image of *The Pleasure that abideth for a Moment*.

Oscar Wilde (*Source:* Small, I. (ed.) *Oscar Wilde: Complete Short Fiction*, Penguin Classics, 1994).

# Preface to second edition

Since the first edition was published in 2003, I have had a good number of opportunities to teach its content. These have caused me again and again to think through ways of explaining the concepts that are the basis of this approach to lighting design. I have satisfied myself that I have a simpler and clearer way of introducing the 'sharpness' of lighting concept, and this has led me to rewrite (and shorten) Section 2.5.

For the example of an applied lighting calculation that I had given in Section 6.1, I followed the procedure of manual calculations using data from lighting manufacturers' catalogues. For this edition I have shown how a computer-based lighting program, in this case DIALux, can be applied for the calculations that I make use of. As well as making the calculations quick and easy (providing we keep our objectives clearly in mind), a great advantage of using this type of software is that it enables on-line searching for luminaires with suitable photometric performance. This is demonstrated in the revised Section 6.1.

There are other additions to the text, such as discussion of opponent colours theory and the colour mismatch vector method of illustrating colour rendering properties in Section 2.2, but the most obvious difference is that this edition is in full colour. I wanted to take the opportunity to make this discussion of lighting much more visual, and while there is no shortage of books that present pictures of 'good' lighting, I wanted instead to illustrate ways in which the appearance of architectural spaces may be affected by lighting. This has led me to add groups of my own colour photographs to introduce each chapter, and generally the aim has been to show comparisons of interior spaces influenced by changes of lighting. I did not take these photographs specifically for this purpose, but rather I use a camera to record my observations of lighting. I do this to develop my own observation-based experience of lighting, and I recommend this practice to anyone who shares this interest.

# Acknowledgments

The most wonderful thing about working in lighting is the people that you encounter. Scientists and artists; engineers and designers; architects and psychologists; optometrists and ergonomists; are all concerned about how people interact with light. It is a topic that is virtually without boundaries, and it has brought me into contact with an extraordinary variety of people from whom I have gathered so much that I know that I cannot properly acknowledge all of them. However, some people have changed the way I think, and these people I particularly want to acknowledge.

David Pritchard pulled me out of the commercial stream of a London luminaire manufacturer and into the technical department. They were a lively bunch and I learned a lot from them, and also I joined the Illuminating Engineering Society. At the London monthly meetings I was encountered speakers of the stature of J.M. Waldram, R.G. Hopkinson, and W.R. Stevens, and lighting became an interest rather than a job.

After five years in London I joined Derek Phillips, a young architect who had taken on the challenge of establishing Britain's first independent lighting consultancy practice. I met clients rather than customers. I learned how to visualize lighting, and what it was to feel responsible for one's own work.

My next move was to join the Daylight Advisory Service of Pilkington Glass at St. Helens, Lancashire. Under the leadership of J.A. (Joe) Lynes, the DAS was developing a quite remarkable reputation for its contributions to daylighting design, and I became increasingly involved in giving seminars on the DAS's design tools at schools of architecture. It was Professor James Bell who encouraged me to study for my Masters degree at the University of Manchester, and at about this time, Harry Hewitt invited me to join the IES Lighting Design Panel. This group of experts had the task of looking ahead to guide the society's work. The panel's meetings were always stimulating, and never more so than when Peter Jay took over the leadership. While I had the good fortune to engage with some outstanding intellects at this time, I have to make special mention of Joe. He literally drew my understanding of lighting into the third dimension, and although we worked together for only two years, I have benefited ever since from the friendship that we have maintained.

In 1976 I emigrated with my young family to join a brand new school of architecture in Wellington, New Zealand. It was a young faculty that developed a collegiate bond that drove all of us. The lack of a lighting community came as a shock, but fairly soon we had the IESNZ up and going, and soon after that New Zealand joined the International Commission on Illumination (CIE). Things seemed to be well on track when Mark Rea invited me to join the Lighting Research Center at Rensselaer Polytechnic Institute in Troy, New York, in order to set up the world's first Master of Science in Lighting degree program. I went to Rensselaer on a three-year contract and stayed for nine years. Once again I was with a newly established outfit where the adrenalin was flowing and my learning curve was as steep as ever. The students were challenging and the faculty was outstanding. Peter Boyce, Howard Brandston, Naomi Miller and Jan Moyer remain firm friends.

I returned to New Zealand and once again I was working with architecture students and getting them to visualize their design concepts in light. Some of the ideas that I make use of have appeared in published papers, and I am grateful to *Lighting Research and Technology* for having given me opportunities to offer my thoughts for peer scrutiny. Also, I want to thank *Lighting Design + Application*, who between 1995 and 1999 published 34 articles of mine in a monthly column titled "Cuttle on Calculations". Opportunities of this sort are enormously valuable for developing one's own ideas, and I need to make particular mention of the writings of Dr. J.A. Worthey, whose studies of light source size have provided the basis for the section on the 'sharpness' of lighting.

I retired from the School of Architecture at the University of Auckland, New Zealand in 2007, and I acknowledge the support that enabled me to write this book. Special thanks are due to the faculty photographer, Lynne Logan, who did all the studio photography for the illustrations. Other illustrations are either acknowledged with due gratitude in the captions, or they are my own.

Kit Cuttle
Auckland, 2008

# Introduction

This book is concerned with devising electric lighting installations for architectural spaces that will contribute towards achieving architectural design objectives. It is written for architects, interior designers and specialist lighting designers. It presumes a basic knowledge of lighting technology, although a brief summary is given in the Appendices for the benefit of those who might need an occasional reminder.

The book comprises three parts. Part One is titled Observation, and the thesis is that the aspects of lighting that concern a designer are those that can be seen to make a difference. The problem is that we all take lighting for granted, and we simply do not notice what lighting can do until we direct ourselves to look for it. If people enjoy the visual experience of a space or the objects it contains, the lighting must have been working well for them. That they remember the architecture or the beautiful art, and they don't remember the first thing about the lighting, is not the issue. To become a lighting designer it is necessary to understand the role of lighting in revealing that experience. This is done by objectively examining interactions of light and matter and developing an extensive range of observation-based experience of lighting.

Part Two is titled Visualization. A lighting design concept develops in the designer's mind, and its strength depends on the designer's ability to visualize three-dimensional space and to bring to that vision observation-based experience of lighting. This use of the term visualization should not be confused with computer-generated renderings. The process described involves mentally applying lighting design criteria to build up a visualization of the design situation in light, and developing the skill to communicate and discuss that concept with a client and other professional designers working on the project.

Part Three is titled Realization. Unlike stage and studio lighting designers, the architectural lighting designer realizes the design concept through the medium of a technical specification. This leap from the cerebral to the technical involves calculations and understanding the performance characteristics of lighting equipment, but the designer must never lose sight of the principle that what matters is what can be seen to make a difference. It is intended that a reader who follows all three parts will become good at seeing small differences of lighting.

# Part One: Observation

All discovery starts with observation. Whether we think of Aristotle leaping out of his bath and startling the Athenian townsfolk with his cries of 'Eureka!', or Newton wondering what caused the apple to fall on his head, or Einstein imagining himself to be sitting on a photon, or Sherlock Holmes' admonishions to Watson: it is all a matter of observation.

The process of visual perception operates throughout our waking hours, continually seeking to make sense of the flow of information being delivered to the brain through the sense of vision. It is obvious that lighting is necessary for vision to operate, and there is a substantial amount of knowledge on ways in which lighting may influence how well the visual process is able to operate. However, this book is more concerned with how lighting may influence our perceptions of our surroundings. There is far less reliable knowledge, and it takes careful observation to identify the aspects of appearance that we rely on to form our perceptions, and how they may be affected by lighting.

While this may seem to be a daunting task, it should be obvious that the essential components of lighting design are there for all to see. The first vital step towards becoming a lighting designer is to develop confidence in the evidence of your own eyes.

# Visible characteristics of objects

1

At first, it seems obvious that we provide lighting to enable people to see, so that all lighting can be assessed in terms of how well it enables people to see. Lighting that maximizes the luminance contrast of visual detail enables very small detail to be accurately detected, and this is the basis of many lighting recommendations and standards. However, observation of our surroundings shows a much larger range of ways in which objects can differ in appearance. Consider for a moment the judgements that we commonly make in deciding whether a surface is clean and dry; whether fresh fruit is good to eat; or whether a colleague looks tired. These judgements are based on observation of appearance, but what are the differences of appearance that are critical in making these judgements? Any of these everyday assessments of appearance can be influenced by subtle aspects of lighting, and so too can our more complex assessments of the appearance of architectural spaces.

A basis of theory enables designers to examine their own observations of the things that surround them. Differences of object appearance have their origin in the physical processes by which light is reflected, refracted, dispersed and scattered by matter. But human vision did not evolve to enable us to observe these processes: it evolved to enable us to recognize our surroundings. Understanding of the roles of these processes requires directed observation, and when we apply observation analytically, we find that the number of physical processes that is responsible for all of the differences that we can discriminate is quite limited. With this insight, we start to gain knowledge of how to control light to achieve a visible effect that we have in mind. It is, in fact, quite remarkable how the astounding range of human visual sensations is governed by so few processes.

Lighting is both the medium that makes things visible, and it is a visible medium. At one level, it reveals the identifying attributes that enable us to recognize the objects that surround us, and at another level it creates patterns of colour, and light and shade, which add other dimensions to the visual scene.

*Facing page:  Union Station, Washington DC.*
*The 1988 renovation of architect Daniel Burnham's Union Station (opened in 1907) included new lighting designed by William Lam Associates. The uplighting in the Main Concourse is by two-to-one combinations of metal halide and high pressure sodium lamps, the sodium lamps having been added to cause the gold leaf decoration to gleam. This is effective both by day and by night, despite the vastly different overall appearance of the terminal*

This chapter examines the role of lighting at the former level, that is to say, its role in making visible the aspects of appearance that enable us to perceive our surroundings. We start by considering what we need to know about the processes of vision and visual perception.

## 1.1 Visual constancy and modes of appearance

The underlying aim of lighting design is to control the luminous environment in order to influence the perceived environment. Figure 1.1 provides a simple model of visual perception, which shows that several stages are involved in making this connection.

**Figure 1.1:**   *A simple model of the human visual perception process. Lighting designers exercise operational control in the luminous environment, with the aim of influencing an observer's perceived environment. A complex series of processes occur between the designer's input and its effect*

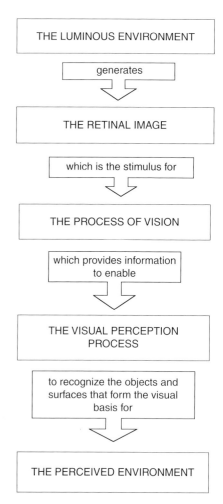

## The luminous environment
This is the physical environment made luminous by light. It is here that the lighting designer exercises control.

## The retinal image
The optical system of the human eye focuses an inverted image onto the retina, shown in Figure 1.2. This image is constantly changing with movements of the head and the scanning movements of the eyes. It is often said that the eye is like a camera, but the only similarity is that it forms a focused image in which, for every pixel, there is a corresponding element in the luminous environment. The main difference is that the eye operates as an instrument of search. Unlike photographic film, the structure of the retina is far from uniform. High-resolution detection occurs only at the fovea, a small area of tightly packed photoreceptors, and except at very low light levels, resolution declines progressively to the periphery of the retina. While the relatively slow movements of the human body occur, more rapid movements of the head enable attention to focus onto things that have been noticed, while still more rapid movements of the eyes within their sockets cause objects of interest to be scanned for detail. The eye is not a picture-making device: it is the optical instrument of search that is actively involved in the process of seeking information of the surrounding environment.

The distribution of luminance and colour that comprises the retinal image is modified by light losses that occur in the optical media of the eye, and these losses are not constant as they increase significantly with age. Here we encounter an interesting conundrum. Because the retinal image is the stimulus for vision, we have no way of examining it. So, we are forced to accept measures of the luminous environment as practical indicators

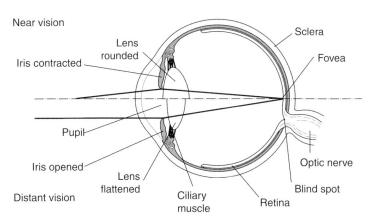

Figure 1.2: *Sectional diagram of the human eye showing lens curvatures for near and distant focus.* (Source: Coaton, J.R. and Marsden, A.M. (eds) Lamps and Lighting, Arnold, 1997)

of the stimulus for vision, which means that we are by default assuming a notion of 'normal vision'. This notion presumes that those who need optical correction to achieve a sharply focused image will have it, and while allowance may be made for reducing image brightness with age, this is often overlooked in practice. This latter point is discussed in Section 2.2.

## The process of vision

The purpose of the visual process is to provide an ever-changing flow of information to the visual cortex of the brain. The retinal image stimulates photoreceptors embedded in the retina, causing a series of minute electrical impulses to flow along the optic nerve pathways to the brain (Figure 1.3). It might seem more appropriate to compare the eye with a television camera than with the more familiar picture-making camera, but even here the comparison falls short. There are millions of photoreceptors in the retina, and processing of their responses occurs at several stages along the route to the brain.

The first level of processing occurs actually within the retina, enabling the optic nerve to transmit the visual information with far fewer nerve fibres than the number of photoreceptors. Further modification of the signals from the two retinas occur in the chiasma, where responses from both left-hand sides of the retinas are channelled to the left-hand lobe of the visual cortex, and the right-hand channel is similarly directed. Further processing occurs in the lateral geniculate bodies before the signals reach the cortex. While there is still plenty that is not understood about the working of these processes, much information on the performance of human vision has been gathered in recent years. The prime

Figure 1.3:  *Schematic diagram of the binocular nerve pathways (adapted from Boyce, P.R.* Human Factors in Lighting, *Applied Science Publishers, 1981)*

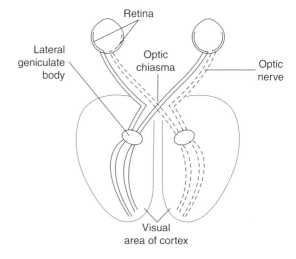

source of this information is studies involving measurements of the ability of an observer to detect small differences of luminance or colour, and this aspect of visual ability is discussed in Section 1.2. Its relevance to this discussion is that if an item of detail is to be part of the perceived environment, then its presence must be indicated by a visually detectable stimulus.

## The visual perception process

The perception of a surrounding environment may be influenced by input from any of the senses, together with memory cues. Although vision is usually the dominant source of sensory information, the perception may be significantly influenced by inputs from other senses, such as auditory, olfactory, and tactile senses, together with memories derived from these senses. This simple model should not be taken too literally, as just how a perception of an environment is assembled from the signals that flow through the optic nerve pathways is much less well understood than the process of vision.

## The perceived environment

This is the construct within the brain that serves as a model for the physical environment, and it has two distinct roles. It is within this mental construct that a person orientates and makes operational decisions, such as how to navigate through the space without colliding with furniture or other objects. Also, the mental construct represents the person's assessment of their environment. If one person finds a space pleasant and another does not, then we can assume that the perceived environments that each of them has formed are different. While some interpersonal differences are inevitable, it is evident that there are broad similarities which enable designers to satisfy both select and random groups of people. Luminous environments can be created that lead to a majority of sighted people generating perceived environments that both enable satisfactory levels of operational decision-making, and which also provide for positive evaluations of their surroundings.

Referring back to Figure 1.1, we can use this model to set lighting design into context. The designer's objective is to bring to life a perceived environment that exists as a mental image in the designer's brain. The image comprises more than a view. Depending on the designer's philosophy, it is likely to incorporate subjective concepts which relate to evaluative responses to the luminous environment, which is to be achieved by applying lighting to a physical environment. This is the essential function that the lighting designer controls. The link between the luminous environment and the perceived environment is the chain of functions indicated in the basic model of visual perception.

Added to this, it is inevitable that past experience will influence an individual's visual perception of their environment, and this gives one more reason why we need to recognize that the luminous environment and the perceived environment are not the same thing. That we have incomplete understanding of how the visual perception functions operate is not an overriding deficiency, as we can employ observation to explore ways in which variations in the luminous environment influence the perceived environment. This is a vital aspect of any design process. At the same time, we should seek theory that confirms observation as this enables us to organize knowledge. It is with this purpose in mind that observation is the central theme of Part One of this book.

## Aspects of appearance

Consider this hypothesis: architectural lighting should provide for reliable recognition of the surfaces and objects that form the environment. The basis of this premise is that every object that is represented within the perceived environment is associated with certain attributes, some of which are essential for recognition of the object, and some of which affect assessment of the object's qualities. A designer can be expected to look for more than lighting that simply makes everything visible. Much design effort may have been expended on selecting materials and specifying colours and textures, and it is important that these selected qualities are effectively revealed.

Examine the four views shown in Figure 1.4. In every case, the objects are instantly recognized, but being able to correctly name an apple, a peach, and a pineapple does not tell us much about these objects. Are they ripe? Are they wholesome? Would they be good to eat? What different impressions do we gain from the various views of the colour and texture of each of these objects? These are the judgements that determine our attitudes towards these familiar objects, but what are the aspects of appearance that influence our assessments?

We have expectations of what good fruit should look like, and we inevitably compare the different views of the objects with our expectations. The perceived objects are more than images: they

Figure 1.4: *(a) The objects are both visible and recognizable, but while the perceived attributes enable recognition they do not necessarily engender favourable assessments of the objects.*
*(b) The spatial distribution of the lighting is the same as for (a) but the spectral distribution is different, and gives more favourable assessment of the chromatic attributes of the objects.*
*(c) The spatial distribution of light contrasts the matt and glossy surfaces of the peach and the apple, and their smooth forms from the rough surface of the pineapple. However, the spectral distribution is as for (a) and does not favour the chromatic attributes.*
*(d) The peach and the apple look ripe, and the foliage of the pineapple appears fresh. Both the spatial and spectral distributions of light reveal differences of object attributes and support favourable assessments of them*

are entities in our minds that are 'coloured' by our expectations. If the fruit appears unattractive in one view, those perceived attributes of the object that do not meet expectations will stand out in the mind of the viewer. The perceived object is not a simple transposition of the retinal image: it carries the viewer's evaluation of the perceived object. A fruit vendor who seeks to meet the viewer's expectations will polish the apples, but not the peaches. However, the apples will not shine unless the lighting has the propensity to reveal that attribute. There is, of course, no such thing as 'shiny lighting', and lighting alone cannot make the peach appear shiny. However, lighting that can produce a pattern of light and shade on the smooth, velvet surface of the peach that differentiates it from both the jagged surface of the pineapple and shiny surface of the apple has properties that meet the expectations of the vendor and his customers. If the lighting also aids discrimination of colours that are associated with fruit that is healthy and ripe, it will gain the customer's approval. The evaluative aspects of perception are primarily concerned with discrimination, and this process is served by lighting that provides for discrimination of object attributes, that is to say, lighting that maximizes differences of object appearance.

Whenever the retinal image stimulates the perception of an object, that object is inevitably perceived to have certain attributes. The apple has the attribute of gloss, and the peach does not. If we doctored the surface of the peach with a clear varnish a viewer might perceive a nectarine, but not a glossy peach. Not all things can be perceived to have all attributes. If the image of the apple appeared to be flickering, this would be perceived to be an attribute of the lighting. We can not perceive an apple that is cyclically altering its surface lightness. If subsequent observation revealed that the flicker was somehow emanating from the object, we might decide that we are looking at a plastic model of an apple with a lamp inside, but we would now have a quite different understanding of the object. In our perceived environment, it would not be an apple.

## Visual constancy

Visual constancy may be described as the process by which perceived objects maintain more or less stable attributes despite changes in the retinal images by which they are recognized. An understanding of how we develop perceptions of our environments and the role that perceived attributes play in enabling us to come to terms with surroundings is crucial to understanding the roles that lighting can play in influencing people's perceptions of their environments.

For all of our lives we are surrounded by objects, and while indoors, our environments are bounded by surfaces. For the moment, we will treat all of these surfaces as objects. The volume of the space is filled with air, but unless it is dusty or misty, we have no visual awareness of the air. It is, however, necessary for us to recognize the objects that surround us. We need to understand why we are in this place, and what is our relationship to these objects. We need to be able to navigate through our environment, and for this we need to have a perception of a stable world, or at least one in which the movements of objects are understandable and reasonably predictable.

The perceptual process works so well that we do not consciously distinguish between the perceived environment and the physical environment, so that 'I saw it with my own eyes' seems to the speaker to be irrefutable proof of an event. Psychologists have developed a number of visual illusions to enable them to study the perceptual process. These are images that reliably confuse the perceptual process, and these confusions can give insight into the workings of the process.

A famous illusion is shown in Figure 1.5. The figure shows two vertical lines. Disregarding their chevron endings, do they seem to you to be the same length? If you need to, use a measure to confirm that they are in fact identical in length. So, why does the one on the left appear to be longer? Could it be that one pair of chevrons is stretching the line by applying tension, while the other is squashing it in compression? That cannot be right, as it is the reverse of the perceived difference. The accepted explanation is rather engaging. It is that the line on the left appears as a receding corner, as if looking into a corner of a room, and the line on the right appears as an advancing corner, as if the external corner of a building. As you perceive the line on the left to be more distant, and its retinal image is of the same size, you perceive it to be larger. Does this explanation seem convincing to you? Try Figure 1.6. Do the black bars seem to you to match in size? You can check that they are identical, but it is almost impossible to see them as equal without obscuring the surrounding lines.

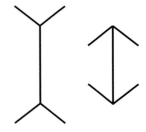

**Figure 1.5:** *The Müller–Lyer figure: the vertical lines are the same length*

Consider something rather closer to everyday life. You meet a couple of friends, and as you walk towards your friends to greet them, their images on your retina enlarge. Why would you not see your friends to be enlarging like a pair of inflating balloons? The answer is that in order for you to be able to navigate your way among people, furniture and other hazards, your brain is continually interpreting your changing retinal images, and updating the model of your environment and your location and movement within it. Your decreasing distance from your friends is an aspect of that perception which is inseparable from your recognition of your friends. Even though the setting in which you meet may be quite unfamiliar, you have developed the skill to orientate yourself within that environment and to navigate your way through it without difficulty. You may have encountered many people since you have developed that skill, and while some of them may have enlarged somewhat during your acquaintanceship, you know that it takes more than a few seconds to achieve this transformation.

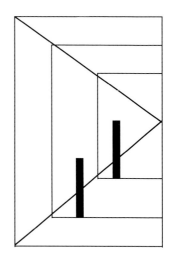

**Figure 1.6:** *Distance–size illusion: in this case, the black bars are the same length*

This discussion has been concerned with the phenomenon of size constancy, which, as we can see from Figures 1.5 and 1.6, is easily demonstrated. This is one aspect of *the visual constancies*, which may be described as perceptual phenomena which enable us to ascribe stable attributes to visually perceived objects. Another of the constancies is lightness constancy which is not as easily demonstrated on the pages of a book. According to Peter Jay (1973), the German physicist Hermann von Helmholtz (1821–94) posed the question, 'Why does a lump of coal in sunlight look black even if it has higher luminance than a sheet of white paper that is in the shade?' You can readily, and quite comfortably, confirm Helmholtz's observation. Lumps of coal are less commonplace household items than in Helmholtz's day, but on a sunny day, place a suitably black object (such clothing is fashionable at the time of writing) in the full sun and settle yourself close by in the shade while continuing to read this book. The sunlit object will not lose its blackness nor will this page loose its whiteness, even if the light level difference is such that a luminance meter would show that the reflected luminous flux density is greater from the coal (or black clothing) than from the paper. What is the explanation? It is easily demonstrated that simultaneous contrast can affect perceived lightness (Figure 1.7), but this is not to be confused with Helmholtz's question. He is asking why it is that recognized objects retain their different identifying visual characteristics even when the effect of lighting would seem to be to cause them to reverse.

Of course, our lives would become chaotic if objects changed from black to grey to white when carried from shade to full light. You could walk out of your house in the morning and find yourself unable to recognize it when you return in the evening. Visual constancy is an essential fact of life. Glancing back to Figure 1.1, the retinal image of the lump of coal may have higher luminance than the image of the paper, but the perceptual process did not

Figure 1.7:   *Simultaneous contrast: the grey squares are identical. This could be confirmed by superimposing a mask with five cut-outs coinciding with the grey squares, so they are all seen against the same background*

evolve to inform us of this photometric fact. It evolved to enable us to develop a mental construct that provides us with a reliable representation of our environment, and that means that objects are perceived to retain their intrinsic characteristics, even where large differences of illuminance occur. The appearance of the lump of coal will not be identical whether it is in sunlight or shade, but it remains unmistakably black.

How do we make sense of this situation? In particular, if your purpose for reading this book is to learn how to plan distributions of illumination, how are you able to cope with the notion that visual constancy operates so that the appearances of objects are more or less unaffected by lighting?

## Modes of appearance

As has been stated, any 'thing' that is recognized is perceived to have certain attributes. The 'modes of appearance' concept explains that the perceived attributes that may be associated with a particular 'thing' depend upon the 'mode' in which it is perceived. This concept provides a theoretical framework for analysing observations of illuminated objects, and it provides a useful concept for examining the roles that lighting can play in influencing the appearance of an illuminated space and the objects it contains.

The originator of the 'modes' concept was David Katz (1935), whose concern was the ways in which the appearances of colours are influenced by the ways in which the stimulus is experienced. He drew distinctions between surface colours and volume colours, and between colours that are perceived to be revealed by illumination and those perceived to be self-luminous. His explorations of the role of colour constancy and the influence of illumination, as well as the work of other contributors, have been reviewed elsewhere (Cuttle, 2004).

In Figure 1.8(a), red and green coloured cards are placed side-by-side on a table top, and a strip of transparent yellow film is laid across them. A colorimeter would indicate four distinct colours, but an observer would perceive three: red and green in surface mode, and yellow in film mode. These modes could be changed. In Figure 1.8(b), a card with four cut-outs is placed on top, and the observer perceives four colours in surface mode. While the names of these modes may seem to describe a physical viewing condition, it is important to recognize that the mode of appearance of an element is determined by how it is perceived by an observer. 'Modes of appearance' may be referred to as a

Figure 1.8:   *(a) A red and a green card are overlaid with a yellow film. The card colours are perceived in surface mode, and the yellow in film mode. A mask with apertures is overlaid in (b), and four colours are perceived in surface mode*

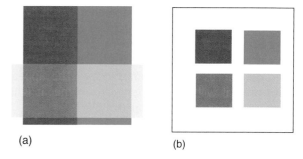

(a)                                           (b)

classification of assumptions that underlie perception. A change of mode may cause the perceived attributes of an object to change from those associated with its physical properties, and this may be described as a 'constancy breakdown'.

It is one of this book's underlying themes that it is a prime purpose of a lighting designer to identify chosen attributes of architectural spaces and the objects they house, and to reveal these attributes. It is, therefore, of high relevance that the 'modes' theory explains that certain attributes may be associated only with objects perceived in certain modes. Perhaps the most remarkable difference concerns the attributes of brightness and lightness. If I shine a spotlight onto a wall, I create a zone that is perceived to have the attribute of brightness. It might be possible for someone to create an identical luminance pattern by selectively spray painting the wall, but it is unlikely that anyone would be convinced that they were looking at a spotlighting effect. The appearance of a spotlight being directed onto a wall is instantly recognized, and the spotlit area is perceived in located illumination mode. It has the attribute of brightness, which may be graded on a bright–dim scale. Meanwhile, the appearance of the wall is essentially unchanged. It is perceived in object surface mode and retains its appearance of uniform lightness, which may be graded on a light–dark scale. This is an important distinction for understanding which are the perceived attributes that may be affected by lighting, and which are the attributes that are not likely to be affected.

The brightness of an element perceived in either located illumination or illuminant modes is largely determined by its luminance relative to the adaptation condition determined by the overall field, and this is discussed further in Section 2.1. The lightness of an element's perceived object surface mode is related to reflectance, and the relationship is fairly well established. The Munsell colour system incorporates a scale of value, which is a subjective scale of lightness. To establish such a

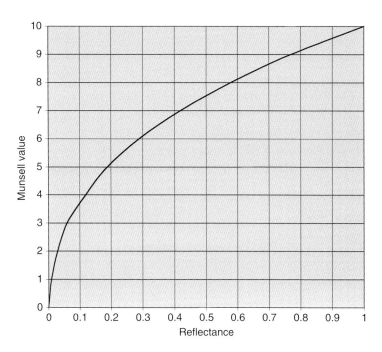

Figure 1.9:  *Munsell value and reflectance*

scale, a subject might be presented with a black and a white colour card, and be required to select from a large number of slightly different grey cards a card that appears to be mid-way between the black and white cards. Then the subject would find cards to fit into the two gaps, and so would proceed to produce a black–grey–white scale of equal perceived intervals. If the black card has a reflectance close to zero and the white card close to one, it might be expected that the mid-way card would have a reflectance around 0.5. This is not so. Munsell's value scale of zero to ten is shown related to reflectance in Figure 1.9, and it can be seen that value 5, which is the subjective mid-point, corresponds to a reflectance of approximately 0.2. In other words, what is perceived to be a mid-grey surface absorbs 80% of incident light. If a designer wants to make use of surfaces that reflect half of the incident light, they will need to have a Munsell value of 7.5 and will be distinctly light in appearance. The point of this discussion is that lightness is a subjective assessment of surface appearance, and while it is related to surface reflectance, it is not a linear relationship. Brightness is also a subjective assessment, but it relates to the emission light from the object rather than to an intrinsic property of an object's surface.

Various authors have proposed their own sets of 'modes' to suit their own purpose, and most have chosen to drop Katz's film mode. This is not because it is wrong, but because it is unlikely

Table 1.1 *Six modes of appearance*

|  | Mode | Examples | | |
|---|---|---|---|---|
| Non-located | Illuminant mode | Sky, ambient fog (Note 1). An illuminated surface viewed through an aperture (Note 2). Integrating sphere. | | |
|  | Illumination mode | Ambient illumination, such as the general lighting within a room. | | |
| Located | Illuminant mode | A lamp or luminaire; a self-luminous object. | | |
|  | Illumination mode | A patch or a pattern of light focused onto a surface or object (Note 3). | | |
|  | Object modes | Surface | An opaque surface; an object seen by reflected light (Note 4). | |
|  |  | Volume | A cloud. A plume of smoke. A transparent or translucent medium. | |

*Note 1*
While we know intellectually that fog is not self-luminous, ambient or pervading fog is likely to be perceived as a luminous body rather than as an illuminated medium.

*Note 2*
Aperture is considered not to be a mode of appearance: it is a viewing condition that causes a patch of a surface to be perceived in a non-located mode although the aperture itself may be perceived in located object mode. Again, an object does not have to be self-luminous to be perceived in an illuminant mode.

*Note 3*
The located illumination mode differs from the non-located illumination mode in that the illumination is perceived to have size, and perhaps outline or pattern. It is not perceived to have three-dimensional form as it takes on the form of whatever it is focused onto.

*Note 4*
It is important to distinguish between the perception of the surface and the perception of the incident light. Consider a surface illuminated by a flickering source: the flicker will be perceived as an attribute of the illumination, not the surface.

to be relevant in design applications. In the 'modes' model used for this text there are six modes of perception, if we consider the two object modes separately, and each has its own set of perceived attributes (Cuttle, 1999). Any 'thing' that is recognized will be perceived in one of these modes, and the mode of perception determines which perceived attributes may be associated with the 'thing'. The modes are listed in Table 1.1, with examples of phenomena that are likely to be perceived in each of the modes. Generally, the examples assume that visual constancy applies.

This table should be read in conjunction with Table 1.2, which shows the modes and associated perceived attributes. A blank indicates that the attribute is not associated with the designated mode of perception, and a cross indicates that there may be an association. This model makes a major distinction between located (perceived to have dimension) and non-located modes. Objects perceived in surface or volume modes are always

Table 1.2 *Matrix of modes of appearance and perceived attributes*

| Perceived attributes | Modes of appearance | | | | | |
| --- | --- | --- | --- | --- | --- | --- |
| | Non-located | | Located | | | |
| | *Illuminant* | *Illumination* | *Illuminant* | *Illumination* | *Surface* | *Volume* |
| Brightness | X | X | X | X | | |
| Lightness | | | | | X | X |
| Hue | X | X | X | X | X | X |
| Saturation | X | X | X | X | X | X |
| Flicker | X | X | X | X | | |
| Pattern | | | X | X | X | X |
| Texture | | | | | X | |
| Gloss | | | | | X | |
| Clearness | | | | | | X |

located, whereas illuminant and illumination modes may be located or non-located. If, upon entering a room, you have an impression of a brightly lit space, this is a non-located illumination mode perception. Alternatively, if you notice that an artwork hanging on the wall is brightly lit, that is a located illumination mode perception. The attributes of brightness and lightness have special roles. Anything that enters conscious perception has either the attribute of brightness or lightness, so that one or the other of these attributes is always associated with the perception. These two attributes are mutually exclusive.

Where visual constancy holds, the objects and surrounding surfaces that comprise a situation to be illuminated are usually perceived in either the surface or volume object modes, although both modes may apply simultaneously. The body colour of a glass vase may be perceived in volume mode while its form is perceived in surface mode. For all visible objects, incident illumination interacts with the physical properties of their materials, providing the visual stimuli for perceptions of their distinctive attributes.

It has been stated that anything that is perceived through the process of vision has either the attribute of brightness or lightness, but not both. It requires careful observation to confirm that this is so. Consider Figure 1.10: what does it show? Of course it shows a suspended matt white sphere. You perceived the sphere instantly, and furthermore you perceived it to be uniformly white. However, this photograph of the sphere is not uniformly white. Instead it shows a shading pattern from light grey to darker grey. Take a sheet of paper and punch a small hole in it. Slide the paper across the photograph, and you will

**Figure 1.10:**   *A simple object in a complex light field*

see how the aperture changes from near white to dark grey. Why did you perceive it to be uniformly white? The answer is that even in this two-dimensional representation, visual constancy is at work. The object depicted in this photograph is simply a Christmas tree decoration that had been sprayed with matt white paint, but just conceivably, the ball could have been cunningly sprayed in shades of grey and photographed in totally diffused illumination to produce an identical image. What you have perceived is the more probable explanation.

In terms of modes of appearance, you perceived the sphere in located, object, surface mode. We will not concern ourselves with how it is that a two-dimensional image causes a three-dimensional object to be perceived. You perceived this object to have the attribute of lightness, and you perceived the lightness to be uniform. If you had the actual object in your hand, you could demonstrate that it retains its appearance of whiteness over a wide range of viewing conditions. It would be possible to confuse a viewer as to the surface lightness, but it takes a contrived viewing condition to do it. If an aperture viewing condition is created, so that the viewer is shown only part of the surface through a hole in another material, such as the sheet of paper that you prepared for viewing Figure 1.10, the viewer is unlikely to be able to make any assessment of surface lightness. In fact, if the surface forming the aperture has a much higher luminance, the visible surface could appear to be black. The point is that such a restricted viewing condition has changed the mode of appearance. It is now perceived in non-located illuminant mode, and it has the attribute of brightness, not lightness. Now that your attention has been drawn to the object-mode perception, what of the shading pattern that is visible in Figure 1.10? This is perceived in the located illumination mode. It has the attribute of brightness, and may have other attributes such as the chromatic attributes of hue and saturation. It is very worthwhile to make yourself one of these devices. Observe it carefully in a variety of lighting conditions and confirm these findings. There is more reference to viewing simple devices of this sort in following chapters.

The concepts of visual constancy and modes of appearance are enormously instructive for lighting designers. Once we have viewing conditions sufficient to enable objects to be recognized, these objects will be perceived to retain their identifying attributes over a large range of lighting conditions. There is limited scope to modify the perceptions of object characteristics while visual constancy applies. For example, the perceived hue and saturation of an object may be influenced by the colour rendering properties of the lamps. If a nominally white light source is used, this will have a quite subtle effect on the appearance of the object, which may nonetheless be appreciated. However, if a distinctly coloured effect is produced, it is likely to be perceived as an attribute of the illumination rather than of the object or surface. It is an important observation to distinguish between aspects of appearance that are perceived in an object mode, that is to say, which are perceived to be attributes of a recognized object, and aspects that are perceived in illumination mode, which means that they are recognized as attributes of the lighting.

The outcome of these observations is quite profound. To think of lighting solely as the medium by which objects and surfaces are made visible is to ignore creative opportunities for influencing users' perceptions. Think of lighting also as a visible medium that may be perceived in illuminant or illumination modes, and which may be located or non-located. It has the attribute of brightness, not lightness, and while the range of attributes is more restricted than for the surface and volume modes, the perception of these attributes is not directed towards recognition of stable, physical characteristics. Herein lies a wealth of opportunities for lighting designers. In the words of Marshall McLuhan, 'The medium is the message.'

## 1.2 Visible properties of materials

When an unfamiliar object is introduced to an infant, it is explored with all the senses. It is handled, and it is held close to the face where young eyes can accommodate the image in fine detail. It is sniffed, shaken and sucked. All of the resulting sensory inputs contribute to the perception of the object. As the infant matures, each new encounter can be referred back to a mental library of sensory experience, and as this develops, so the sense of vision becomes the dominant source of the perceived environment.

For every visible element in the perceived environment, there is a corresponding element in the luminous environment that is either self-luminous, or it is the result of an interaction between light and matter. It is the light and matter interactions that provide the bulk of the information that enables us to recognize the vast array of materials that comprise our environments. To understand the interactions that we initiate when we illuminate an object, we need to take a look at the nature of light.

## The spectrum of light

It can be physically demonstrated that light is a stream of photons, where a photon is an elementary energy particle. In vacuum, all photons travel at the same velocity, this being the great universal constant, the speed of light. It is equal to approximately 300,000 kilometres per second, or in scientific notation, $3 \times 10^8$ m/s. Photons differ only in their energy levels, where the photon energy level $e$ (Joules) is given by the expression:

$$e = h\nu \text{ Joules}$$

where $h$ = Planck's constant and $\nu$ = frequency (Hz).

Life would be more simple if every observed property of light could be explained by this simple model, but such is not the case. It is, in fact, slightly embarrassing to have to admit that this book, entirely devoted to lighting, will not attempt to provide a comprehensive explanation of the physical nature of light, although some suggestions for further reading are offered in the Bibliography. It is sufficient to say that some of the commonly encountered properties of light are more conveniently explained by treating light as waves of radiant energy rather than as a flow of particles, and it is for this reason that the visible spectrum is usually defined in terms of the wavelength of light. As has been shown, photon energy and frequency are directly proportional. Frequency and wavelength are inversely proportional, and are related by the expression:

$$\nu = c/\lambda$$

where $c$ is the velocity of light (m/s), and $\lambda$ is wavelength (m).

In this way, the visible spectrum is conventionally defined as extending from 380 to 770 nanometres (nm), where $1\,\text{nm} = 10^{-9}\,\text{m}$ or one billionth of a metre, although it would be equally

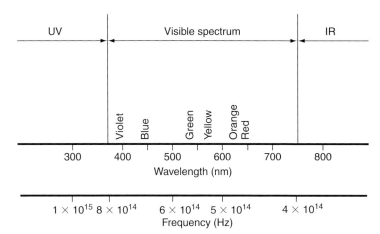

**Figure 1.11:** *The range of the visible spectrum is 380–770 nanometres, or approximately $4 \times 10^{14}$ to $8 \times 10^{14}$ hertz. It is therefore an octave of wavelength or frequency*

valid to define the spectrum in terms of photon energy levels or frequency, as is shown in Figure 1.11.

## Light meets matter: the gaseous state

Light travels in vacuum without loss of energy, and (as far as we need be concerned) it obeys the law of rectilinear propagation, which means that it travels in straight lines. Things change when light encounters matter. The first state of matter that we will consider is the gaseous state, in which the atoms or molecules are free to move, subject only to very small intermolecular forces. Some scattering of photons occurs as they travel through such a medium. Where the gas molecules are small in relation to the wavelength of light, *diffraction scattering* occurs as photons interact with these particles. Each particle acts as a centre of radiation and scatters light in all directions. The degree of diffraction scattering is proportional to the fourth power of the frequency of the light ($\nu^4$), so that the shorter visible wavelengths are scattered much more strongly than the longer wavelengths. Outside the earth's atmosphere sunlight has a colour temperature of 5,800 K, but down at ground level, sunlight has a yellowish appearance and a colour temperature of around 3,000 K. The difference is due to the scattering of shorter wavelengths which occurs in the upper atmosphere, the effect of which is evident as the blue sky.

Larger particles are encountered in the lower atmosphere, such as water droplets, dust particles, and atmospheric pollutants. These may cause *reflection scattering*, where the particles act as tiny mirrors, and having random orientations, they produce randomly distributed reflections. Reflection scattering occurs also in liquid-state and solid-state matter, and is dealt with more thoroughly later in this section.

Alternatively, the effect of interactions with larger particles may be *absorption*, where the particles convert the photon energy into some other form of energy. Usually this is heat, but other forms may occur as in photochemical reactions. The loss in intensity of a parallel beam of light in a homogeneous medium (not necessarily gaseous) follows an exponential decay function:

$$I = I_0 \exp(-\alpha\chi)$$

where $I_0$ is the initial beam intensity, $I$ is the intensity after travelling a distance $\chi$ in the medium, and $\alpha$ is the linear absorption coefficient, which usually varies with wavelength.

For the moment, we may note that while scattering and absorption in the atmosphere have much to do with both natural and artificial outdoor lighting, it is generally disregarded from considerations of indoor lighting. Over the short distances involved, and with the expectation of a clean atmosphere, it is usually practical to assume that photons travel indoors as they do in vacuum, that is to say, without visible effect. Where some visible effect does occur, as when artificial smoke is added to the atmosphere, this is generally the result of reflection scattering and absorption.

## *Liquid-state matter*

The next state of matter to consider is the liquid state, in which the freedom of molecules to move with respect to each other is more restricted by cohesive forces. Liquids have fixed volumes: they assume the shape of the vessel containing them; and in the absence of other forces, the surface to the atmosphere forms a planar boundary. With the exception of metals in the liquid state, liquids are generally transparent, but differ from the previously considered gaseous-state media by having much higher densities. There are some materials that do not have definite fusion temperatures as they cool from the liquid state, and they become more viscous until they assume the rigid cohesion of a solid-state material without losing the molecular structure of a liquid. Glass and the transparent plastics are examples, and these materials may be described as either amorphous solids or supercooled liquids. Optically they behave as liquids, although we describe them as transparent solids. Both diffraction and reflection scattering occur, and there is a marked reduction in

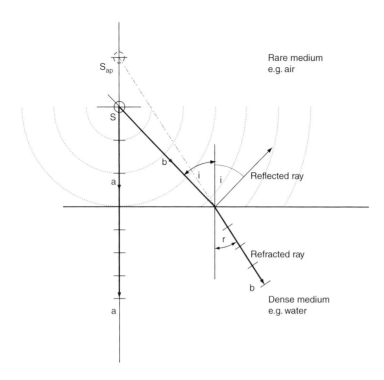

**Figure 1.12:** *Two rays from S passing from a rare to dense medium. The rate of propagation is lower in the dense medium, causing the wave fronts to close up, and for the oblique ray to change direction*

the velocity of light. To examine the effect of velocity change, we employ the light wave model.

Figure 1.12 shows wavefronts of light radiating outwards from source S, and the direction of any ray from S is normal to the wavefront. Two rays are shown, a and b, and as they pass through the rare-to-dense medium boundary, the reduced velocity of light in the dense medium causes closer spacing of the wavefronts. Ray a is incident normal to boundary, and passes through without deviation, but b is refracted towards the normal. The direction of the ray is still normal to the wavefronts, but now the origin of the waves is the apparent source $S_{ap}$.

The angles of incidence and refraction are related by Snell's law. The velocity of light in air is not significantly different from its velocity in vacuum, and in practice, it is so common for the rare medium to be air that the difference in velocity may be considered due only to the effect of the dense medium. This enables the refracting power of a transparent medium to be expressed by its refractive index $\mu$, and for Snell's law to be expressed as:

$$\sin i = \mu \sin r$$

This expression assumes that the angle $i$ is measured relative to the normal in air, and the angle $r$ occurs in the dense medium.

Table 1.3 *Refractive index values and critical angles for some transparent materials*

| Material | Refractive index $\mu$ | Critical angle (degrees) |
|---|---|---|
| Water | 1.33 | 49 |
| Acrylic | 1.49 | 42 |
| Soda (common) glass | 1.52 | 41 |
| Polystyrene | 1.59 | 39 |
| Flint glass | 1.62 | 38 |

Values of $\mu$ for several dense transparent media are given in Table 1.3.

Refraction at a medium boundary is accompanied by reflection (Figure 1.12), and where the boundary is optically smooth, this is *regular reflection* which is governed by two laws:

- the angle of incidence equals the angle of reflection

- the incident ray, the normal and the reflected ray all lie in the same plane.

The proportion of the incident light that undergoes regular reflection is defined by Fresnel's equations, and depends upon the angle of incidence and, for a ray incident in air, the refractive index of the dense medium. Figure 1.13 shows the directional dependence of reflectance for a typical glass surface, so that as the angle of incidence increases, the proportion of reflected light increases only gradually at first, and then sharply. Regular reflection is sometimes called specular reflection, and where both regular and diffuse reflection occur, the portion of reflected light that is due to regular reflection may be called the specular component.

In Figure 1.14(a), a ray encounters a boundary to a dense medium and is refracted towards from the normal. It is a principle of optics that every ray is reversible, so if the arrows were to be reversed, the figure would show a ray incident in the dense medium and being refracted away from the normal. Case (b) shows a ray incident in the dense medium at an increased angle $r$, and in this case the refracted ray is coincident with the boundary. This is the critical angle for the dense medium, which is equal to $\sin^{-1}(1/\mu)$. Some values of critical angle are given in Table 1.3. What happens if we further increase the angle $r$? This is shown in case (c), where total internal reflection occurs. This is regular reflection, and is 'total' because it occurs without loss of energy. This is the principle of the fibre optic, so that a ray that enters the end of the fibre not too far out of parallel with the axis of the fibre may undergo repeated reflections from the internal surface.

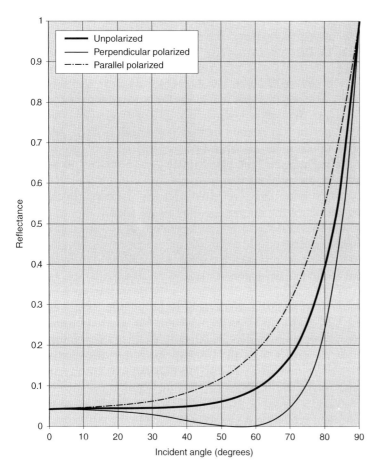

**Figure 1.13:** *Fresnel reflection at an air/glass boundary*

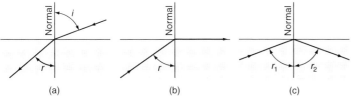

**Figure 1.14:** *Refraction and total internal reflection at a dense/rare boundary (Source: Bean, A.R. and Simons, R.H. Lighting Engineering: Applied Calculations, Architectural Press, 2001)*

## Solid-state matter

The third state of matter is the solid state, in which atoms and molecules are not free to move, but vibrate about fixed positions. The model for inorganic materials has these particles geometrically arranged in a crystalline lattice. Such solid materials are opaque, but as has been explained, some materials that are described as amorphous possess the transparency property of liquids while having other physical characteristics of solids.

Except in rather unusual situations, the great majority of the objects and surfaces that form architectural interior spaces comprise opaque solid materials. Whereas these materials appear to us to have distinct boundaries, if we could reduce our scale of dimensions to that of an arriving photon, the molecular structures would present a view of an open lattice comprising an ordered array of molecules with an abundance of clear space between them. Arriving photons would be likely to penetrate some distance into the lattice before interacting with particles. These particles are large in relation to the wavelength of light, and while some photons will be absorbed, others will undergo reflection scattering whereby the particles act as tiny mirrors. In this way, some of the photons that have entered the surface layer of the crystalline lattice are re-emitted by back-scattering. Because the alignments of the mirrors are effectively random, the re-emitted light is totally diffused and independent of the direction of the incident photons and for this reason the process is known as *isotropic re-emission*. Such a surface is a *uniform diffuse reflector,* and is said to obey Lambert's law.

Figure 1.15 shows a small element of uniform diffuse reflector. The reflected light from this element has a cosine distribution, that is to say, the luminous intensity varies as the cosine of the angle measured from the normal. Also, the projected area of the surface from any viewing direction varies as the cosine of the same angle, so that element has the same luminance from all directions. A uniform diffuse reflector that reflects all of the incident light would be a *perfect diffuse reflector.* Although no real materials achieve this, some come close to it. Reference white surfaces used in photometry laboratories may reflect 99% of incident light at all visible wavelengths, and fresh white paint may be

**Figure 1.15:** *The perfect diffuse reflector*

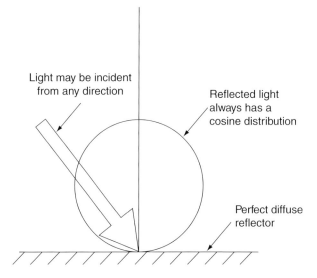

Light may be incident from any direction

Reflected light always has a cosine distribution

Perfect diffuse reflector

as high as 95%. It is often assumed that a surface must be shiny to have high reflectance, but that is not so. Matt white paint reflects a higher proportion of incident light than does a silvered glass mirror or a polished metal surface, but of course the distribution of reflected light is quite different. More importantly, the diffuse reflector does not form a reflected image. If the reflected images formed by shiny surfaces include images of bright light sources, this can cause those surfaces to appear much brighter than adjacent diffuse reflectors and give rise to the misconception that they are reflecting more of the incident light.

Photons incident on diffuse reflectors are either back-scattered (diffusely reflected) or absorbed. The reflectance of the surface is the ratio reflected to incident light, and this may be strongly wavelength-selective. Low-lightness surfaces absorb high proportions of the incident photons, and coloured surfaces may be described as wavelength-selective absorbers. This concept will be discussed further in the following section, but we should not lose sight of the fact that although we may describe some saturated surface colours as 'bright', particularly when referring to primary hues such as red or green, this 'brightness' is not achieved by red or green light being added to the sum of reflected light. It is due to the surface layer of the material strongly absorbing the complementary hues from the incident light spectrum. Our sensations of brightness are not simply determined by the amount of light arriving at the eye.

The crystalline lattice structure applies generally to inorganic materials, but organic solid materials may take up different forms of structure with more scope for randomness. For example, white paper viewed through a microscope is seen to consist of a mass of fine fibres, which individually may be almost transparent. Although the molecular structure is quite different from the crystalline lattice, reflection occurs by isotropic re-emission and the matt surface of high-grade unglazed white paper is another close approximation of the perfect diffuse reflector.

The effect of applying glaze to paper, or polish to flooring or furniture, is to add regular reflection to isotropic re-emission. The glaze and the polish are amorphous substances overlaying the structure of the solid material, and incident photons undergo a rare-to-dense medium transition, with some reflection loss, before undergoing the back-scattering and absorption that characterize the attributes of the perceived object. There are many examples of this combination of reflection characteristics. Paint comprises particles of pigments, which are wavelength-selective light absorbers, suspended in a clear vehicle, which traditionally

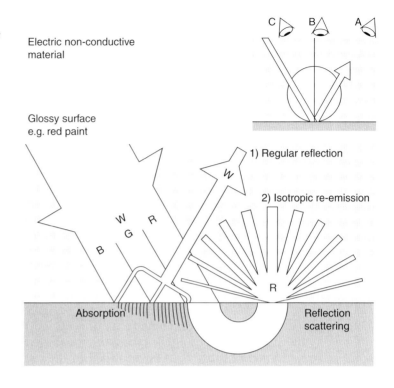

**Figure 1.16:** *Reflection from a shiny dielectric surface, in this case gloss red paint (after Hebbelynck, 1987)*

was an oil-based varnish and now is more often a clear plastic coating material. The difference between gloss and matt paint is the vehicle. For a gloss paint, the vehicle dries out to a smooth, hard surface where regular reflection occurs.

Figure 1.16 illustrates the processes at work when a beam of white light (W, comprising a combination of red, green and blue (R, G and B) components) is incident on a glossy red painted surface. The paint layer comprises particles of pigment suspended in a transparent amorphous vehicle that cures to form a smooth, non-electro-conductive surface. Both regular reflection and isotropic re-emission occur, giving differences of appearance to the observers A, B and C.

For the regular reflection:

- direction is in accordance with laws of regular reflection

- quantity is in accordance with Fresnel's reflection laws

- colour is the colour of the source

- luminance = source luminance × directional specular reflectance determined by Fresnel's laws (Figure 1.13).

Note that the luminance of the reflected source image is independent of the distance of the source, and that this image will be seen by observer A but not observers B and C.

For the isotropic re-emission:

- direction is in accordance with Lambert's law
- quantity is determined by reflectance $\rho$, where $\rho = 1 - \alpha$
- colour is determined by wavelength selective absorption
- luminance = illuminance $\times$ reflectance/$\pi$.

Note that luminance is proportional to illuminance, and so is dependent on distance from the source. Observers B and C see the full saturation of the red pigment, but for observer A the redness is diluted, or even obliterated, by the regular reflection, depending on the relative luminances. A large diffuse light source would dilute the colour saturation equally for all observers.

As shown in Figure 1.13, the proportion of incident light reflected from the surface of an amorphous material varies strongly with the angle of incidence. If the surface is smooth, regular reflection occurs and an image is formed, but generally this effect is apparent only for oblique viewing angles. Greatly increased levels of regular reflection can be achieved when an electro-conductive material is polished to an optically smooth surface, to the point where the high reflectance due to Fresnel reflection at high angles of incidence is achieved for all incident directions, so that variation with incidence angle is effectively eliminated. Examples of this have been referred to: polished metals such as silver, aluminium and chromium provide regular reflection that is independent of wavelength, while gold, brass and copper have wavelength dependent characteristics.

Figure 1.17 illustrates the processes for an electro-conductive surface, in this case polished brass. There is no isotropic re-emission, and all reflection is regular. Nonetheless, some absorption occurs, selectively at the shorter wavelengths, and this accounts for the characteristic metallic yellow colour of brass.

In this case:

- direction is in accordance with laws of regular reflection
- colour is the colour of the source less the absorption losses
- luminance = source luminance $\times$ reflectance, where $\rho = 1 - \alpha$.

**Figure 1.17:** *Reflection for an electro-conductive surface, in this case polished brass (after Hebbelynck, 1987)*

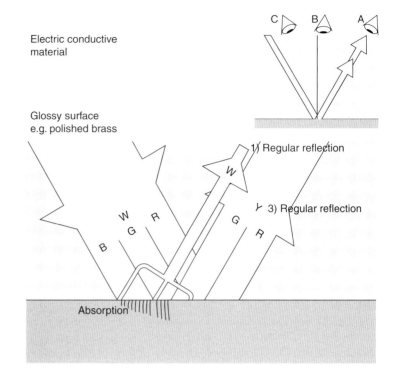

Note that in this case the source image luminance is largely independent of direction, as well as being totally independent of source distance. Roughened or textured surfaces may partially or totally eliminate the reflected image, giving rise to various impressions of surface quality ranging from shiny, through sheen, to matt. Even so, the reflection process is quite different from isotropic re-emission, and so is the impression of colour. The metallic colours cannot be achieved by mixing pigments. Their appearance depends on modifying the source image, rather than the incident illumination.

## Interaction processes of light and matter

To summarize the foregoing, the basic purpose of visual perception is to enable recognition of object attributes. The source of the information flowing through from the visual process is the interactions that occur when light encounters matter. The foregoing paragraphs describe the interaction processes that concern us, and in fact, they are quite limited in number.

We can reduce the number further. Although *diffraction scattering* was mentioned, it involves interactions with very small particles and is not of concern for indoor lighting. This leaves the following processes:

- **Absorption** is almost inevitable; in fact, the only process mentioned that does not involve some degree of light absorption is total internal reflection. It is easy to dismiss absorption as an unfortunate source of inefficiency, but it should be recognized that this is the basis of surface lightness, and selective absorption is the origin of surface colour.

- **Regular reflection:**
  - from the surface of liquid-state (including amorphous) materials, the Fresnel reflection enables us to distinguish glossy from matt surfaces
  - from electro-conductive surfaces, which give us reflected sparkle and the metallic colours.

- **Refraction and dispersion** within liquid-state materials, which give shape clues and may reveal spectral colours.

- **Reflection scattering:**
  - from particles in gaseous-state or liquid-state materials, giving cloudiness or translucency
  - isotropic re-emission in surface layer of solid-state materials, which reveal lightness, hue and saturation attributes.

This is not a complete list of ways in which light may interact with matter, but it covers the interaction processes that concern us. Lighting is the source of energy that stimulates these optical phenomena, and provides much of the information that enables the perception process to discriminate differences of opaque, transparent and translucent materials. Ways in which lighting may be controlled to selectively promote or suppress these processes will be discussed in the following chapter, and that discussion will include recognition of object attributes such as form and texture.

In the meantime, it should be noted that phenomena such as diffraction and polarization can be demonstrated in an optical laboratory, but it would be unusual for these to be of concern to an architectural lighting designer.

## 1.3 Object characteristics and perceived attributes

The processes of interaction of light and matter described in the previous section cause the events in the luminous environment that are the stimulus for vision (Figure 1.1). The visual process is the source of information for the perceptual process, which gives rise to the sensation of a perceived environment in the viewer's brain, and comprises recognized objects with distinct characteristics. Whereas a single pixel in the luminous environment can be specified completely in terms of luminance and chromaticity, the object that contains this pixel may be perceived to have characteristics of substance, utility, beauty, value, affection, and so forth. These interpretations which occur during every moment of our waking hours derive from recognition of perceived attributes. The perceived attributes that may be associated with any 'thing' that is seen depend on the mode of appearance in which it is perceived (Tables 1.1, 1.2).

We are so dependent on vision for understanding our surroundings that it is difficult, or even impossible, to imagine the world as perceived by less vision-dependent species. A bat is, quite simply, 'as blind as a bat', and yet it can navigate at speed through forests and within caves. We know that it employs a sonar system similar in principle to that used by ships to locate submarines or shoals of fish, but what does the world 'look' like to a bat? Obviously they cannot experience colour, but we are able to recognize black and white images. However, can we even imagine a three-dimensional world with no light or shade? What is the image in a bat's brain as it swoops between obstacles to intercept an insect in mid-air? Although this is not a lighting issue, it may cause us to think about how we perceive our environments, and the role of lighting in that process.

It is important to appreciate that something that has the physical properties of an object is not necessarily perceived in one of the 'object modes'. Figure 1.18 shows two views of a luminaire. In case (a), the surface form, texture and lightness of the glass shade are all clearly visible. We could assess its lightness on a scale of zero to ten. We could make a reasonable guess of its reflectance. We perceive this shade in object surface mode. However, our perception of the shade is different in case (b). We recognize that it is still the same shade, but now that it glows we really have no idea of its texture, and it is quite meaningless to discuss its lightness. We could certainly discuss its brightness, and this lies at the heart of our changed perception of the shade. We are now perceiving it in illuminant mode, and as indicated in Table 1.2, the range of associated attributes is different, and furthermore, the number of attributes is

Figure 1.18:   *In view (a) the glass shade is perceived in object mode and has attributes of lightness and texture. In view (b) the shade is perceived in illuminant mode and has the attribute of brightness*

Figure 1.19:   *(a) and (b) How do we perceive transparent media? This glass vase is perceived in both surface and volume modes, and it can be seen in (a) that the directional lighting reveals the surface attribute of gloss while hue is perceived in volume mode. For view (b) only the background has been changed. The surface highlights are still evident, but it can be seen that the chromatic attributes visible in (a) are revealed not only by transmitted light but also by internally reflected light*

reduced. Of course we know that the glass shade is not self-luminous, but nonetheless, the 'thing' that our intellect informs us is a trans-illuminated object is perceived as if it is the source of light.

Furthermore, an object may be perceived simultaneously in more than one mode. The glass object shown in Figure 1.19 is perceived to have both surface and volume attributes. The two cases show how a change of background can give a different balance of the perceived attributes. Without disturbing the light sources, the object can be presented to give emphasis to its internal colour or to the smooth glossiness of its surface. Differences of this sort are explored in the following chapters, but we should note that throughout these changes our understanding of the object's fundamental nature remains intact. The differences of appearance may influence our sense of appreciation of the object, but basically it remains a coloured glass vase. Such is the power of the perceptual system to recognize object attributes that, providing there is sufficient light to enable the visual process to operate effectively, viewing conditions have to be severely constrained for viewers to be confused over object recognition. Consider for a moment; if we could present the glass vase in Figure 1.19 so that the surface attributes were completely invisible, what would a viewer perceive? Is it possible to imagine the volume attributes without a bounding surface? Fortunately the perceptual process very rarely presents us with such confusion.

The basic purpose of visual perception is to enable recognition of object attributes. Each attribute is associated with certain optical properties of the object, and is recognized by a characteristic interaction with light. Generally, the prime purpose of indoor lighting is to enable recognition of stable environments comprising recognized objects within which people can orientate themselves and navigate with confidence. However, the perceptual process is very adept at doing this, and copes well over a vast range of visual conditions. On one hand, this permits many lighting solutions that provide for no more than sufficiency of illumination to be found acceptable. On the other hand, it offers opportunities for designers to apply imagination to selecting object attributes for emphasis without compromising the basic requirements that lighting for occupied space must fulfil.

It needs to be noted that the perceptual process involves placing interpretations upon the visible effects of optical interactions. Every 'thing' that we perceive in our surroundings is recognized to have certain attributes, and the range of attributes that may be associated with a 'thing' depends upon the mode in which it is perceived. Objects perceived in the surface and volume modes have the greatest range of associated attributes, and this is where lighting designers often look to for opportunities to influence the appearance of surroundings. In Figure 1.19, the light that is reflected towards the viewer from the surface has undergone a different reflection process from the light that has been reflected or refracted within the volume of the object. While some lighting designers work on the basis of an intuitive understanding of this difference, a designer who understands the optical nature of this difference is in a stronger position to control the processes, and to select attributes for emphasis. To explore how this is done, we move on from characteristics of objects to characteristics of lighting, which opens up more opportunities for influencing the appearance of surroundings.

# Visible characteristics of lighting

2

Visual constancy requires that we are able to differentiate between changes of surface lightness and surface illuminance. According to the 'modes of appearance' model, 'things' that are perceived in surface or volume object modes have the attribute of lightness but not brightness. Helmholtz's paper appeared white and the lump of coal black regardless of their relative luminances. Nonetheless, he would have been conscious that the coal was more brightly lit than the paper. While he perceived the stable attributes of these objects in surface mode, he would have perceived the different attributes of their lighting in localized illumination mode. While a luminance meter would measure the combined effects of illumination and surface lightness, a human observer assesses these independently. This chapter examines perceived attributes of lighting.

## 2.1 Ambient illumination

Upon entering a space, the first obvious characteristic of the lighting is an overall sense of the space appearing to be brightly lit, or dimly lit, or something in between. This may be accompanied by an impression that the lighting imparts an overall sense of warmth, or alternatively coolness. Referring back to the modes of appearance concept, these are non-located illumination-mode perceptions, for which the principal associated attributes are brightness, hue and saturation (Tables 1.1, 1.2).

An initial impression will be influenced by one's previous state of exposure to light. As we enter an illuminated room from outdoors, the sense of brightness is quite different by day and night. It takes some while for one's eyes to adapt to the new surroundings, and this adaptation process is crucial for understanding human response to light.

### Adaptation level

Adaptation is the process by which the response of the visual system adjusts to suit different conditions of ambient illumination.

*Facing page: Hong Kong International Airport. Sir Norman Foster's design provides for a smooth and gradual transition from daytime to night time. Triangular skylights are arranged for indirect illumination of the soaring roof shells by day, with metal halide light sources taking over to provide a similar light distribution by night*

Human vision can operate in conditions ranging from starlight to bright sunlight, albeit with varying levels of performance, which is a vast luminance range of around 10 decades (1:10,000,000,000). The only part of that range that concerns us for interior lighting is the photopic range, being the range in which retinal cones are operative, so enabling colour vision. The *adaptation level* is a measure of the luminance of the visual field as it affects a viewer's state of adaptation. If the range of luminance values is not more than 1:100, it is acceptable to assume that the average luminance of the field of view defines the adaptation level. The low end of the photopic range corresponds to an adaptation level of around $3\,cd/m^2$, and in bright sunlight the adaptation level can be as high as $10,000\,cd/m^2$, giving a photopic range of approximately 3.5 decades. Although this is a much more restricted range, it is still far too big for us to be able to cope with it simultaneously. Moving from sunlight to a well-lit indoor space where the adaptation level might be $30\,cd/m^2$, the initial impression will be of dim space with subdued colours. It may take several seconds for surfaces and objects to take on their familiar appearance, and it should be noted that our adaptation rate slows down with age.

If we further restrict the range of adaptation levels to include only conditions that are likely to be encountered indoors, we come down to just 2 decades, or a range of just 1:100, being the lower part of the photopic range and extending from 3 to $300\,cd/m^2$. For this range, the simple model of brightness adaptation shown in Figure 2.1 is adequate. The solid line indicates how people's subjective estimates of overall brightness vary as their adaptation level changes. It is important to understand the difference between the two scales being used. Brightness is a sensation that occurs in the human brain. For a researcher to record an observer's response on a scale of brightness, the observer might be instructed, 'If the target on your left has a brightness of ten units, what brightness score do you give to the target on your right?' A rating of twenty should indicate that the observer judges the right target to be twice as bright as the left target. As well as recording the observer's rating, the researcher would record the luminance of both targets. Luminance is a photometric unit, and a doubling of target luminance means a doubling of the luminous flux density arriving at the eye. Figure 2.1 shows that there is not a one-to-one relationship between luminance and brightness. This has led some people to conclude that the eye is a poor judge of brightness, but that completely misses the point. Human vision did not evolve for the purpose of measuring luminous flux. It would be more sensible to say that the luminance meter gives a poor

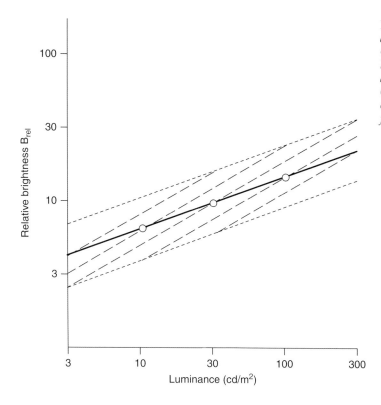

**Figure 2.1:** *A simple model of the adaptation process. The heavy line (gradient 0.37) indicates relative brightness of the overall appearance of a space, and the dashed lines (gradient 0.58) indicate the relative brightness of elements within the space. See text for explanation*

measure of brightness, but again this is off target. The fact is that there is not a simple and reliable relationship between the subjective sensation of brightness and the amount of luminous flux arriving at the eye. However, that does not mean that they are entirely unrelated.

Figure 2.1 shows that as the adaptation level increases, brightness increases at only about one third of the photometric rate. Once a person is adapted to a condition, the brightness of different elements within their field of view varies more strongly with luminance differences, as indicated by the steeper dashed lines passing through various adaptation points. Studies by researchers around the world have confirmed this type of luminance/brightness relationship, and the slopes of the lines shown are based on studies by Marsden (1970), which give overall relative brightness as varying with luminance to the power of 0.37 ($B_{rel} \propto L^{0.37}$), and for the relative brightness of elements within the field of view, $B_{rel} \propto L^{0.58}$.

With this model in mind, we can apply introspective observation to the everyday process of moving from one room to another, or experiencing changes of illumination that occur within a room, such as the diurnal variations of daylight. Consider for a moment: if the solid line in Figure 2.1 had a 45° slope, then our impression of illumination brightness would be in accord with illuminance, that is to say, twice as much light would appear twice as bright. If the line was horizontal, then adaptation would be total, so that we would adapt completely to any change of illuminance, and we would be unaware that a change had occurred. What we have involves at least two adaptation states. As we move from one space to another, or as the light level changes within the space that we are in, our non-located illumination mode perception of brightness changes more slowly than the change in illuminance. When fully adapted to the new condition we are conscious of being in a space where the illumination is brighter or dimmer, but as we look around us, our located illumination mode perceptions promote stronger impressions of brightness difference.

Referring to Figure 2.1, consider a person whose adaptation level is $30 \, cd/m^2$ and this condition is accorded a relative brightness rating of 10 units. If the ambient light level in the space is raised tenfold to give an adaptation level of $300 \, cd/m^2$, the person's overall brightness rating can be expected to increase to 23 units. If the light level is reduced to give an adaptation level of $3 \, cd/m^2$, the overall brightness rating reduces to around 4.3 units. Alternatively, if no change is made to the lighting so that the adaptation level is steady at $30 \, cd/m^2$, and the person looks around within the space, a perceived source of brightness (perceived in illuminant or illumination mode) having a luminance of $300 \, cd/m^2$ would be rated at 38 relative brightness units. A source of brightness at $3 \, cd/m^2$ would be rated at 2.6 units. When we look for these effects we can see them, but it requires the conscious effort of looking. It is necessary to do this, as it is the only way to understand the important role of adaptation level in lighting design.

To make this observation process objective it should include measurement, but this raises a problem: how do we measure the adaptation level? Luminance meters (see Section 3.2) are quite expensive devices, and generally they measure luminance in a narrow cone, so that an average measure of the field of view would involve working out the mean of many spot measurements. The practical solution is to measure eye illuminance. An illuminance meter is a more simple instrument which measures the density of luminous flux incident at a point on a surface in lux, where one lux is one lumen per square metre. Its usual use is to measure illuminance on a work surface, such as a desk or bench top, but to measure eye illuminance you simply hold the meter up to your eye so it is normal to your direction of view.

Even so, there is still a problem. The aim is to measure how much light arrives at the eye from the surfaces and objects that make up our surroundings, but the meter may also be receiving light directly from the luminaires. Consider for a moment that you are in a room that has ceiling-mounted luminaires that concentrate their light output in the downward direction. The only light that reaches the ceiling and upper walls is light that is reflected from the floor or furniture, and if these are low in reflectance, the adaptation level and brightness impression will be correspondingly low. It is important, therefore, that the meter is not exposed to direct light from the luminaires, as this light is glare and does not add to the impression of room brightness.

A technically feasible way of measuring the adaptation condition would be to mount a wide-angle calibrated CCD camera on a tripod for the appropriate viewpoint and direction of view, to give a screen image of the field of view. The operator would use a light pen of similar device to identify those areas of the image that represent self-luminous elements, and mean luminance at the viewpoint would be computed for the remainder.

David Loe and his colleagues have taken a more straightforward approach, and have adapted an illuminance meter by adding a shield that restricts the field of measurement to a 40° horizontal band (Figure 2.2), and have found satisfactory agreement with people's assessments of the appearance of a room with several different distributions of overhead lighting (Loe et al., 2000). Depending upon the type of lighting, it can be sufficient to simply shield the meter from direct illumination as shown in Figure 2.3. An outcome of this research was that whichever type of lighting was used, people found the

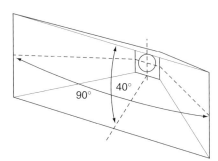

Figure 2.2: *Loe's illuminance meter shield to restrict response to a 40° horizontal band (adapted from Loe, D., Mansfield, K. and Rowlands, E. A step in quantifying the appearance of a lit scene,* Lighting Research and Technology, 32(4), 2000, 213–22)

Figure 2.3: *Measuring eye illumination using the hand to shield the meter from direct light from luminaries*

Table 2.1 *Appearance of ambient illumination related to adaptation level and eye illuminance*

| Adaptation level cd/m² | Eye illuminance lux | Appearance of ambient illumination |
|---|---|---|
| 3 | 10 | Lowest level for reasonable colour discrimination |
| 10 | 30 | Dim appearance |
| 30 | 100 | Lowest level for 'acceptably bright' appearance |
| 100 | 300 | Bright appearance |
| 300 | 1000 | Distinctly bright appearance |

overall brightness to be sufficient when the adaptation level was greater than 30 cd/m², and this corresponds approximately to an eye illuminance of 100 lux. (More precisely in a uniform luminance field, 1 cd/m² corresponds to $\pi$ lux.) This approximate relationship has been used to draw up Table 2.1. An eye illuminance of 10 lux corresponds to the low end of the photopic range, and if the level falls below this value, colour discrimination starts to decline rapidly. The upper end of this scale is less easily defined, but an illuminated room that produces an eye illuminance of 1000 lux will appear distinctly bright.

It is important when taking eye illuminance readings to ensure that the meter is responding to the light arriving at the eye from the room surfaces and the objects in the room. Direct light from luminaires or windows must be avoided. Loe's device is not a universal solution as it does not block light from task lights, standard lamps or windows. Where high brightness elements occur within the field of view, their effect will be to raise the adaptation level above the luminance level of the room surfaces, causing those surfaces to appear darker. This is an aspect of glare, where more light arriving at the eye can have the effect of inducing an impression of gloom. It is important that any-one who seeks to engage in architectural lighting design gains first-hand experience of the role of adaptation in influencing the appearance of illuminated spaces.

## Room surface inter-reflection

Now let's try a thought exercise. Imagine a room in which all surfaces are of uniform reflectance $\rho$. We place a can-dle, or some other luminaire, in the room. The Principle of Conservation of Energy requires that *the rate at which lumens are released into the room equals the rate at which they are absorbed by the room surfaces.* If this famous principle does not mean much to you, think about it this way: if the lumens were absorbed more slowly than they were released, they would stack up and the room would become brighter and brighter the longer light is left on. The converse is more difficult to imagine: lumens would have to be absorbed before they had been emitted! So accepting the principle, we can write:

$$F_L = F(1 - \rho_{rs}) \text{ lumens}$$

where $F_L$ = the luminous flux (lumens) emitted by the luminaire(s);

$F$ = the total luminous flux incident on all the room surfaces, both directly and by inter-reflection;

$\rho_{rs}$ = room surface reflectance, so that $(1 - \rho_{rs})$ equals the room surface absorptance, $\alpha_{rs}$.

Note: Refer to Appendices A1 and A2.

Rearranging the expression for total flux:

$$F = F_L / (1 - \rho_{rs}) \text{ lumens}$$

Illuminance is luminous flux divided by area, so if the total room surface area is $A_{rs}$, the mean room surface illuminance:

$$E_{rs} = \frac{F_L}{A_{rs}(1 - \rho_{rs})} \text{ lux}$$

This is sometimes referred to as Sumpner's principle (Cuttle, 1991), or the radiosity principle (Simons and Bean, 2001).

$E_{rs}$ is the sum of direct and indirect components:

$$E_{rs} = E_{rs(d)} + E_{rs(i)}$$

and

$$E_{rs(d)} = F_L / A_{rs}$$

so

$$E_{rs(i)} = \frac{F_L}{A_{rs}(1 - \rho_{rs})} - \frac{F_L}{A_{rs}}$$

$$= \frac{F_L - F_L(1 - \rho_{rs})}{A_{rs}(1 - \rho_{rs})}$$

$$= \frac{F_L \rho_{rs}}{A_{rs}(1 - \rho_{rs})}$$

This is an important expression, and we will return to it in later sections. The first thing to note is that $E_{rs(i)}$ is the illuminance that all the room surfaces receive by inter-reflected flux, and so it will equal the average illuminance at your eye due to light from these surfaces, that is to say, your average eye illuminance excluding direct light. It is equal to the average exitance of the room surfaces in lm/m$^2$, and so we may rewrite this expression for mean room surface exitance:

$$M_{rs} = \frac{F_L \rho_{rs}}{A_{rs}(1 - \rho_{rs})} \text{ lm/m}^2$$

The next thing to note is that the top line of the expression, ($F_L \rho_{rs}$), is the *first reflected flux*, FRF. This is sometimes called the *first-bounce lumens*, and these lumens are the source for all the inter-reflected light within the room.

Finally, the bottom line, $A_{rs}(1 - \rho_{rs})$, is the *room absorption*, which may be indicated by the symbol $A\alpha_{rs}$ (See definition of

$\rho_{rs}$ on previous page). It is a measure of the room's capacity to absorb light. A perfect absorber would have a surface reflectance $\rho_s = 0$. A surface with a reflectance $\rho_s = 0.67$ absorbs one third of the light incident upon it, so that $3\,m^2$ of this material has the same capacity to absorb light as $1\,m^2$ of a perfect absorber. In this way, $A\alpha_{rs}$ is the number of square metres of perfect absorber that has the same capacity to absorb light as all of the room surfaces.

So, to obtain the mean room surface exitance, we divide the first-bounce lumens by the room absorption.

$$M_{rs} = FRF/A\alpha_{rs} \ \mathrm{lm/m^2}$$

This looks easy, but of course we started with a case that was too simple to be true: real rooms do not have uniform reflectances. Nonetheless, the principle can be applied to real rooms.

For a room that comprises $n$ surface elements, where a surface element might be a wall, ceiling or partition, the first reflected flux is the sum of the products of direct surface illuminance, surface area, and surface reflectance:

$$FRF = \sum_{s=1}^{n} E_{s(d)} A_s \rho_s$$

The room absorption is the sum of products of surface areas and absorptances:

$$A\alpha_{rs} = \sum_{s=1}^{n} A_s (1 - \rho_s)$$

We can apply these expressions in the previous formula, and for real rooms we can conclude that average eye illuminance equals mean room surface exitance, which equals first-bounce lumens divided by room absorption. It may be noted that the only assumption being made here is that the reflected lumens are uniformly distributed. There will be situations where this obviously is not valid, such as where only one wall at the end of a corridor is illuminated, but otherwise these expressions are widely applicable for relating ambient illumination to the sense of overall brightness.

These expressions are also very informative. Look again at the equation for $M_{rs}$ which can be slightly expanded to:

$$M_{rs} = \frac{F_L}{A_{rs}} \frac{\rho_{rs}}{(1 - \rho_{rs})}$$

This shows that $M_{rs}$ is equal to the direct illuminance, $F_L/A_{rs}$, multiplied by the term $\rho_{rs}/(1 - \rho_{rs})$, and this term shows us the influence of reflectance in providing eye illumination. It is conventional for lighting people to refer to surface reflectances, but as has been explained, $(1 - \rho_{rs})$ is the surface absorptance $\alpha_{rs}$ of an opaque material. In this way, the $\rho_{rs}/(1 - \rho_{rs})$ expression is termed the reflectance/absorptance ratio $\rho/\alpha$. Its function is shown in Figure 2.4, where it can be seen that when $\rho_{rs}$ has a value of 0.1 or less, there is practically no room surface exitance as almost all the light is absorbed upon incidence. It is not until $\rho$ has a value of 0.5 that room surface exitance equals the direct illuminance. As has been explained in Section 1.1, this surface reflectance corresponds to Munsell value 7.5, which is quite a high value of lightness. Even so, if we increase reflectance above this value, we gain a bountiful return of room surface exitance and eye illuminance. Increasing $\rho_{rs}$ from 0.5 to 0.67 doubles the eye illuminance, and increasing from 0.67 to 0.8 doubles it again!

This emphasizes the value of taking an illuminance meter and walking from space to space, first assessing overall brightness and then measuring eye illuminance. It would be reasonable to expect that overall brightness would be determined by how much light is being put into the space, but this is soon shown

**Figure 2.4:** *The room surface reflectance/absorptance function*

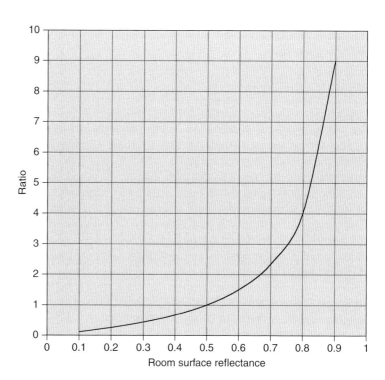

to be false. An installation of recessed downlighters over a dark floor may be putting plenty of light into a space, and this could be confirmed by holding the meter horizontally as if measuring illuminance on the working plane. However, overall brightness would be judged low, and this would accord with measured eye illuminance. What if we could redirect the light onto light-coloured walls or ceiling? Obviously, it would raise eye illuminance and transform our assessment of overall brightness.

The $\rho/\alpha$ ratio provides a theoretical link between direct illuminance and room surface exitance, and we will return to these equations in Part Three. However, the important thing at this stage is to employ observation to develop experience of how overall brightness relates to eye illuminance, as this becomes important knowledge in visualizing the design concept. It is not enough to rely on the simple descriptions given in Table 2.1, as these provide no more than outline guidance. Observation-based experience is essential for visualizing and realizing a lighting design concept.

## Ambient illumination colour

Thus far we have considered ambient illumination only in terms of overall brightness, but there is also the important aspect of ambient illumination colour. This is not a discussion of the use of coloured light, but rather how to employ the various shades of white light that may be used in architectural lighting. When choosing a white paint or a white fabric, we can opt for subtle tints of virtually any hue, but for illumination, the choice is more restricted. People do not look good or feel good in lighting that imparts even the most delicate shade of green or mauve. However, there is substantial latitude for differences of illumination colour appearance on a yellow–blue axis. This probably is due to the naturally occurring variation of illumination under which the human race has evolved. It is common experience that bright midday daylight gains a strong component from the blue sky, even if it has been diffused by a cloud layer, while for lower solar altitudes the balance of daylight shifts towards yellow and then reddish hues.

The range of illumination colour appearance from yellowish-white to bluish-white is indicated by the *correlated colour temperature CCT* of the ambient illumination, expressed in kelvins. This is the temperature of a 'black body' or total radiator for which the emitted light most closely matches the colour appearance of the illumination produced by the light source. Table 2.2 shows the association of 'warm' and 'cool' colour

Table 2.2 *Correlated colour temperature and colour appearance*

| Correlated colour temperature | Colour appearance |
|---|---|
| $\geq$5000 K | Cool (bluish white) |
| <5000 K; $\geq$3300 K | Intermediate (white) |
| <3300 K | Warm (yellowish white) |

**Figure 2.5:** *The colour appearance of ambient illumination. Correlated colour temperature CCT in kelvins is compared with the reciprocal mega kelvin MK⁻¹ scale*

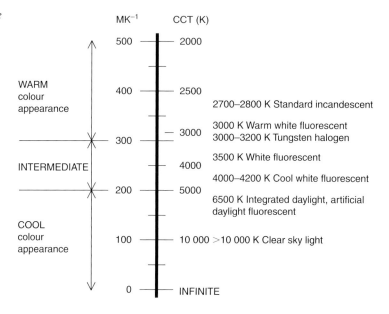

appearance with CCT, and it should be noted that, counter-intuitively, warm is associated with low colour temperatures, and cool with high K values.

There is an alternative scale for specifying the colour appearance of ambient illumination. The unit is the *reciprocal mega kelvin MK⁻¹*, and to convert a CCT into MK⁻¹ you divide the kelvins by one million and take the reciprocal. Figure 2.5 shows the very tidy scale that results. The range of intermediate colour appearance is 200 to 300 MK⁻¹ and increasing values correspond to increasing apparent warmth. More than that, equal intervals on this scale correspond to approximately equal perceived differences. What does a difference of 300 K look like? The difference between 2700 and 3000 K is the difference between standard incandescent and tungsten halogen lamps, which is distinctly visible, whereas the difference between 5000 and 5300 K is a small difference that probably would not be detectable under normal viewing conditions. However, the difference between incandescent and halogen is 37 MK$^{-1}$. Figure 2.5 shows that a 5000 K source is 200 MK$^{-1}$, so to experience a visually similar difference of colour appearance we need to compare it with a 163 MK$^{-1}$ source, and such a source would have a CCT of 6100 K. Lamp engineers make use of the MK$^{-1}$ scale because it relates to visual experience so much better than CCT, but unfortunately it has not spread into more general use.

Measurement of colour temperature is less straightforward than for illuminance. There is a type of instrument called a chroma meter that gives measures of illuminance, chromaticity and CCT, but if such a meter is not available, the only way of being sure about CCT is by examining the manufacturer's markings on the lamps. We need to consider two subjective aspects of ambient illumination. The colour appearance of nominally white light sources can be rated on a warm–cool scale, that is to say, the appearance of the overall colour cast imparted by the lighting ranges from distinctly warm to distinctly cool, with a neutral condition that is neither warm nor cool in appearance. Table 2.2 shows how the terms 'warm', 'intermediate', and 'cool' are often used to describe the colour appearance of lamps, but lighting designers should establish their own experience of this relationship by observation. Additionally, we need to assess at the same time the overall sense of brightness. As has been discussed in the previous subsection, this aspect of appearance can be rated on a dim–bright subjective scale. We need to assess both of these subjective aspects of appearance as they are related. However, attempts to define that relationship have encountered difficulties that make an interesting tale.

It was way back in 1941 that A.A. Kruithof, a lamp development engineer with Philips Lighting in the Netherlands, wrote an article describing the fluorescent lamp. This lamp had been introduced in the USA in 1938, and despite the turmoil of the Second World War, it was finding its way into Europe. Among the many unfamiliar aspects of this new technology that Kruithof described was that lighting specifiers would be able to select the CCT of their lighting, which previously had not been possible. To provide guidance on how to do this, he included the diagram reproduced in Figure 2.6, where the white zone indicates acceptable combinations of illuminance and CCT. Within the lower shaded zone, which includes combinations of low illuminance and high CCT, the effect was described as 'cold and harsh', while in the upper shaded zone, which includes combinations of high illuminance and low CCT, the effect was described as 'unnatural' (Kruithof, 1941).

**Figure 2.6:** *The 'Kruithof effect' is illustrated by this chart. As explained in the text, it relates subjective assessment of ambient illumination to Illuminance E and correlated colour temperature $T_c$*

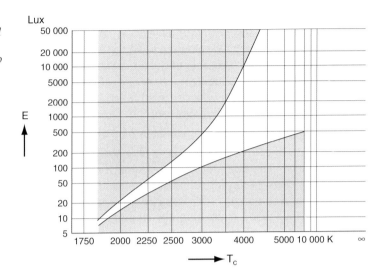

The article gives little information on how this diagram was derived, but Kruithof has told the author that it was a 'pilot study' based entirely on the observations by himself and his assistant. For low colour temperatures, incandescent lamps were switched from series to parallel, but as the halogen lamp had not been invented, those conditions would have been limited to 2800 K. For higher CCTs, they used some special fluorescent lamps that were currently under development, but even with the resources of the Philips research laboratories, the range of phosphors available at that time would have been restricting. For some parts of the diagram, Kruithof relied on a common-sense approach. It is obvious that outdoor daylight with a CCT of 5000 K at an illuminance of 50,000 lux is very acceptable, so he extrapolated to that point. It was in this way that the diagram of the 'Kruithof effect' was put together.

Since that time, several researchers have sought to apply scientific method to defining a sound basis for this phenomenon, but this has proved an elusive goal. Some have reported a much weaker effect than that indicated by Kruithof (Bodmann, 1967; Davis and Ginthner, 1990), while others have reported no effect at all (Boyce and Cuttle, 1990). Despite these research findings, the Kruithof effect lives on, and the diagram continues to be published in guides for good lighting practice (for example, IESNA, 2000). Lighting designers continue to refer to it with reverence, and perhaps more convincingly, you are unlikely to find opportunities to carry out observations of lighting installations that occur in the shaded areas of the diagram. You will find that the higher lighting levels provided in commercial and industrial locations, whether by fluorescent or high intensity discharge lamps, make use of CCTs corresponding to the intermediate or cool ranges shown in Table 2.2. Even where CCTs higher than 5000 K are used, if the illuminance also is high (say more than 1500 lux), the effect is more inclined towards a bright and colourful appearance reminiscent of daylight, rather than a noticeably 'cool' effect. Conversely, where lighting is deliberately dim, the low CCTs of incandescent lamps, or even candles, are likely to be the chosen light source. If you practise observation coupled with measurement, you will find ample confirmation of the Kruithof effect.

## 2.2 Visual discrimination

While ambient illumination strongly influences the overall impression of a space, it is obvious that illumination also influences how well we are able to see. When we need to read small print, or we want to see the fine detail of an object, we switch on a task light or carry the object across to a window. We are particularly likely to choose the window option when we want to be sure of the colour of an object, such as an article of clothing that we are thinking of buying.

There is no simple measure of how well lighting enables us to see. A lot of factors can become involved, such as what it is that we are trying to see and how good our eyesight is, and even then, there is no objective basis for comparing how well two different people have seen the same thing. However, it may be noted that performance measurements of subjects engaged in simulated office tasks over extended periods have sought to assess the influence of comfort factors, such as task-surround luminance gradients and discomfort glare, and have found no significant effect. At a lighting seminar in 2006, Dr P.R. Boyce commented, 'Only lighting that affects task visibility can be relied upon to change performance.'

Initially, studies of human vision examined people's ability to discriminate small differences; in particular, small differences of detail and of colour. These studies have provided the basis for the concepts of *visual performance* and *colour rendering*, which we will examine in this section.

### *Visual performance*

Everyone has seen a chart like Figure 2.7. Optometrists use them to test eyesight. The letters are black on a white background to

Figure 2.7:   *A Snellen type visual acuity chart. At a*
*6 m viewing distance, the smallest size of letters that can be*
*recognized gives a measure of the viewer's acuity*

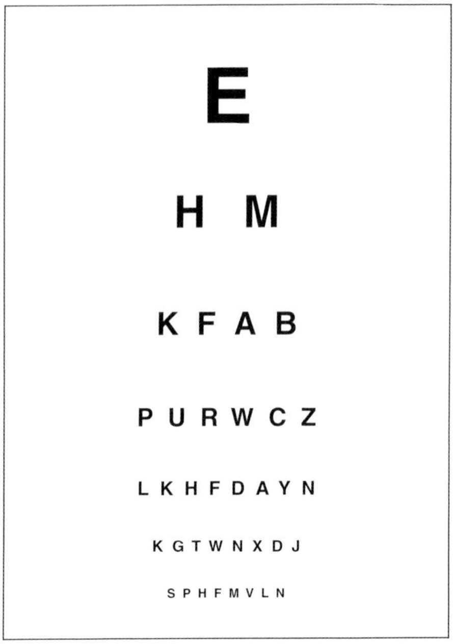

maximize contrast, and the chart is viewed at a distance of six
metres. The lines of letters are designated by a series of numbers, 6/4, 6/6, 6/8 and so on, from the bottom of the chart. If
a person can read down to the 6/8 line but no lower, this fraction may be used to classify their eyesight, as it indicates that at
a distance of 6m, this person can only discriminate detail that
would be visible to a person with normal sight at 8m. In this
way, normal eyesight for a healthy young person is 6/6 vision,
although this is still often referred to as 20/20 vision because
the chart's inventor, Dr Snellen, stated that the chart should
be viewed at 20 feet. A person with 6/4 vision has better than
average eyesight.

While Snellen's system satisfies optometrists, scientists prefer to
measure the ability to discriminate small detail in terms of *visual
acuity*. The smallest detail that has to be discriminated in order
to identify an object is termed the *critical detail*, and for a letter
on the Snellen chart, this might be the gap that distinguishes a
'C' from an 'O'. When an observer is just able to discriminate
the critical detail, this is described as a *threshold condition*. The
size of the critical detail may be measured in terms of the angle
that it subtends at the eye, as shown in Figure 2.8, and for a
threshold condition, visual acuity is calculated from the expression VA $= 1/\alpha$, where $\alpha$ is the angular size of the critical detail
in minutes of arc. For example, if the critical detail at threshold
subtends an angle of 2.5 minutes, visual acuity is 0.4.

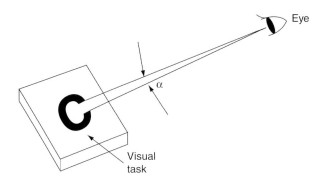

Eye

**Figure 2.8:** *The angular size of the critical detail at threshold determines visual acuity*

α

Visual
task

It can be seen that the Snellen chart is a simple device for measuring a person's ability to discriminate detail, and it can be applied quite readily for the needs of optometrists or visual scientists who are seeking to measure a person's visual ability. The crucial factors are the contrast of the detail against its background and the angular size of the detail, and when the chart is viewed at the correct distance, both of these are controlled. So, what is the role of lighting in all this? The answer is that providing that the ambient illumination is 'acceptably bright' (note the discussion in the previous section) it makes no practical difference. If the optometrist's room appears to be generally well lit, the test conditions are satisfied if the chart is fixed onto a wall and viewed from six metres, using a mirror if necessary. This is not to deny that scores would be affected by providing noticeably high or low light levels, but nonetheless, consistent scores can be expected over the broad range of illuminances that is commonly encountered in well-lit rooms.

This might seem to be a rather strange conclusion, as it implies that illuminance makes little difference to how well we can see. The answer to that is that there is more to seeing than visual acuity, and it is for this reason that vision scientists have devised the concept of visual performance.

Human performance in carrying out various types of work tasks can be measured in several ways. The most obvious measures are how long it takes to complete the task or how many times the task can be completed in a set time. After that, various measures that have been devised for quality control may be applied, and for any work task, there will be a range of factors that influence performance. One of these is likely to be the visual conditions, but tasks differ greatly in the extent to which they are vision-dependent, ranging from tasks that require 6/6 vision to ones that can be performed 'with one's eyes shut'.

Scientists have devised visual tasks that are highly dependent upon vision, an example being the Numerical Verification Task (NVT) for which the experimental subject scans two similar columns of numbers and has to identify any differences. The researcher measures both the time taken and the number of mistakes made in completing a NVT, and this test is repeated under different visual conditions. The data are processed to give scale of visual performance, which takes account of both speed (the inverse of time taken) and accuracy (the inverse of mistakes made). This enables the experimenter to measure the effects of alternative visual conditions in terms of visual performance. As has been noted in the previous paragraph, overall performance may be influenced by many other factors, so that application of visual performance data to actual work performance requires assessment of both the visual task difficulty and the extent to which overall work performance is vision dependent.

The *Relative Visual Performance (RVP)* model is due to Rea (1986) and Rea and Ouellette (1991). A RVP value of 0 represents a 'readability threshold', which means that the visual conditions are just sufficient to enable a normally sighted person to read slowly, and a value of 1 corresponds to an experimentally determined level of performance that is 'unlikely to be exceeded in practice'. It is worth taking a careful look at this model as it reveals the underlying factors that govern how visual performance is influenced by the visual conditions.

Figure 2.9 illustrates four examples of how RVP varies with visual conditions, where the visual conditions are represented by just three factors:

- *Target size*, being the angular size of the detail to be seen, measured in microsteradians (μsr), and represented by the four different diagrams ranging from 1.9 μsr (very small detail) to 130 μsr (large detail).

- *Luminance contrast* of the detail against its background which, for a small target seen against a brighter background, may have a value somewhere between zero (no contrast) and one (hypothetical perfect black on perfect white). A contrast value greater than one indicates that the detail is brighter than its background.

- *Retinal illuminance* for the observer, measured in trolands, which provides an indication of the level of the stimulus to the retinal photoreceptors.

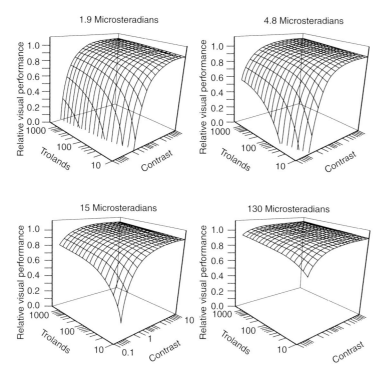

The terminology may seem formidable, but do not be discouraged. While scientists need measures that ensure controlled conditions, these can be related to practical, everyday concepts. In every case shown in Figure 2.9, the vertical scale is relative visual performance, and the first thing to note is that for even the smallest detail, RVP approaches the maximum value providing both contrast and illuminance are high. The important differences between the four examples concern what happens when either or both of these factors are less than optimum.

Boyce and Rea (1987) have described the RVP model as a 'plateau and escarpment' landscape, and this topography can be seen in Figure 2.9. As noted, high contrast and high retinal illuminance correspond to high RVP, and this will always be so unless the detail is so small that the resolution capability of human vision is challenged. The principal difference between the four cases of task size is the plateau area. Providing that illuminance is sufficient to provide for a high level of RVP for a given visual task, increasing the illuminance does not enable that task to be performed better, but rather enables better performance of more difficult visual tasks. If there are no visual tasks of smaller detail or lower contrast present, there is no performance advantage to be gained from increased illuminance.

For large-detail visual tasks there is a correspondingly large, flat zone within which neither contrast nor light level have to be high to provide for a high level of RVP. This is the big plateau: the RVP high country where the seeing conditions are good. Providing contrasts and light levels are maintained at reasonable levels, visual tasks are easily performed. As visual tasks diminish in size, the level of the plateau drops only very slightly; but far more threatening is the diminishing area of the plateau. The brow of the escarpment draws close enough to be a source of concern, and we become conscious that if we have to cope with either small task size or low task contrast, or worse still a combination of them, there could be a real problem in providing light levels sufficient to keep a footing on the high ground.

The security of being on the plateau comes from the fact that when you are there, RVP is not a problem. More to the point, providing you know that you are there, you do not need to know the value of RVP precisely. Even so, in order to have any notion of where we are, we have to cope with those microsteradians and trolands. So let's look at those, and we will start with *target size:*

This is 14 point print. It is easy to read except at very low light levels. If you hold this page 350 mm from your eyes and normal to your direction of view, the size of detail is approximately 20 μsr.

This is 10 point print. Unless you have very good eyesight, you will want to ensure that you have reasonably good lighting to read this for any length of time. At 350 mm, the size of detail is approximately 10 μsr.

This is 6 point print. Although the luminance contrast is high, it is fairly difficult to read. Unless the lighting is good, you probably will find yourself moving your head closer to increase the angular task size. At 350 mm, the size of detail is approximately 3.5 μsr.

This gives a reasonable notion of target size. Although the researchers measured the detail size in microsteradians, from now on we will refer to these as 6-, 10- and 14-point tasks, and you can use your imagination to apply these measures to the sizes of detail that you may encounter in whatever aspect of lighting concerns you.

*Luminance contrast* (C) is a measure of the luminous relationship between a task (t) seen against a relatively large background (b), and is expressed as $C = |(L_b - L_t)|/L_b$. For perfectly matt surfaces, luminance values are directly proportional to their reflectances, so that for black ink, where $\rho_t = 0.04$, on white paper for which $\rho_b = 0.8$, $C = 0.95$. Such high contrasts are quite common for office work, and although small detail may be encountered (particularly in law practices), contrasts less than 0.5 are quite rare (Dillon et al., 1987). Industrial tasks are often of a different type. The detail to be seen may be a scribe mark or an undulation in a homogeneous material that is made visible only by its interaction with directional lighting, and the gloss or sheen of the material plays an important role in making this happen. Accurate measurement of contrast is very difficult under these circumstances, but the people who work with these materials become very adept at turning the object or adjusting their viewing angle to maximize contrast. The last thing that they want is diffuse lighting, as this eliminates their scope to manipulate the task contrast. We will have more to say about contrast.

The final factor defining the visual conditions is *retinal illuminance*. As a measure of the stimulus for vision, the illuminance that is actually incident on the retina would seem to be the obvious metric, but there is a problem: how to measure it? Obviously we cannot measure it directly, and so an indirect means has been devised. There are three determinants of the illuminance at a point on the retina: these are the luminance of the corresponding element in the field of view, the area of the pupil, and the light losses due to the imperfections of the optical media of the eye. The *troland* is referred to as a unit of retinal illuminance, but it takes into account only the stimulus luminance and the pupil area. The light losses within the eye are not taken into account, and they are not constant as they increase with age. Also, there is a tendency for pupil diameter to reduce as people get older, so that compared with a 20-year-old, retinal illuminance has dropped to a half by age 50 and to one third for a 65-year-old (Weale, 1963).

To cope with these problems, scientists have prepared an interactive RVP program that models the pupil response and light scattering as functions of age, so that all that is left to do is to define the brow of the escarpment. Where is the edge of the plateau?

It is important to appreciate that a RVP value of, say, 0.95 does not mean that a person in that situation will perform their work with 95% efficiency. As has been explained, many factors determine overall work performance, and the role of vision as a determinant of overall performance varies from one activity to another. In practical situations, people will readily adapt to difficult circumstances in order to be able to see what they need to see. When they reach a situation in which there is a measurable deterioration in performance as a result of visual shortcomings, even small reductions of RVP are significant. Accordingly, it is reasonable to take the 0.98 RVP contour to represent the boundary of the high RVP plateau.

Figure 2.10 shows the plateau boundary for the three point tasks. The horizontal scale of contrast has been discussed, and the vertical scale shown here represents the illuminance to provide the required background luminance, assuming a background reflectance of 0.8. This corresponds to the three point tasks illustrated previously, but to apply these notions of target size to situations where the background reflectance is lower, the illuminance value has to be increased accordingly. For example, if the background reflectance is 0.2, then the illuminances read from Figure 2.10 must be multiplied by 4.

*Figure 2.10: The high RVP plateaux for the three point-size tasks, for a 60-year-old observer. Each plateau extends from the top right-hand corner to the escarpment edge, which is defined as RVP = 0.98 for each of the tasks*

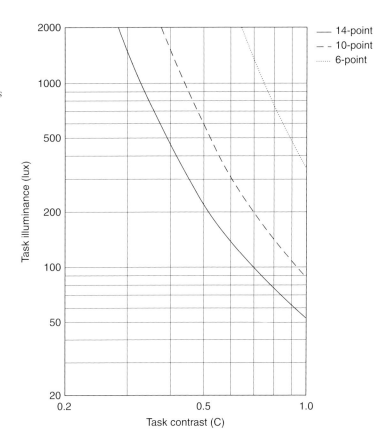

Figure 2.10 indicates that at 500 lux we can cope well with the 10-point task down to contrast values of around 0.5, and even lower for 14-point tasks, but that for the 6-point task we must have high contrast of 0.9 to avoid visual difficulties. Increasing the illuminance up to 2000 lux pushes back the escarpment, enabling us to cope with 6-point tasks having 0.6 contrast, but note that for the same task contrast, 10-point tasks require only 300 lux and 14-point tasks just 130 lux. The slope of the boundary line should be noted carefully: it takes a lot of illuminance to compensate for reduced contrast. Table 2.3 compares two currently recommended scales of task illuminance for different categories of visual task, and although there are differences in the descriptions given for the tasks, the overall level of correspondence to the RVP model may be noted.

As the RVP model is specified in terms of retinal illuminance, it takes more task illuminance to provide for a given RVP as people

*Table 2.3  A comparison of two recommended scales of illuminance and visual tasks*

| Characteristic visual tasks (CIBSE, 1994) | Illuminance (lux) | Illuminance category (IESNA, 2000) |
|---|---|---|
| | 30 | **A** Public spaces |
| Confined to movement and casual seeing without perception of detail. | 50 | **B** Simple orientation for short visits |
| Movement and casual seeing with only limited perception of detail. | 100 | **C** Working spaces where simple visual tasks are performed |
| Involving some risk to people, equipment or product. | 150 | |
| Requiring some perception of detail. | 200 | |
| Moderately easy: i.e. large detail, high contrast. | 300 | **D** Performance of visual tasks of high contrast and large size |
| Moderately difficult: i.e. moderate size, may be of low contrast. Colour judgement may be required. | 500 | **E** Performance of visual tasks of high contrast and small size, or low contrast and large size |
| Difficult: details to be seen are small and of low contrast. Colour judgements may be important. | 750 | |
| Very difficult: very small details which may be of very low contrast. Accurate colour judgements required. | 1000 | **F** Performance of visual tasks of low contrast and small size |
| Extremely difficult: details are extremely small and of low contrast. Optical aids may be of advantage. | 1500 | |
| Exceptionally difficult: details to be seen are exceptionally small and of low contrast. Optical aids will be of advantage. | 2000 | |
| | 3000 | **G** Performance of visual tasks near threshold |

get older. Figure 2.10 is based on a 60-year-old observer, but some recommendations assume younger eyes, and others suggest that design should be based on the average age of the occupants. This approach is inappropriate. Most workplaces comprise people who range in age from around 18 to 65, but it is not satisfactory to assume that anyone aged more than 41.5 years does not need adequate provision for the visual component of their work. The lighting installation should be designed to provide for all normally sighted people in the workplace, whatever their ages, with separate provision being made for people with visual disabilities. Sometimes the school classroom situation is cited as an example of a young working population, but it should be noted that every school classroom can be expected to contain at least one adult person upon whose performance everyone else depends.

Even so, it is interesting to use the RVP model to examine how big the age factor really is. Figure 2.11 shows the plateau boundary for the 10-point task for three ages. It shows how well young people can cope with low illuminances providing contrast

*Figure 2.11:  Hight RVP plateaux for the 10-point task and three observer ages*

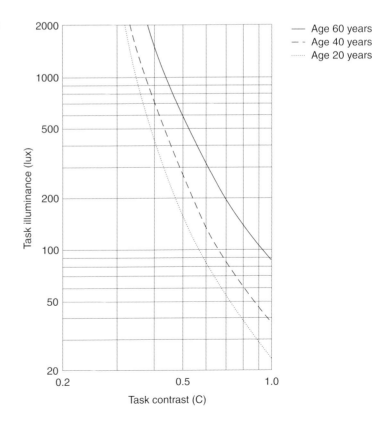

is high; but note that for moderate contrasts, the curves become quite close together. As we aim to provide illuminances sufficient to ensure that people can cope easily with some contrast reduction, the age differences in ability to cope with moderate contrasts appear to become fairly marginal. Even so, the message is clear: in the world of RVP, life is an eroding plateau.

The role of contrast requires further examination. The numerical verification tasks used in the research studies comprised black print on white or grey paper, so that task contrast was determined by the reflectance values of the ink and the paper. In practice, the effective task contrast may be influenced by the lighting in two distinct ways.

*Disability glare* occurs where a bright source within the field of view produces a veil of scattered light within the eye (Figure 2.12). The optical media of the eye are never perfectly transparent, and become increasingly cloudy with age. The detrimental effects of disability glare increase as the illuminance at the eye due to the glare source increases, and as the angle θ reduces. To experience the effects of disability glare, concentrate your attention onto an item of detail and try shielding surrounding sources of brightness from your view. It is quite easy to find both indoor and outdoor conditions for which the visibility of the page that you are now reading is noticeably affected by shielding your eyes in this way. While it is common sense to

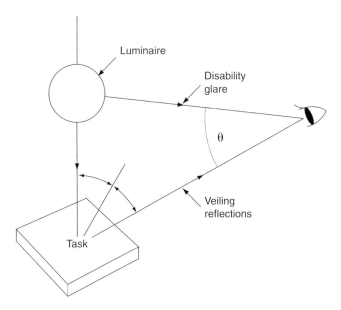

**Figure 2.12:** *Effective task contrast may be reduced by disability glare, which may be received directly or by reflection, or by veiling reflections*

shield lamps and luminaires from direct view where good seeing conditions are required, it should be noted that shiny or
glossy elements within the field of view can also become significant sources of brightness.

*Veiling reflections* occur where specular reflections obscure
the information to be gained from diffuse reflections. Specular
reflections reveal the colour and brightness characteristics of
the light source, whereas diffuse reflections reveal the reflection properties of the task materials. Visual conditions that provide for discrimination of contrasts due to differences of task
materials are said to achieve good *contrast rendering*, but some
caution should be applied here. As has been explained, there
are circumstances in which the visual detail is revealed by the
specular component of reflection.

Procedures have been devised for predicting and evaluating
the effects of both disability glare and veiling reflections. While
these procedures may be useful in some specialized applications,
such as industrial inspection, for general design purposes it is
much more important that the designer is alert to these problems, and rather than numerically evaluating them, takes sensible steps to avoid them. The effect of both of these phenomena
can be equated to a loss of task contrast, and as has been noted,
it takes a lot of illuminance to compensate for even a small loss
of contrast.

While 'plateau and escarpment' is a useful concept for visualizing the distribution of RVP, we should be careful not to over-
dramatize the situation. An observer does not plunge over
a precipice at the plateau boundary and descend into the abyss
of gloom. Everyone has coped with RVP of less than 0.98 many
times without sensing pain or suffering. The difference comes
when people are put in the position of routinely having to cope
with such conditions. This occurs not only in workplaces, but
also in many sports, recreational and leisure activities, and it
should be expected that users will be adversely affected by the
experience and will react accordingly. Wherever people require
good seeing conditions, the lighting designer should have it in
mind that the combination of task size, contrast and illuminance
needs to provide visual conditions that are on the high-RVP plateau, and at a comfortable distance from the escarpment.

The RVP model identifies the factors that are important and
indicates their relative effects, and it is not necessary to carry
out calculations to apply these concepts. However, it is necessary to appreciate that RVP predicts what people need, not

what they want. If the users are firmly on the plateau, they will be able to see what they need to see. However, if the combination of large target size and high contrast means that little light is necessary for this to happen, it does not follow that they will happily accept the low light level. Even if they can see everything that they need to see, they do not want their surroundings to appear dim. Alternatively, if unavoidable conditions have them in the vicinity of the escarpment, this is where seeing ability changes quickly. Small differences in viewing conditions can make a big difference in RVP, which may or may not be realized in practice. The best solution is to keep off these slopes, but if that is not possible, think through carefully what are the things that can be controlled that will make a difference. Is small target size the problem? If it is practical to use magnifiers, these are likely to be far more effective than high lux levels. Low contrast is very detrimental, and as discussed, the specular component of reflection from the task may or may not be helpful. It is necessary for the lighting designer to examine the visual task carefully, and to tease out how lighting could be applied to maximize the available contrast. However, the difficulty in reading those credit card dockets in restaurants is simply the worn-out printer ribbon. Is this a factor that can be controlled? Identifying the cause of the problem is the really important step in devising an effective solution.

## Colour rendering

Scientists tell us that a human subject can discriminate more than 10 million differences of colour, and that fact is made all the more remarkable when we realize that we discriminate colour by the differential responses of just three types of retinal cone photoreceptors. Although there are more than 120 million photoreceptors in each retina, it is only the seven million cones that we use for daytime vision and which provide us with sensations of colour. These cones are of three different types, according to the photopigments that they generate. Each of these pigments has maximum absorption in a different zone of the visible spectrum, and they are best classified as long, medium and short wavelength cones (L-, M-, and S-cones) although they often are referred to as the red, green and blue cones. This is misleading because they would not appear to have these colours, as these terms refer to the spectral components that they absorb rather than those they reflect.

Our ability to experience colour is entirely due to differentials in stimulation of these three cone types, and it might be supposed that the colour perceived would be determined by their proportional responses. Recent research has shown that this is not the case, and interestingly, this research has confirmed observations dating back more than one hundred years. It had been pointed out that the spectrum does not appear to be a continuous transition, but that within the range of spectral colours there are some clear and distinct hues separated by zones which appear to be mixtures of these hues. The four 'pure' hues are red, yellow, green and blue, and only certain mixtures are possible. For example, yellowish-reds and bluish-reds are possible, but greenish reds are not, and this led to an opponent-colours theory which seemed for some while to be in direct opposition to the established principles of trichromacy, being the principle that any hue may be matched by a combination of three primary hues.

Figure 2.13 shows the responses of the three retinal cone types feeding into three channels which convey information to the visual cortex of the brain. The achromatic channel signals the level of stimulation at a given zone of the retina, which is represented by the sum of responses of the L- and M-cones and may be seen as a luminance response. The two chromatic channels are opponent channels, and signal the balance of yellow–blue and red–green responses as illustrated in Figure 2.14. The connections of the three cone responses, shown in Figure 2.13, provide the inputs to these three channels, two of which are

**Figure 2.13:** *The three retinal cone types and the visual response channels, comprising an achromatic non-opponent channel and two chromatic opponent channels*

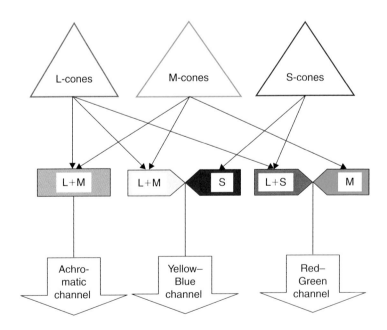

chromatic opponent channels, and this quite recent understanding of the process of colour vision enables both the trichromatic and the opponent-colours theories of colour vision to co-exist. This is the process that enables human observers to distinguish differences of colour, and these two figures give a graphic illustration of its workings. However, one absolute requirement for this to occur is that the incident radiant power on the retina is sufficient to effectively stimulate the cone receptors, and that means that the viewer is in a state of photopic adaptation.

In order to achieve a visual match to a certain colour, it is not necessary to match the spectrum of light associated with that colour. A different spectrum which stimulates similar responses from the three types of retinal cones under a similar state of visual adaptation may be visually indistinguishable. A colour LCD screen comprises thousands of tiny red, green and blue luminous dots which, as we know, can provide a wide range of colour experiences, even if not quite all of the 10 million possibilities.

As was explained in Section 1.2, our surroundings comprise mainly opaque dielectric materials that reflect light by isotropic scattering. The colours that we associate with these materials are due to selective absorption spectra, but this is counter-intuitive. When we describe a material as 'bright red', we perceive it to be adding brightness to the scene. It is difficult to accept that the surface layer of this material is heavily absorbing over the short and medium visible wavelengths, and that only a fraction of the incident light is being reflected. Every colourant, whether a pigment or a dye, can be thought of as a selective absorber, and the more saturated is the appearance of their hue, the more effectively the colourant absorbs complementary hues.

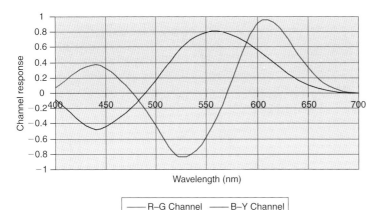

*Figure 2.14: Schematic illustration of the channel responses for the two chromatic opponent channels (courtesy of X-Rite, Inc.)*

Figure 2.15 shows spectral reflectance curves for several strongly coloured pigments. The red pigment curve is as described in the previous paragraph, with strong absorption (i.e., low reflectance) at medium and short wavelengths, but note the curve of the yellow pigment. This material does not reflect only the 'yellow' portion of the spectrum: it reflects all but the shorter visible wavelengths. An important point emerges here. Yellow is not a colour of light, but is a sensation that occurs in the brain when the medium- and long-wavelength receptors within one or more receptive fields are more or less equally stimulated, while the short-wavelength receptor is substantially less stimulated. There are many spectra of light that will do this, ranging from monochromatic (single wavelength) radiation of around 580 nm to a continuous spectrum through the long and medium wavelengths, but which is devoid of radiation at wavelengths shorter than 490 nm. The RGB dots of a LCD screen stimulate the sensation of yellow by mixing R and G components with little or no B component. The wavelength of the spectrum that we describe as yellow (around 580 nm) does not have to be present.

The spectral reflectance curves in Figure 2.15 are the chromatic fingerprints of these pigments. If we were to illuminate surfaces coloured with these pigments with an equi-energy light source (constant radiant energy at all visible wavelengths) the spectrum of light reflected back from each surface would be a replica of its spectral reflectance curve. Average noon sunlight with a correlated colour temperature CCT of 5250 K is a close approximation of the equi-energy light source, and common experience tells us that this is an illuminant that 'renders'

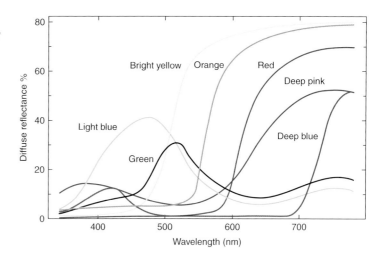

*Figure 2.15:  Spectral reflectance curves for typical pigments (courtesy of the Society of Light and Lighting)*

colours well. Saturated colours appear rich; pastel shades are readily distinguished; and above all, colours appear natural. Is this the ideal colour rendering source? If a cloud obscures the sun, and we have illumination predominantly from a clear blue sky, the illuminant spectrum will become strongly biased towards shorter wavelengths, and the CCT may rise as high as 25,000 K. A change to overcast sky would also increase the CCT, although less dramatically. Alternatively, later in the day, as solar altitude declines, CCT will reduce and the spectrum will become biased towards longer wavelengths. All of these changes will affect the spectrum of light being reflected from illuminated surfaces, but we do not perceive the surfaces of these materials to have undergone colour changes. We are conscious of differences between a sunny day and an overcast day, and between noon and late afternoon sunlight, but we do not perceive the colours of the flowers in our garden to change, nor the illustrations in the book that we are reading in these changing conditions to take on different hues. We adapt readily to variations of daylight, and while we may revel in our appreciation of the magnificent colours generated by a sunset or the intensity of a blue sky, over a large range of conditions the phenomena of lightness constancy and colour constancy ensure that we perceive the things that surround us in object surface mode, and to have stable and recognizable attributes.

We have to apply some care in translating these outdoor experiences to indoor situations. Light produced by incandescence, which includes candles and electric filament lamps, have continuous spectra, but the CCTs are much lower than those of daylight for all but very low solar altitude conditions. The colour temperatures of filament lamps are limited to around 3200 K by the melting temperature of tungsten (3695 K), and compared with the equi-energy source, radiant power is strongly biased towards long wavelengths. Nonetheless, the conclusions drawn from the outdoor observations generally hold. If we see a filament lamp in use in an indoor space that is illuminated by daylight, the lamplight appears noticeably yellow. Note, by the way, that it does not appear red even though there is more radiant power at the 'red wavelengths' than at the 'yellow' ones. The reason is that the radiant power at the mid-wavelengths has higher luminous efficiency, so that the mid- and long-wavelength receptors are more or less equally stimulated. Anyhow, returning to the filament lamp example, if we enter the same space at night, the lamplight seems to have lost its yellowness. It washes surfaces with illumination that appears to brighten the warm hues (red, orange, and yellow) while somewhat dulling dark greens and blues. You might notice mauve and lavender hues gaining a slight pink cast, but you are sure to appreciate the warmth given to the appearance of timber and leather objects, and the kind of things done to the human complexion. It is a very pleasant light source, and while you are fully adapted to it, you are both able to recognize objects from their daytime appearance while appreciating the particular colour qualities that this source imparts.

If this example gives you the feeling that colour rendering is not a simple topic, how are we to cope with the utterly unnatural range of spectral power distributions that have been developed by the lighting industry? Figure 2.16 shows some examples of the amazing variety of spectra that is available. Starting from the equi-energy source and phases of daylight having similar colour temperatures, we move on to the much lower colour temperatures of the filament lamps. After these continuous spectra, we are looking at a collection of spikes and bulges, and it is obvious that the light that will be reflected to the eyes when any of these sources are in use will have practically no resemblance to spectral reflectance curves in Figure 2.13. Before giving up in despair, think of the example of the yellow surface described earlier in this section. Any colour sensation depends on the adaptation state of the eye and the differential responses of the three cone types.

*Figure 2.16: Spectral power distributions for light sources of similar correlated colour temperatures and differing colour rendering properties. (a) Tungsten filaments of the same wattage and different temperatures. 2700 K is the CCT of standard incandescent lamps and tungsten halogen lamps are generally in the range of 2950–3200 K. In every case the CRI is 100. (b) A halophosphor fluorescent lamp for which CCT = 2900 K and CRI = 51. (c) A tri-phosphor fluorescent lamp; CCT = 2900 K, CRI = 82. Some metal halide lamps have fairly similar SPDs and CRIs. (d) A multi-band phosphor fluorescent lamp; CCT = 3000 K, CRI = 96. ((a) IESNA, 2000; (b), (c), (d) courtesy of Philips Lighting)*

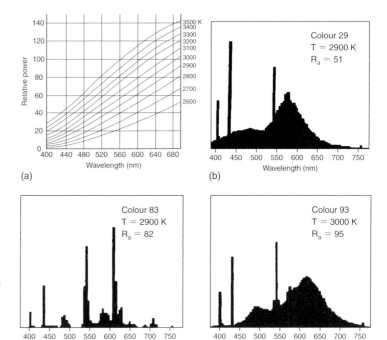

In 1965, the International Commission on Illumination (CIE) addressed this thorny issue by introducing the Colour Rendering Index (CRI, or $R_a$). The basis of the index is that a light source is scored out of 100 for how closely it makes the colour appearance of a set of standard colours match their appearance when illuminated by a reference source of the same CCT. For reference sources, the CIE have taken a family of daylight distributions for CCTs equal to or greater than 4800 K, and an incandescent black body for CCTs less than 4800 K. In this way, CRI always compares the source with a reference that has a continuous spectrum and for which the colour rendering should appear 'natural' for that colour temperature. The success of CRI is that any 'white' light source can be given a simple merit score. The problem is that this simplicity has the effect of obscuring the complexity of colour rendering, and has led to lamp selections being made without warning of possible, and even likely, pitfalls.

An understanding of how the appearances of coloured surfaces in an indoor space are affected by the choice of the light source requires some careful observation. A reference range of surface colours is needed. The type of chart given away by paint manufacturers can serve the purpose, but particularly suitable is the 'ColorChecker' chart produced by the GretagMacbeth Corporation. This comprises 24 matt surface colour samples arranged on a rigid board. It is a valuable experience to spend some time looking carefully at the chart under midday daylight. Figure 2.17 shows the chart being used in this way, and the colour descriptions of the individual samples are given in Table 2.4. The bottom row of samples is a grey scale. Seen under daylight, they appear absolutely devoid of hue, and equally spaced

**Figure 2.17:** *Viewing the ColorChecker chart in daylight (courtesy of Munsell Colour Services)*

Table 2.4 *Diagram of the ColorChecker Color Rendition Chart. The neutral values are Munsell Values, and D values are optical density (courtesy of X-Rite, Incorporated)*

| Dark skin | Light skin | Blue sky | Foliage | Blue flower | Bluish green |
|---|---|---|---|---|---|
| Orange | Purplish blue | Moderate red | Purple | Yellow green | Orange yellow |
| Blue | Green | Red | Yellow | Magenta | Cyan |
| White | Neutral 8 | Neutral 6.5 | Neutral 5 | Neutral 3.5 | Black |
| D 0.05 | D 0.23 | D 0.44 | D 0.70 | D 1.05 | D 1.50 |

in steps of greyness. The row above comprises clear, saturated colours. The blue, green and red samples are, as closely as can be achieved by pigments, the primary colours of additive colour mixing. The yellow, magenta and cyan samples are the primaries of subtractive colour mixing, that is to say, they are anti-blue, anti-green and anti-red respectively. Observe carefully the relative brightness of these samples under daylight. The upper two rows comprise a range of colours for which we may have various associations, and particularly those which people associate with natural materials are likely to influence for assessments of the acceptability of the colour of lighting. Whether a furnishing fabric or an ornament appears to have an attractive colour is less important than whether flowers, or fruit, or in fact anything to be eaten, appear natural and wholesome. Note particularly the two skin tones at the upper left. Critical assessments of people's state of health and attractiveness are readily and routinely made from the appearance of their complexions, and lighting that imparts an unnatural or unhealthy pallor to these samples will be disliked. As you scan these samples, think carefully about the objects that may be associated with these colours, and how your assessment of their appearance might be influenced by colour rendering.

Now take the chart indoors and view it under electric lighting. Perhaps your first reaction will be that it does not look any different, but observe more carefully. Does the grey scale still appear to be completely devoid of hue? Sometimes it is the mid-greys that show a colour cast more clearly than the white sample. As discussed in Section 2.1, a colour cast with a touch of blueness is associated with 'cool' colour appearance, and a yellow cast has a 'warm' effect. These are ambient conditions that we readily adapt to, but that does not mean that we are unaware of a difference, and we can expect to see a changed brightness balance in the appearances of the saturated colours. There are some colour casts that we do not readily adapt to. If the grey scale is showing a touch of greenness, or perhaps a hint of mauve, you should look carefully for how this affects the 'associated' colours, such as skin tones or foliage. Lighting that make these surfaces appear unnatural will not be liked.

It is important that these assessments are made with the observer fully adapted to the light source being evaluated. Side-by-side viewing cabinets with different lamp types show clear differences of appearance, but they do not show the colour appearances that will be experienced by an adapted observer. While the 'ColorChecker' chart is particularly well suited for colour rendering observations, what really counts is that the user has a chart for which time has been taken to learn how the appearances of the colour samples are affected by the illumination. While these observations are being made, it is instructive to refer to the spectral power distribution charts given in the lamp manufacturers' catalogues. It sometimes happens that strange-looking SPDs give quite acceptable colour rendering, while other more likely-looking curves produce unacceptable distortions.

So what use is the colour rendering index? The first thing to be understood about CRI is that it means nothing without the CCT. Daylight and incandescent sources have CRI scores of 100, and widely different colour rendering. There are artificial daylight sources with CCTs around 5000 K that are widely used in industry where critical colour judgements have to be made, and even if they have CRI values that are less than 100, it would be disastrous to replace them with incandescent lamps. Whatever type of 'white' light is to be used for a particular application, the CCT is an important aspect of the ambient illumination, as has been discussed in Section 2.1.

Once the CCT has been decided, CRI indicates in general terms how closely the colour appearances of illuminated surfaces will seem natural for a person who is fully adapted to ambient illumination having that CCT. Table 2.5 shows colour rendering groups where the ranges of CRI scores indicate effective categories of difference. For Group 1A, differences in colour appearance for sources of the same CCT are too small for one source to be preferred to the other. Even for Group 1B, differences are slight and are unlikely to be significant except where critical assessments of colour rendering apply. The difficulties emerge when sources of lower CRI are to be used. Lamps with improved colour characteristics come onto the market all the time, but for various reasons, there continue to be applications for which Group 2 or even 3 lamps are the best choice. To know that a certain lamp type is, say, in Group 2 and has a CRI of 65, is to know that some distortion of colour appearance will

Table 2.5 *Colour rendering groups*

| Colour rendering group (CRG) | Colour rendering index (CRI) |
| --- | --- |
| 1A | 90–100 |
| 1B | 80–89 |
| 2 | 60–79 |
| 3 | 40–59 |

occur. What is not indicated is whether all colours are slightly affected or just one or two colours are strongly affected, and if the latter, which are the colours?

The reality of the situation is that CRI addresses the needs of specifiers who want to be able to state 'Colour rendering index shall be not less than 85', and feel confident that whatever lighting is installed in that location, it will not cause the appearance of coloured materials to be unacceptable. Lighting designers are often faced with a different need. They are aware that colour rendering qualities of lighting are not simply good or bad, but that the rendering of colours may influence the appearance of objects or the space in which they are located in ways that support certain design objectives. For example, the choice of certain colours by the interior designer could be enhanced by lighting that gives some emphasis to those colours, so that while the lighting may not rate highly on the CRI scale, it may nonetheless suit the particular setting. Where does a lighting designer turn to for information on how different light sources interact with the gamut of surface colours?

The Colour Mismatch Vector (CMV) chart was proposed by van Kemanade and van der Burgt in 1988 as a means of providing more information on the colour rendering properties of lamps than is given by CRI. The mismatch vector is the measure of chromaticity difference between the test source and its reference source for a given colour sample. CRI is based on the average mismatch vector for eight standard test colour samples (TCS), but the averaging process loses all information about which samples are most affected, and the directions in which the colour shifts occur. The CMV chart presents the mismatch vectors for 215 colour samples which cover most of the chromaticity chart. The vectors are shown plotted on a CIELAB chart (while this is a more up-to-date and uniform colour space than the UCS chart used in the CRI system, it has since been superseded by charts based on even more uniform colour space), and an example is shown in Figure 2.18. The colour rendering characteristics of this ceramic metal halide are beautifully revealed.

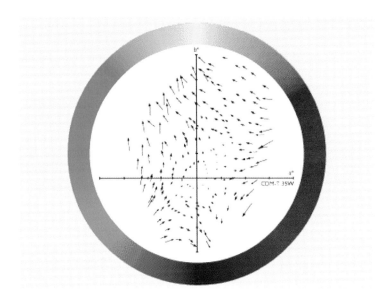

**Figure 2.18:**  *A chromatic mismatch vector (CMV) chart, where the vector arrows represent the differences in CIE LAB space for 215 test colour samples under a test source, compared with a reference source. Rotational directions indicate hue differences, and radial directions indicate saturation differences*

Vectors pointing towards the centre of the chart indicate hues that will be desaturated by the lighting, and this occurs for reds and, to a lesser extent, blues. Arrows pointing away from the centre indicate increased saturation, which occurs for yellow-greens. Radial arrows indicate hue shifts, and strong red-purples are shifted towards blue. Generally, less saturated colours are less affected. This example has been taken from the Philips Lighting website, and it may be noted that the two authors of CMV were Philips staff members. It is to be regretted that the lighting industry has not seen fit to standardize this highly informative form of presentation.

A lighting designer's concerns for colour rendering are much more demanding than those of a specifier. It is not a matter of whether colour appearance will be affected by lighting, but how it will be affected. What sort of chromatic impact is wanted for a public library, or a late-night bar, or an ice hockey stadium? Careful observation of the 'ColorChecker' chart can enable a designer to build up experience of different light sources, and for a specific design application, this can be taken a stage further by examining samples of the selected materials and surface finishes under alternative sources. This is the most reliable approach to developing the ability to advise clients and other designers on lamp choices. Regrettably, the information issued by lamp man-ufacturers is quite uninformative, with the exception of the CMV charts previously mentioned.

## 2.3  Illumination hierarchy

Most forms of life are attracted towards light, and humans are no exception. Phototropism is the process by which attention is drawn towards the brightest part of the field of view. It can be detrimental, as when a glare source creates a conflict between itself and what the person wants to see. For lighting designers, it is a powerful tool, enabling them to selectively direct illumination, drawing attention to what they want people to notice and away from things of secondary or tertiary significance. It forms an underpinning basis for structuring a lighting design concept.

It is important to spend some time looking carefully at how our perception of space and objects are influenced by selective illumination. Provided that illumination is generally adequate, we can make a good job of recognizing differences of object attributes such as lightness, hue and saturation over a very wide range of lighting conditions. If high contrasts are achieved, and particularly where an object that is small in relation to its surroundings receives selective illumination without the source of light being evident, the perception of object attributes may be significantly affected. The object may appear more colourful, or more glossy, than it would appear without the selective illumination. This occurs when visual constancy is overcome, at least to some extent.

### *Illuminance ratios*

Less dramatically, we can more often observe situations in which lighting itself can be seen to vary locally in brightness, hue and saturation. This located illumination-mode perception is distinct from the non-located perception of ambient illumination discussed in Section 2.1. When we place an attractive object, such as a vase of flowers, beside a window to 'catch the light', we do not transform the appearance of the object, but rather we provide a pool of local illumination that identifies this object as having been selected for special attention. Similarly, a distribution of electric lighting can be devised to provide a planned gradation of lighting that expresses the designer's concept of layers of difference. Emphasis is not achieved only by hard-edged contrasts, and may be as effectively achieved by a build-up of light levels that leads the eye progressively towards the designer's objective. High drama requires that surroundings are cast into gloom, but in architectural situations surroundings must remain visible at all times even though they do not demand attention. Planning such a distribution is more than simply selecting a few objects for spotlighting. It involves devising an ordered distribution of lighting to achieve a *hierarchy of illuminance*.

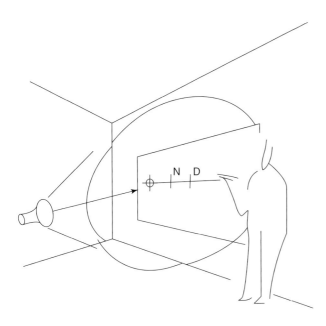

The concept of a hierarchy of illuminance has been developed by J.A. Lynes (1987), who introduces his students to the topic through an exercise in perceived difference of illuminance. His simple procedure is illustrated in Figure 2.19. He stands in front of his class with a spotlight shining onto a white screen. Point 0 is the brightest spot, and he obtains the consensus of the class where to mark 'N' so that it corresponds to a 'noticeable difference of brightness'. Then D is a distinct difference, S a strong difference, and E an emphatic difference. Then he takes an illuminance meter, measures the level at each point, and calculates the illuminance ratios.

The author has conducted this exercise with students on numerous occasions. Perhaps the first surprise is to find how easy it is to obtain consensus, and the second is how well the results are repeated year after year. Typical results are given in Table 2.6. Of course this is not good science, and proper experimental control would no doubt reveal significant inter-personal differences, as well as aspects of the viewing conditions that could exert influence over the results. Even so, it is worth doing. It is a revealing exercise in observation, and furthermore, it gives useful guidance for lighting design. The designer's aim is not that people will think (let alone say), 'That's a noticeable difference of illumination brightness.' However, if the aim is to achieve a difference that is sufficient to be noticed, then you can forget about 10% or 20% differences. Unless you provide a difference of at least 1.5:1, you might just as well stay with uniform illumination. To achieve a difference that could be described as distinct

Table 2.6  *Perceived differences of illuminance*

| Perceived difference | Illuminance ratio |
| --- | --- |
| Noticeable | 1.5:1 |
| Distinct | 3:1 |
| Strong | 10:1 |
| Emphatic | 40:1 |

or strong, you have got to be quite purposeful about what you are doing, and unless the object is small, an emphatic difference is difficult to achieve in an architectural setting without casting the surroundings into gloom. We will return to this last point, but before we move on, let it be repeated that this is a revealing exercise in observation. Actually doing it, and measuring your own assessments of perceived difference, is instructive. Then following up with observation and measurement in real locations is enormously valuable. The meter tells you nothing useful until you have related its readings to your own experience. The data in Table 2.6 is not offered as a robust guide for lighting design. When you, as a designer, have in mind what is the effect that you want to achieve, the illuminance ratios that you specify should be based on your own observation-based experience.

## Maximum attainable contrast

It's time for another thought exercise. Let us suppose that you are designing a setting in which a white marble sculpture will be presented, and you want to achieve a stunning effect. You want the sculpture to stand out from its background so strikingly that it appears to glow. You want the highest possible target/background contrast. Peter Jay has examined the condition of *maximum attainable contrast* (Jay, 1971), for which the objective is that every lumen provided is incident on the target, and the background is illuminated only by light reflected from the target.

Let us examine this situation analytically. We are going to use mathematics to learn something about lighting, but first we need to be clear about what it is that we are trying to do. The contrast $C$ between a target and its background is defined by the expression $C = (L_t - L_b)/L_b$, where $L_t$ and $L_b$ are target and background luminances respectively. For this exercise we will assume all surfaces to be diffusing reflectors, so we can define contrast in terms of exitance values:

$$C = \frac{M_t - M_b}{M_b}$$

In any enclosed space, the total room surface area $A_{rs}$ is the sum of the areas of the enclosing surfaces and any objects contained within the space. If we direct all of the light from the luminaires onto a target area $A_t$, then the remainder of surface area, which forms the background to the target, is $A_b$, so that $A_{rs} = A_t + A_b$. The background receives only indirect illumination, and the contrast for this condition will be the maximum attainable contrast, $C_{max}$. Target and background illuminances and reflectances are $E_t$, $E_b$, $\rho_t$ and $\rho_b$ respectively.

The target is completely enclosed in a space of exitance $M_b$, and the indirect component of its average illuminance will be equal to $M_b$. The direct component of the target illuminance is therefore $(E_t - M_b)$, and the total luminous flux from the luminaires is $A_t(E_t - M_b)$. As we have done previously, we apply the conservation of energy principle to state that this flux must equal the rate of absorption by both the target and background areas, so that:

$$A_t(E_t - M_b) = A_t E_t (1 - \rho_t) + A_b E_b (1 - \rho_b)$$

$$A_t E_t - A_t M_b - A_t E_t + A_t M_t = A_b E_b (1 - \rho_b)$$

$$A_t(M_t - M_b) = A_b E_b (1 - \rho_b)$$

Divide through by $M_b$, noting that $M_b = E_b \rho_b$:

$$\frac{M_t - M_b}{M_b} = \frac{A_b}{A_t} \frac{1 - \rho_b}{\rho_b} = C_{max}$$

This is Jay's expression for maximum attainable contrast (Jay, 1971). It shows that $C_{max}$ is the product of two factors, one being the ratio of the surface areas $A_b/A_t$, and the other factor, $(1 - \rho_b)/\rho_b$, being dependent only on the background reflectance. Now think back to the white marble statue. These two factors tell us that to maximize the contrast, we need to put the statue into a large space with low surface reflectance. There is nothing surprising about that, until we notice that there is no mention of target reflectance. If we were to replace the white marble statue with a black one, all the exitance values would be reduced proportionately, but the contrast would be unchanged.

Let's look at this expression a bit more carefully. The $(1 - \rho)/\rho$ term is the absorptance/reflectance ratio $\alpha/\rho$, and we found in Section 2.1 that the inverse of this ratio, the reflectance/absorptance ratio, describes the influence of reflectance upon

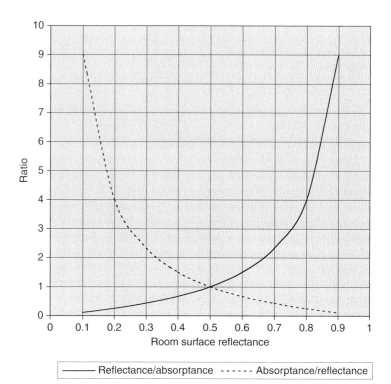

Reflectance/absorptance ------ Absorptance/reflectance

ambient illumination. Both of these ratios are plotted in Figure 2.20, where it can be seen that they mirror each other. This figure breaks down into three zones. Where $\rho$ has a value less than 0.3, room surface exitance will be substantially lower than direct illuminance. Here we have the potential to achieve high target/background contrasts, even where the target area is not much smaller than the background area. Moving to the other side of the chart, where $\rho$ has a value more than 0.7, room surface exitance exceeds direct illuminance by some margin, and while this will give an enhanced sense of overall brightness, high contrasts can be achieved only with targets that are much smaller than their surroundings. For $\rho$ values in the range 0.3 to 0.7, room surface exitance values will be fairly similar to direct illuminances. This equal balance of direct and diffuse illumination components gives scope for providing distinct illumination differences while avoiding strong contrasts, including unwanted shadows. It is also a prescription for practical room surface reflectance values, and guides for good lighting practice invariably recommend reflectances within this range. However, this should not inhibit a creative designer. The important thing is for the designer to have experienced the impact that room surface reflectance can exert upon illumination, and to know when to step outside recommended practice.

Jay's study extended beyond a target object surrounded by a background, to examine the limitations for contrast when the target is part of the space itself. Examples would be a demonstration area in a teaching space, or a dance floor in a restaurant. It must not be lost sight of that the expression is based on the assumption that 100% of the provided luminous flux is incident on the target, so that ambient illumination outside the target area is due only to reflected flux. As the target becomes a larger part of the total surface area, so it becomes more realistic to assume that there is negligible spill light onto the background, and also more probable that the ambient illumination will not need to be supplemented to meet requirements for safe movement.

## Colour contrast

There is another dimension of contrast that is routinely exploited by stage lighting designers, and which has the potential to be influential in architectural lighting design. People are sometimes surprised by the appearance of colour photographs taken outdoors in sunny conditions. Areas in sunlight appear to have a yellow cast, and particularly for snow scenes, shadows appear noticeably blue. The response of daylight colour film is set to render colours for integrated daylight having a colour temperature of 6500 K, but direct sunlight has a CCT around 3000 K while the skylight that is illuminating the shadowed areas has a much higher CCT, perhaps more than 20,000 K. If you look for it you can see it, and many artists, particularly the Impressionists, have recorded their observations of this 'sun and sky' lighting effect.

Stanley McCandless incorporated the effect into his method for stage lighting (McCandless, 1958). The essential feature of McCandless' approach is that all objects on stage are illuminated from opposite sides, with the light from one side having lower CCT to give a sunlight effect, and the light from the other side having higher CCT, perhaps of lower intensity, to give a skylight effect. In this way, a distinct and coherent 'flow of light' is achieved without strong shadows being cast. This means that an actor can have his face in the shadow without losing visibility.

When you are aware of this 'sun and sky' lighting effect, it is surprising how often you can find examples of it in retail display lighting. Car showrooms can achieve very effective display by flooding the space with diffuse light using a 'daylight' type fluorescent lamp which might have a CCT of 5000 K, and providing highlighting from tungsten halogen spotlights having a CCT of 3000 K. Demands to limit lighting power loads have encouraged more use of fluorescent lamps in retail stores, and examples of 'sun and sky' are becoming more common. A clothing store might use halogen spotlights to strongly highlight selected items that are arranged as vertical displays, while relying on the cooler appearance of fluorescent lighting to reveal the daylight colours of the merchandise that the customers handle. Blue is a frequently used colour for the internal surfaces of display cabinets that have internal spotlights, and of course it gives the sky effect to the shadows. Everybody sees effects of this sort, but it takes a lighting designer to observe the visual effect and to mentally analyse it.

## 2.4 The 'flow of light'

Thus far we have considered illumination as a two-dimensional quantity, and that is its status in illumination engineering where it is often defined in terms of the luminous flux density 'at a point on a surface'. The implication is that light has no visible effect in space, unless it is dispersed by particles such as mist or smoke, so we need concern ourselves only with light that is incident on a surface.

In this section we explore a quite different way of envisaging light. Consider for a moment: the room in which you are currently located is full of light. Look around yourself. There is no part of the room where things could disappear through lack of light. There are no black holes on this planet, let alone in your room. Think now of your room as being a three-dimensional light field. Get a friend to walk around the room, facing you all the time, and carefully observe how the changing balance of lighting within your light field affects your friend's appearance. Look for changes in how directional or diffuse the light is. Differences will be particularly noticeable if your friend passes by a window or a table lamp, as this will generate pronounced differences in your impression of both the directional strength and the direction of the lighting effect. Now think about what it is that you actually look at in this room. Do you spend much time gazing at the walls and ceiling, or are you more interested in the things inside the room? It should be clear that the directional nature of lighting has a lot to do with how lighting affects the appearance of three-dimensional objects.

### The three lighting patterns

The three objects in Figure 2.21 are all small in relation to the light field in which they are located, and it can be assumed

Figure 2.21: *Three objects in a light field*

that their lighting conditions are very similar. However, they have interacted with the light field in three very different ways. The peg on a disc reveals a sharply defined shadow pattern, which is quite different from the pattern of reflected highlights revealed by the glossy black sphere. Different again is the shading pattern revealed by the matt white sphere. The terms shadow pattern and shading pattern tend to be confused, but their appearances are distinct, as are the means by which they are formed. The shadow pattern requires a shadow caster and a receiving surface, whereas the shading pattern is formed by the changing orientation of a convex three-dimensional surface.

These three lighting patterns: the *shadow pattern*, the *highlight pattern*, and the *shading pattern*, are the directional lighting effects of a three-dimensional object interacting with a light field (Cuttle, 1971). Turning back to Figure 1.4; the peach forms a shading pattern; the apple a highlight pattern; and the pineapple a shadow pattern. Although the patterns are quite distinct on these familiar objects, the three objects in Figure 2.21 have been devised to achieve maximum separation of the three lighting patterns. The appearance of your friend's face is rather more complex than these objects, but if you observe carefully, you will see the three patterns superimposed on his or her features. The eyebrows, nose and chin are shadow casters, and shadow patterns will be formed if the lighting has the right characteristics. Healthy skin has some gloss which will reflect bright elements in the surrounding field, but if these elements are lacking, the result will be a dead pallor. The shading pattern is moulded by the form of the head, bringing out the best (or worst) of your friend's features. If you cannot see all these aspects of appearance, ask your friend to move to a better-lit space. When the lighting is right you will see all three of the lighting patterns.

Now let's take a closer look at the three objects in Figure 2.21. The peg on a disc forms a sharply defined shadow, and slightly above this shadow we can see a much more softly defined shadow. The situation is more easily understood when we examine the glossy black sphere. We can see the reflected highlight of a large light source, and above it the highlight of a much smaller and more intense source. But where is the evidence of these two sources in the shading pattern? The graded illumination distribution that is visible on the surface of the matt white sphere has the appearance of a single direction of light. You could draw an arrow across the sphere indicating this direction, and it does not coincide exactly with your impression of the direction of either of the two light sources. Actually, it lies closer to the direction of the larger, lower source, which is not what you might expect from the appearance of the shadow pattern.

There are requirements for both the object and the lighting for a lighting pattern to be evident. For the object requirements, no shadow pattern will appear without a shadow caster. There can be no highlight pattern without either transparency or surface gloss. No object reveals more simply and clearly the potential of lighting to form a shadow pattern than a matt white sphere. But what do these patterns tell us about the lighting?

The critical lighting factor in producing shadow and highlight patterns is the angular size of the light source, that is to say, how big is the source in relation to its distance from the object. Look again at the shadow pattern in Figure 2.21. The shadow that we notice is not the one due to the source that is producing the highest illuminance, but the one that produces a sharply defined shadow. This is the light source that subtends a small angle at the object. The photograph cannot show the relative brightness of the two highlights on the black sphere, but in the real situation the highlight that gave lustre to the glossy black sphere was, as for the shadow pattern, the highlight that was sharply defined. This subjective characteristic is termed the *sharpness of lighting,* and it relates to the potential of lighting to produce distinct, sharply defined shadow and highlight patterns.

The shading pattern generated by the matt white sphere is quite clear, but it could never appear sharp. In order to describe this impact of the lighting, we have to use different terms. The sphere has the appearance of intercepting a directional flow of light. We could rate this flow on a scale of very weak to very strong: in the case shown, we might describe it as moderately strong. We could describe its direction: from the right, about 30° above the horizontal. Together, these subjective characteristics are termed the *flow of light*, and this term relates to the potential of lighting to produce distinct shading patterns. By the way, if you have not worked it out already, the objects were photographed about two metres back from a window, with a tungsten halogen spotlight located above the window. Perhaps this is not a frequently encountered lighting condition, but it is one that served well to introduce differences between sharpness and flow of light.

The characteristics of lighting that generate shading patterns are quite distinct from those that form highlight and shadow patterns. Figure 2.22 shows the three objects in three different lighting conditions, and this time the lighting conditions were set up in a studio. For case (a), the light source is a compact, high intensity spotlight, and all three lighting patterns are strongly evident. The peg-on-a-disc shows a dense and sharply defined shadow pattern; the highlight pattern revealed by the glossy black sphere is bright and sharply defined so that it gleams; and you could easily place an arrow on the figure to show the direction of the strong flow of light across the matt white sphere. This is unambiguous directional lighting that has the characteristics of both sharpness and flow.

Case (b) shows the effect of adding more spotlights randomly distributed about the object. The shadow pattern cast by the peg-on-a-disc has become more complex, and it has lost some density but not its sharpness. The highlight pattern on the black sphere has lost none of its gleam, although it too has become more complex. What has changed dramatically is the shading pattern. No longer is there a clear sense of a flow of light. The matt white sphere has lost its definition. This lighting has sharpness, but not flow.

Case (c) is another single light source situation, but this time the light source is a diffuse source with a large angular subtense at the object. The shadow and highlight patterns have both softened. The shadow pattern has been diluted almost to the point of vanishing, and the highlight pattern has lost its gleam: but the shading pattern is almost as strong and as definite as it was in case (a). This is lighting that lacks sharpness, but has flow.

Ideally, a fourth case would be shown. You would see the three objects in an integrating sphere. Such lighting provides diffuse,

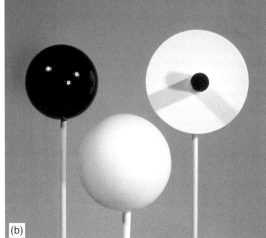

**Figure 2.22:**
*(a) Single point source lighting has both sharpness and flow.*
*(b) Multiple point source lighting has sharpness but not flow.*
*(c) Single diffuse area source lighting has flow, but not sharpness*

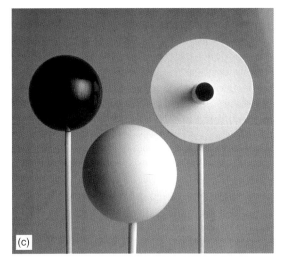

isotropic illumination which is totally lacking in both sharpness and flow. If, like the author, you lack the facility of an integrating sphere, the next best situation in which to observe this condition is the white-out experience of a blizzard.

It requires some careful observation to make the step from these generic objects to the objects that surround us in our daily lives, but a sound understanding of the distinction between the sharpness and the flow of light is essential for describing the spatial characteristics of lighting. The glass-mosaic-covered column shown in Figure 2.23(a) used to form part of Louis Comfort Tiffany's house in Long Island, New York, and now stands in New York's Metropolitan Museum of Art. As it is not susceptible

**Figure 2.23:**
*(a) This column is decorated with glass mosaic, and the lighting generates a brilliant highlight pattern. The column is the work of Louis Comfort Tiffany, and is on display at the New York Metropolitan Museum of Art.*
*(b) Another column displayed at the New York Metropolitan Museum of Art, this time from a 4th century BC Greek temple, has similar lighting which produces a sharply defined shadow pattern.*
*(c) Also from ancient Greece, the Venus di Milo on display at the Museé de Louvre, Paris, has a different quality of lighting that produces a distinct shading pattern*

to damage due to light exposure it is located in a part of the museum that receives ample daylight from a large skylight, although the skylight has been designed to avoid direct sunlight penetration and to admit only diffuse skylight. Nonetheless, the column has a spotlight directed onto it. This has nothing to do with illumination: the role of the spotlight is to provide sharpness. The photograph shows the reflected highlights, and as the column is beside a walkway, these highlights glitter and sparkle as people walk past the column. The skylight provides ample ambient illumination, but the spotlight is needed to provide sharpness.

Figure 2.23(b) shows another column, which stands nearby in the Metropolitan Museum of Art, although its origins are more distant as it comes from a fourth century BC Greek temple. There are no signs of highlights here as there is no gloss to enable it, but sharpness abounds. This architecture developed in a sunny climate, and the sharply incised forms were designed to interact with sunlight. If the museum ceiling could be raised a few metres, a single light source could simulate sunlight and give this artefact something closer to its intended appearance. As it is, several smaller sources are used, and even though they illuminate from opposite directions, they provide the sharpness of lighting that produces the crisp shadow patterns evident on the ancient Greek artisan's handiwork.

For Figure 2.23(c), we stay with carved stone from ancient Greece, but we move to the Louvre in Paris to view at what is probably the world's most famous statue, the Venus di Milo. There is no sharpness of lighting here, but there is a beautiful interaction of form and light. This is flow of light. The large angular size of light source avoids sharp-edged shadows appearing on the Venus' smoothly rounded forms, and the low surrounding reflectances ensure a flow of light that has the strength to give depth to the shading patterns.

The terms 'sharpness' and 'flow' describe subjective characteristics of lighting. Now we need to move on to objective characteristics, that is to say, what are measurable and predictable aspects of lighting that relate to these subjective characteristics? Sharpness of lighting is examined in the following section, and the remainder of this section is devoted to the flow of light.

## The illumination solid

The concept of the 'flow of light' has been proposed by J.A. Lynes (1966) to describe the potential of lighting to produce

Figure 2.24: *The flow of light being examined by using a small matt white sphere to reveal the shading pattern*

distinct shading patterns. Figure 2.24 shows a matt white sphere comprising a table-tennis ball cemented to a cocktail stick and sprayed, and the reader is strongly recommended to make one of these devices. Within a light field, it reveals simply and clearly the variation of the potential of lighting to produce shading patterns. It is evident that a shading pattern is a distribution of surface illuminance produced by the sphere's interaction with the three-dimensional illuminance distribution generated by the light field. The notion of being able to measure or predict this varying quantity might seem to be a formidable problem, but fortunately a solution is to hand.

We need a form of measurement that characterizes the three-dimensional illuminance distribution at a point in space. How might you envisage such a distribution? Let's suppose that you mount a conventional illuminance meter (more on these in Chapter 3) onto the head of a tripod that enables you to rotate the meter through 360°. Figure 2.25 shows the contour for a single small source S without any reflected light. The maximum illuminance occurs in the direction of the source, for which the angle of incidence on the plane of measurement is 0°, and for other directions it declines in accordance with the cosine of the angle of incidence. The contour appears as a circle, but the three-dimensional illuminance distribution is a sphere with P on the surface of the sphere. This is a three-dimensional cosine distribution.

In a real illuminated space, not only does every light source contribute its own spherical illuminance distribution to the total, but also every luminous point visible from P. The total is a sum of spheres of varying magnitudes, and such a distribution is shown

Figure 2.25:   *The spatial illuminance distribution due to a single point source is a three-dimensional cosine distribution*

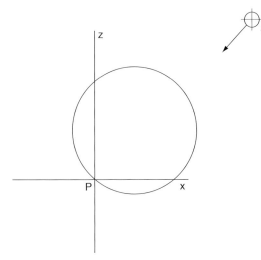

Figure 2.26:   *The illumination solid in a real space. The cosine distribution defines the illumination vector, and for any axis through P, the vector value equals the illuminance difference in the opposite directions*

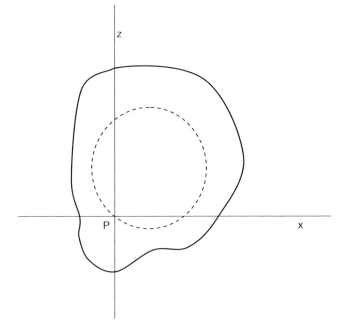

in Figure 2.26. You can think of this distribution as a lumpy but smoothly rounded potato, as it is a sum of spheres, with three long needles pierced through it, representing the x, y and z axes and intersecting at P. In every direction from P, the distance to the skin of the potato is proportional to the illuminance measured at P on a plane normal to that direction. If the intersection point is near the middle of the potato, the appearance of the flow of light at P will be weak, and the shading pattern on an object placed at P will be indistinct. If the intersection point is near the potato's skin, the flow of light will appear strong, and the direction of flow will appear to be from the direction of most potato.

A cosine distribution is shown within the illumination solid. This is the resultant vector of the solid, and we will go into this more deeply in Part Three. In the meantime, it should be noted that this distribution accounts for the asymmetry of the illumination solid about point P. It is the sum of illuminance differences in opposite directions, and is due to light arriving from every direction. Although it appears similar to the cosine distribution shown in Figure 2.25, it is not due to a single source, and in fact, there may be no light source at all in the location corresponding to S in Figure 2.25.

Here we are using measurement to create a model that characterizes a subjective aspect of lighting. Even so, we cannot specify lighting in terms of pierced potatoes. We can start by eliminating vegetable references and instead think in terms of an *illumination solid,* being the three-dimensional form whose contour represents the illuminance distribution. However, it is still an awkward device to use for specifying lighting. We need a way to characterize the illumination solid mathematically, and for this we employ the *illumination vector.*

A familiar use of vectors is to represent lines of force. In Figure 2.27(a), P is a point in a bridge or some such structure. F1 indicates the gravitational force at P due to the mass of the bridge. F2 is the lateral force to support the span of the bridge. F3 is the resultant of these component forces, indicating the magnitude and direction of force acting at P. In this scheme of events, parallel components in the same direction are additive, and in opposite directions they are subtractive.

We have observed that the flow of light appears to act towards the point of concern 'from the direction of most potato', and for this reason we adopt a quite different way of depicting the illumination vector. Figure 2.27(b) is the equivalent of Figure 2.27(a), where two small light sources provide the component vectors, and they, as well as the resultant vector, are shown acting towards the point. This form of representation coincides more readily with the impression of a 'flow of light' when an object is located at P, but apart from this difference of representation, the illumination vector is a regular, law-abiding vector. There is, however, a difference in how we treat source vectors that do not contribute towards the resultant illumination vector. Equal and opposite forces that cancel out are of no concern to the bridge

*Figure 2.27:   (a) Perpendicular lines of force and the resultant acting at P. (b) An object intercepts the flow of light, and the illumination vector components and the resultant are represented acting towards the point*

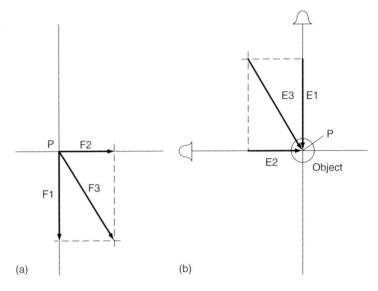

(a)                                                     (b)

*Figure 2.28:   x, y and z axes intersecting at P. Always the z axis is vertical, and generally the y axis is arranged to be parallel to the long axis of the room*

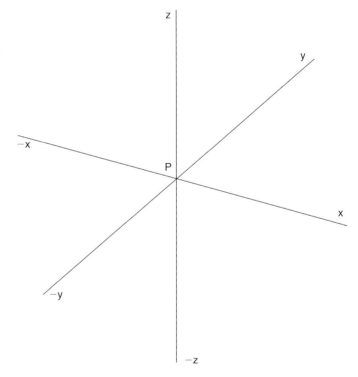

engineer, but equal and opposite components of the illumination solid do concern the lighting designer.

Figure 2.28 shows the point P defined in space by the intersection of dimensions on *x*, *y* and *z* axes. By convention, the *x* and *y* axes are horizontal, and the *z* axis is vertical. While it

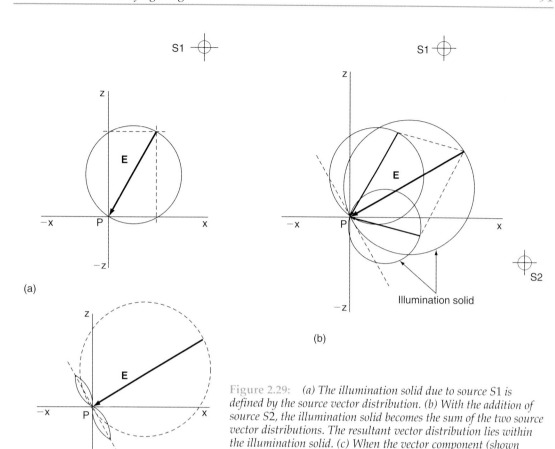

(a)

(b)

(c)

Figure 2.29: *(a) The illumination solid due to source S1 is defined by the source vector distribution. (b) With the addition of source S2, the illumination solid becomes the sum of the two source vector distributions. The resultant vector distribution lies within the illumination solid. (c) When the vector component (shown dashed) is subtracted from the illumination solid the remainder is the symmetric solid (shown solid). The illumination solid comprises these two components, one totally asymmetric and one totally symmetric about P*

is convenient to show the following examples on a two-dimensional vertical plane through P, we should not lose sight of the fact that we are concerned with three-dimensional illuminance distributions.

Figure 2.29(a) shows the illumination vector **E** due to source S1, which equals the diameter of the cosine distribution and terminates at P. (Note that a bold symbol is used to indicate a vector.) It may be noted that both the magnitude and direction of **E** are defined by the components $E_{(x)}$ and $E_{(z)}$. Source S2 is added in Figure 2.29(b), and the individual source vectors are added to give the resultant vector **E**. The distribution of **E** is still a cosine distribution whose surface passes through P, and again **E** may be defined by components on the *x* and *z* axes. However, the illumination solid, indicated by the perimeter contour, extends beyond the vector distribution. The dashed line through P that is normal to **E** shows the illuminances normal to the vector direction, and *these are equal and opposite.* In Figure 2.29(c), the illumination vector distribution has been subtracted from the illumination solid (its former position is indicated by the dashed circle) and what remains is a rather oddly shaped distribution that has the property that the distance from P to its surface in any direction is exactly equal to the distance to the surface in the opposite direction. We have broken the illumination solid into two components:

- A *vector component*, which has a cosine distribution, whose diameter is equal to the vector magnitude |**E**|, and whose surface passes through the point P so that it is totally asymmetric about P.

- A *symmetric component,* which is totally symmetric about P in that its magnitude in any direction is equal to its magnitude in the opposite direction.

In Figure 2.30(a), we leave S1 where it is, but we swing S2 round to a different location. It is at the same distance from P, so the vector component that it provides is of the same magnitude, but it comes from a different direction. Although the amount of light arriving at P is unchanged, **E** is greatly diminished. So where has the light gone? Figure 2.30(b) shows the vector component subtracted from the illumination solid, and it can be seen that we now have a much larger symmetric component. We could proceed to add a third, fourth or fifth light source; we could continue until we have an infinite number of light sources; and always the contribution of an individual source can be assessed by adding its vector to the illumination solid.

This exploration leads us to a remarkable conclusion. The illumination solid at any illuminated point in space can be separated into two components: the vector and symmetric components.

- The cosine distribution of the *vector component* could be reproduced by a single small light source in the direction of the vector. In an actual situation there may be no light source at all in the vector direction, but the asymmetric component of the illumination solid will be as if such a source does exist.

- The *symmetric component* is the sum of equal and opposite components. An integrating sphere would provide a uniform symmetric distribution, but this is a special case. The distribution of the symmetric component is not necessarily uniform, but it is in equilibrium about the point.

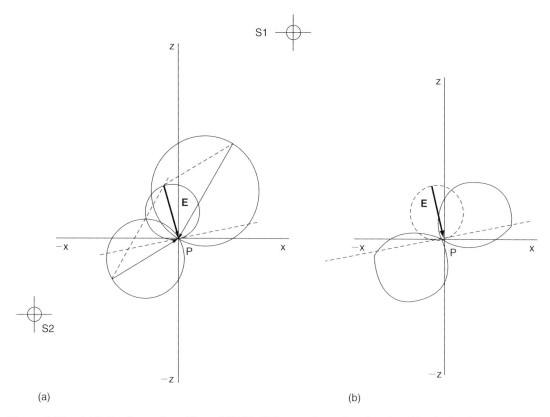

(a)    (b)

**Figure 2.30:** *(a) Following on from Figure 2.23(b), S2 is moved round to the other side of P but kept at the same distance so that it produces the same illuminance at P. The resultant vector is much reduced. (b) When the vector component is subtracted, the remainder is a much increased symmetric component. A spherical object at P would have the same quantity of luminous flux incident on its surface as in the previous case, but it would now be more uniformly distributed and the flow of light would appear much weaker*

In Part Three we will work through an application that involves these insights, but for the while the important thing is to recognize that, no matter how many light sources are involved or how complex is the light field, the illumination solid can be envisaged as comprising these two components, each having distinctive and opposite characteristics.

No object reveals the illumination solid more clearly than a matt white sphere. It is a rewarding experience to carry a sphere (Figure 2.24) through spaces that have distinct directional qualities of lighting, particularly spaces with wallwashing or side windows, and to observe the above-mentioned changes of the flow of light. If a flow of light is visible, it is due to the asymmetry of the illumination solid. This asymmetry cannot occur in more than one direction, no matter how the light sources are distributed. The asymmetry of the illumination solid is due to the vector component, and the spatial illumination distribution that reveals it is identical to the illuminance distribution of a single, small spotlight. If you are able to mentally extract this component, you are left with the symmetric component. While this component may be quite non-uniform, because it is symmetric, its distribution on the hemisphere that faces you is mirrored on the hemisphere that is facing away from you. If you fix the location of the sphere and walk around it through 180°, the only difference of appearance will be due to the vector component. These findings are not intuitive. First and foremost, the illumination vector concept promotes understanding of the principles that govern the formation of shading patterns, but it takes observation to develop the experience to make use of this insight in lighting design.

For the symmetric component to have a distinctly non-uniform distribution, there has to be a directional 'equal and opposite' distribution of incident light. An example would be outdoors at night on a lit walkway, and mid-way between luminaires. For indoor situations, indirect light will often make non-uniformity of the symmetric component barely visible. Where the level of indirect illuminance equals or exceeds the direct illuminance ($\rho > 0.5$ for $\rho/\alpha > 1$; see Section 2.1), the symmetric component usually is defined adequately by its average value. As you walk around a fixed sphere, you see a different hemisphere from every direction of view. The average illuminance of your visible hemisphere due to the vector component obviously will change with direction of view, but not so for the average illuminance due to the symmetric component. Notice again that the vector component has a simple cosine distribution, so that variation of the appearance of the shading pattern on the sphere with changing direction of view is simple and predictable. Again, these findings are not intuitive, and it requires careful observation to be convinced of their validity. However, this is the key to understanding what visual effects can be achieved, and what can not be achieved, by shading patterns.

While the balance of asymmetric and symmetric components is an excellent way to envisage the three-dimensional illuminance distribution, it is conventional to employ the vector/scalar ratio as the indicator of the apparent strength of the flow of light.

## *Vector/scalar ratio*

Scalar illuminance is mean spherical illuminance, so if you bring back into view the small matt white sphere, it is the average illuminance over the whole surface of the sphere. Light is evaluated without regard for the direction from which it has come, so that scalar illuminance may be thought of as a measure of the ambient light level at the point. Note that a scalar quantity has only magnitude, unlike a vector which has magnitude and direction. For comparison, air temperature is also a scalar, as the measured value does not depend on the direction in which you point the thermometer.

Scalar illuminance is equal to the average value of the illumination solid, which is the sum of the vector and symmetric solids. While the illumination vector is the vectorial sum of individual source vectors, scalar illuminance is their arithmetical sum. Figure 2.31(a) shows a disc of radius $r$ illuminated by source S. The disc intercepts $F$ lumens, so that the illuminance of the disc $E = F/(\pi r^2)$, and in the absence of any other light, this equals the magnitude of the illumination vector $|\mathbf{E}|$. In Figure 2.31(b), the disc is replaced by a sphere that is also of radius $r$ and intercepts $F$ lumens. The average illuminance of the surface of the disc $E = F/(4\pi r^2)$, which is the value of the scalar illuminance $E_{sr}$. It can be seen that the vector component contributes one quarter of its value to the scalar illuminance, so that the maximum possible value for the vector/scalar ratio, which would occur with a collimated beam of light in a totally black room, is $|\mathbf{E}|/E_{sr} = 4.0$. In this way, we can arrive at the general expression that applies to any illumination solid:

$$F_{sr} = |\mathbf{E}|/4 + {\sim}E_{av}$$

where ${\sim}E_{av}$ is the average value of the symmetric component.

It is time for another thought exercise. As a first step towards envisaging how the vector/scalar ratio is influenced by the surrounding luminous field, consider the 'sphere-in-a-sphere'

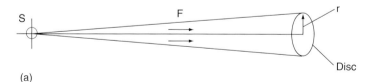

(a)

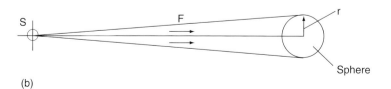

(b)

Figure 2.31:   (a) A disc illuminated by source S. (b) A sphere illuminated by source S

**Figure 2.32:** *A spherical object is surrounded by a diffuse spherical source, the angular subtense of the source being defined by the semi-subtense angle $\gamma/2$*

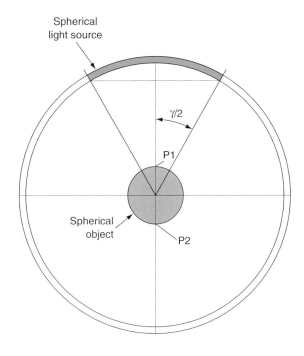

shown in Figure 2.32. The object is surrounded by a spherical light source of variable subtense, so that when the semi-subtense angle $(\gamma/2) \rightarrow 0°$ the object is illuminated by a point source, and when $(\gamma/2) = 180°$ it is at the centre of an integrating sphere. As the light source enlarges, its luminance reduces to maintain the illuminance at point P1 at a constant value. For the point source condition $(\gamma/2) \rightarrow 0°$, Figure 2.33 shows the illumination vector **E** to have a relative value of one so that the scalar illuminance $E_{sr} = 0.25$, and $|\mathbf{E}|/E_{sr} = 4$. For this condition, half of the object is in darkness. As the source enlarges, no light reaches P2 until $(\gamma/2) > 90°$, and as $|\mathbf{E}| = E_{P1} - E_{P2}$, it retains its value up to this point. However, as the boundary of the illuminated area creeps towards P2, $E_{sr}$ rises and $|\mathbf{E}|/E_{sr}$ gradually falls. As $(\gamma/2) \rightarrow 180°$, $E_{sr}$ climbs to equal $E_{P1}$, and $|\mathbf{E}|/E_{sr}$ reduces to zero.

The next stage is to pursue observation with measurement in a variety of spaces. Measurement of the illumination vector and scalar illuminance is discussed in Section 3.1, and it has to be admitted that it is made slightly tedious by the lack of commercially available meters developed for this purpose. However, a procedure is described for taking measurements on the six faces of a cube using a conventional illuminance meter, enabling the direction and magnitude of **E** and the value of $E_{sr}$ to be calculated. To actually experience the correspondence between

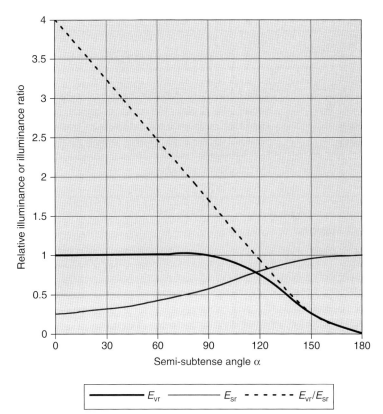

observation and measurement in real situations is enormously valuable. In particular, to 'see with one's own eyes' how the visible effect of multiple light sources is integrated into an over-all direction of flow, and the crucial role of interreflected light on the apparent strength of the flow, is to gain understanding of the workings of the three-dimensional light field.

These observations may be compared with the results of studies of people's preferences for the appearance of the human features. In an interview situation, it has been found that $|\mathbf{E}|/E_{sr}$ values in the range 1.2 to 1.8 are preferred (Cuttle, 1967). More generally, correspondence between $|\mathbf{E}|/E_{sr}$ and subjective assessments of the strength of the flow of light are indicated in Table 2.7. The preference studies also indicated that people like the flow of light to be from the side rather than from overhead, with a preference for a vector altitude between 15° and 45°, as shown in Figure 2.34.

While the flow of light is primarily determined by the three-dimensional illuminance distribution, colour can add a subtle

Table 2.7  *Vector/scalar ratio and the flow of light*

| Vector/scalar ratio | Assessment of appearance | Application |
|---|---|---|
| 4.0 (max) | | |
| 3.5 | Dramatic | |
| 3.0 | Very strong | Strong contrasts, detail in shadows not discernible |
| 2.5 | Strong | Suitable for display; too harsh for human features |
| 2.0 | Moderately strong | Pleasant appearance for distant faces (formal) |
| 1.5 | Moderately weak | Pleasant appearance for near faces (informal) |
| 1.0 | Weak | Soft lighting for subdued effects |
| 0.5 | Very weak | Flat shadow-free lighting |
| 0 (min) | | |

Figure 2.34:  *Observers preferences for vector altitude when viewing human features*

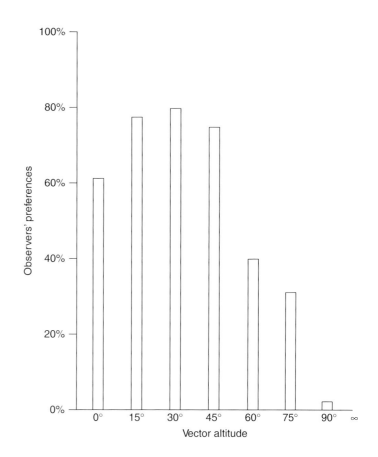

but significant effect. The stage lighting method devised by Stanley McCandless (1958) in which modelling effects are accentuated by colour differences has been described in Section 2.3. The illumination provided by a sunny day comprises a diffuse, high colour temperature component from the blue sky and a directional, low colour temperature component of sunlight. McCandless employed this effect, at much lower illuminances, to give the appearance of a distinct flow of light without creating shadows that would obscure detail, such as an actor's facial expression. Some architectural lighting designers have made use of this approach. An example would be to provide indirect lighting using 4000 K fluorescent lamps, and to add selective highlighting using 3000 K tungsten halogen spotlights. Skilfully done, the combination is an attractive effect reminiscent of warm sunlight and cool daylight, and may cause the flow of light to appear stronger than would be expected from the vector/scalar ratio.

## 2.5 The 'sharpness' of lighting

As explained in the previous section, the concept of 'sharpness' refers to the potential of lighting to create sharply defined highlight and shadow patterns. Three-dimensional objects that have appropriate forms to generate shadow patterns, or surfaces with properties that may generate highlight patterns, must be present for these lighting patterns to occur, but it needs to be kept in mind that sharpness describes a characteristic of lighting rather than of object appearance. As stated above, lighting that has 'sharpness' has the potential to form sharply defined shadow and highlight patterns, but such patterns will occur only if suitable objects are present.

Figure 2.35 shows a surface illuminated by a disc-shaped light source. Imagine that we can vary either the luminance or the area of this source, and suppose that we want to double the illuminance at P. Unless the source becomes very large (i.e., the angle $\gamma$ subtended at P exceeds 70°), it makes little difference whether we keep the light source the same size and double its luminance, or keep the luminance the same and double its area.

However, if an object at P has properties which reveal highlight or shadow patterns, the appearance of the object may be strongly affected by the angular size of the light source. In the previous section we examined in some detail the difference between the three lighting patterns that may be formed on the surface of different types of three-dimensional objects. As illustrated by the 'sphere in a sphere' example (Figure 2.32), the shading pattern is only gradually affected by the angular size of the light source until the source becomes distinctly large. In this section we examine the much more dramatic effect of source subtense upon the highlight and shadow patterns. It is

Figure 2.35:  *Surface illuminated by a disc-shaped light source*

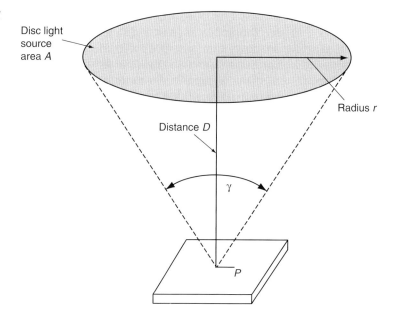

Figure 2.36:  *Comparison viewing panel*

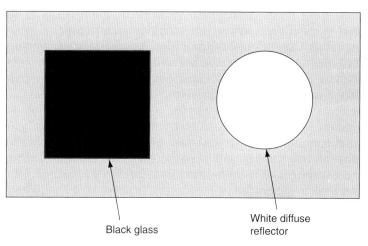

the potential of lighting to produce these patterns that may be described as the 'sharpness' of lighting.

## Light source angular size

The influence of light source size has been explored by J.A. Worthey (1990), who has proposed a thought experiment that involves viewing side-by-side the black glass and the white diffuser panel shown in Figure 2.36. Imagine that you place this reference viewing panel onto the surface at P shown in Figure 2.35. This is the two-dimensional equivalent of the glossy black and matt white spheres examined in the previous section. The question is: How does the brightness of the reflected image of the light source seen in the black glass compare with the brightness of the white diffuser?

Let's suppose that we maintain the illuminance at a constant value. The luminance of the light source is $L$, and the approximate size of the solid angle $\Omega$ that it subtends at P is given in steradians by dividing its area $A$ by the square of distance $D$ ($\Omega \approx A/D^2$). To maintain the illuminance at a constant value, we need to ensure that $L\Omega = $ const, so that if we reduce $\Omega$, $L$ must be correspondingly increased. The brightness of the white diffuser will not change because the illuminance does not change, but the image in the black glass will become progressively brighter. But that's not all. The image also becomes smaller, so that as it becomes more intensely bright, it becomes easier to avoid the reflection in the glass by moving your head. If there are no other sources of light and the surround to the light source is dark, the glass now looks completely black. We need to think more carefully about this.

One of the measures used by lighting engineers to evaluate alternative lighting systems is the Contrast Rendering Factor (CRF). Research has shown that the visibility of reading tasks may be adversely affected if light sources are located in the 'offending zone' (Figure 2.37), as this situation has the potential to produce 'veiling reflections' which have the effect of reducing the contrast between the white paper and the text (Section 2.4). If the paper could be a perfect diffuser and the text a perfect absorber, the source location would make no difference, but this does not occur in practice. All practical reading matter exhibits some degree of gloss, and some, particularly graphic material, is printed on high-gloss art paper. The standard for CRF is the level of contrast for the task concerned that would be obtained under sphere lighting. If we place a reading task at P in Figure 2.35, and we increase the source size so that the subtense angle $\gamma = 180°$ (for this condition, $\Omega = 2\pi$ str), then CRF = 1.0 whether the material is matt or glossy. Lighting engineers strive to achieve this condition. For many situations where visual performance is a concern, such as an open plan office, there really is no practical way of providing lighting that does not involve locating luminaires in the offending zone. For reading tasks that exhibit even small degrees of gloss, this will have the effect of reducing the task contrast and lowering the CRF to less than one. To minimize this effect, lighting systems that have low luminance in the offending zone are favoured. Unfortunately, this has become a hallmark of lighting quality

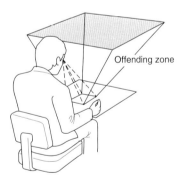

**Figure 2.37:** *Luminaires located within the 'offending zone' are likely to produce veiling reflections, and for clerical tasks, these will have the effect of reducing the task contrast*

even in situations where reading performance is of little or no importance.

Why unfortunately? Figure 2.38 shows three views of a glass tumbler which contains some water. Both of these substances are transparent, so why are they not invisible? In Section 1.2 we saw that while glass and water both transmit light, they also reflect some of it, and the transmitted component is refracted. In Figure 2.38(a), we can see that the tumbler and the water act both as a distorting lens and as a distorting mirror. In Figure 2.38(b), the lens effect has been largely obscured by eliminating the background pattern, but the mirror effect is still evident, and this is mostly due to distorted images of the light source. From this viewpoint, the flat air/water surface does not catch one of these bright images, but the curved surface of the glass picks up highlights from all around. It is at the zones of sharpest curvature, particularly the base and the top rim, that the highlights are compressed and simply pile up. To reveal this point clearly, we take away the exitance of the background diffuser in Figure 2.38(c) and see the object revealed by highlights. These highlights are specular reflections (Section 1.2) and they are produced in the same way as the veiling reflections, but these reflections are giving us the visual information that makes the tumbler and its contents visible. They inform the viewer, and for fine glassware, they may give pleasure or even delight. How else could we experience the sparkle of cut crystal or the glitter of jewellery?

Let us return to the thought experiment and the reference viewing panel. If we reduce the source size so that the solid angle $\Omega$ becomes a very small angle, we have to increase $L$ to a very high value in order to maintain the illuminance at P, and we will see a sharp, bright reflected image in the black glass. If it obscures detail that we want to see, it requires only a small movement of the head to avoid the effect. Now replace the black and white object with a glossy two-dimensional task, such as a page of text from an art magazine, or a glossy photograph. In the area where the highlight occurs, the task contrast is obliterated and CRF = 0. However, adjacent to this area, the appearance of the task is excellent: the black ink of the text looks truly black, and the colours of the photograph appear saturated and rich. Imagine that we leave these materials in place and enlarge the source, in this case lowering its luminance to maintain constant illuminance. We watch the zone of obliterated detail expand like a growing amoeba. As its brightness continues to diminish, some details become faintly visible, but at the same time the zone of high visibility is vanishing.

Figure 2.38:   *(a) The glass and the water can be seen to act both as a distorting lens and as a distorting mirror. (b) The lens effect is largely obscured by eliminating the background pattern. (c) The lighting is unchanged, but by eliminating light diffused by reflection the pattern of light source reflections is clearly revealed*

If we extend to the point where the 'task' is surrounded by a luminous hemisphere, we have sphere lighting, and CRF = 1.0. We can read the detail and we can recognize the photograph, but they lack the depth of contrast that we saw before, and no amount of head movement can restore that level of visibility.

Worthey's example is described as a thought exercise as it is unlikely that any reader would be able to rig up and control a light source to provide the viewing conditions. Even so, it is very worthwhile to set up a situation in which you can compare the effects of diffused and directional lighting upon the appearances of matt and glossy materials involving text and colour. Much of conventional lighting practice has developed in response to lighting problems in workplaces, particularly offices, and the solutions have then become universally accepted as 'good lighting practice'. It is wonderfully instructive to actually see what is the potential for lighting to achieve contrasts of brightness and colour, and to compare this with the lifeless appearance that often passes for good lighting practice.

## *The role of gloss*

It is appropriate to ask: Why are glossy magazines glossy? Why is it usual for colour photographs to be printed on glossy paper? Such materials are shunned for office stationery, and laboratory studies confirm that these materials have the potential to lead to serious visibility loss. The answer to this mystery is there for all to experience. Pick up a glossy magazine, and if the sun or your desk lamp produces a bright reflection on the page, without consideration or hesitation you will tilt the page, move your head, or perhaps a bit of both, to improve the contrast rendering. For the best effect, not only do the sources of light need to be small and of high luminance, but they need to be surrounded by areas of relatively low luminance. In short, to achieve high contrasts in the material that you are looking at, you need high contrasts in the surrounding light field.

It is necessary to experience this by observation in order to be convinced, because recommendations for good lighting practice invariably advise against providing such conditions. We are assured that these recommendations are based on experience, and so no designer should thoughtlessly ignore them. High-contrast environments may cause discomfort, particularly for people who are subjected to prolonged exposure, and where high-luminance light sources or their images occur randomly in the visual field, they represent unwanted distractions. The difference comes when the images of high-luminance sources, whether due to reflection or refraction, impart meaning to the scene, and also when it is practical to adopt a viewing geometry that enables detail and colour to be experienced without veiling reflections. A decision to fly in the face of experience needs to be undertaken with a clear understanding of both the advantages and the pit-falls that may be involved.

## The highlight ratio

In Section 1.2 it was noted that most of the materials that make up the surfaces and objects that surround us are dielectric materials, and for a broad range of angles of incidence, approx-imately 4 per cent of incident light is specularly reflected from the surface. Worthey has defined three '4 per cent rules' which he describes in terms of the black/white reference object.

1.  If light is incident more or less normal to an air–dielectric interface, such as the black glass, about 4 per cent will be reflected at the surface.

2.  If a source is imaged in a shiny dielectric surface, the lumi-nance of the veiling reflection (or highlight) is about 4 per cent of the source luminance.

3.  Under sphere lighting, the veiling reflection in the black glass is about 4 per cent of the luminance of the white sur-face next to it.

(Worthey, 1989b)

These three rules provide a basis for analysing the occurrence of highlights. Whether the light source is large or small, the luminance of its image in the black glass:

$$L_{bl} = 0.94L_s$$

where $L_s$ is source luminance.

The exitance of a surface is given by the product of its illumi-nance and its reflectance, $M = E\rho$, and for a perfectly diffusing surface, luminance is given by the expression $L = E\rho/\pi$. The illu-minance due to a diffusing disc source of luminance $L$ is given by the expression $E = \pi L \sin^2(\gamma/2)$, where $\gamma$ is the subtense angle of the source (Figure 2.35). If we assume that our white comparison surface is not only perfectly diffusing but also is a total reflector (i.e., $\rho = 1.0$; some reference white surfaces come very close to this), then the luminance of the white surface is given by:

$$L_w = E/\pi$$
$$= L_s \sin^2(\gamma/2)$$

We can express this difference in terms of the highlight ratio (HLR):

$$HLR = L_{bl}/L_w$$

$$= 0.04/\sin^2(\gamma/2)$$

We should examine this expression with care. Perhaps the first surprise is that HLR depends only on the subtense angle, $\gamma$. One might suppose that the way to increase highlights would be to increase the luminous intensity, but that affects $L_{bl}$ and $L_w$ equally, leaving HLR unchanged. So, what is the effect of varying $\gamma$? If we start with a full hemisphere of light source, so that $\gamma = 180°$, HLR has a value of just 0.04, meaning that, for dielectric surfaces, a specular image of the light source has a luminance of just 4 per cent of the luminance of a diffusing white surface. These images can hardly be described as highlights, as they would barely be visible even on black surfaces. If we progressively reduce $\gamma$, it has to be brought down to a value of just 23° before HLR = 1.0, at which point 'highlights' have the same luminance as matt white surfaces, which may be visible, but will hardly be a striking visual effect. We have to reduce $\gamma$ down to 7° for HLR = 10, and down to 2.25° for HLR = 100. Now we are getting some visual effects that can legitimately be described as highlights, but it can be seen that the effect of $\gamma$ is very non-linear.

We can take this study one step further by expanding the above expression so that subtense is stated in terms of solid angle $\Omega$, rather than degrees of angle, using the formula $\Omega = 2\pi[1 - \cos(\alpha/2)]$, so that:

$$HLR = 0.04/\sin^2\left[\cos^{-1}\left(1 - \frac{\Omega}{2\pi}\right)\right]$$

At first this looks like an unwarranted complication, but actually, the relationship is simplified by the fact that HLR is a linear function of $\Omega$ as shown in Figure 2.39. This makes it relatively straightforward to consider sources with very small angular subtense which have correspondingly high HLR values, and Table 2.8 lists HLR values for a variety of familiar light sources, all at a standard distance of 2 m. Note that the subtense solid angle is measured in microsteradians, where 1 $\mu$str = $10^{-6}$ str.

We now have a theoretical basis to explore various practical options, enabling us to examine how HLR influences the sharpness lighting, evident in the appearance of highlight and shadow

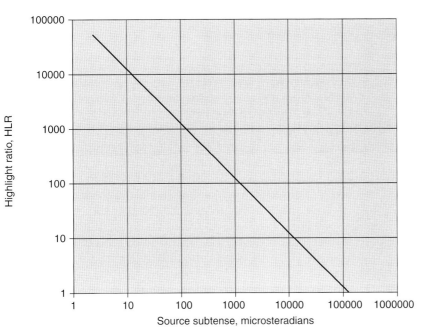

Figure 2.39: *Highlight ratio HLR relative to source subtense*

Table 2.8 *Light source sizes and HLR values for 2 m viewing distance (after Worthey, 1990)*

| Light source | Area, m² | Solid angle subtense at 2 m μstr | Highlight ratio HLR |
|---|---|---|---|
| **Lamps** | | | |
| 60 W clear incandescent GLS | $2.0 \times 10^{-5}$ | 5 | 25 000 |
| 60 W pearl incandescent GLS | $3.1 \times 10^{-4}$ | 78 | 1600 |
| 60 W 'soft white' incandescent GLS | $2.4 \times 10^{-3}$ | 600 | 210 |
| 1200 mm T12 fluorescent | $4.6 \times 10^{-2}$ | 12 000 | 10 |
| 1200 mm T8 fluorescent | $3.0 \times 10^{-2}$ | 7500 | 17 |
| 1150 mm T5 fluorescent | $1.8 \times 10^{-2}$ | 4500 | 27 |
| 18 W 2-arm compact fluorescent | $4.7 \times 10^{-3}$ | 1200 | 110 |
| 18 W 4-arm compact fluorescent | $2.7 \times 10^{-3}$ | 680 | 190 |
| Candle flame | $7.5 \times 10^{-5}$ | 19 | 6700 |
| **Reflector lamps** | | | |
| PAR 38 (120 mm diameter) | $1.1 \times 10^{-2}$ | 2800 | 45 |
| MR 16 (50 mm diameter) | $2.0 \times 10^{-3}$ | 500 | 250 |
| MR 11 (35 mm diameter) | $1.0 \times 10^{-3}$ | 250 | 500 |
| MR 8 (25 mm diameter) | $5.0 \times 10^{-4}$ | 130 | 1000 |
| **Luminaires** | | | |
| 250 mm diameter opal sphere | $5.0 \times 10^{-2}$ | 12 000 | 10 |
| 600 × 600 mm fluorescent diffuser | $3.6 \times 10^{-1}$ | 90 000 | 1.4 |
| 1200 × 600 mm fluorescent diffuser | $7.2 \times 10^{-1}$ | 180 000 | 0.7 |
| Luminous ceiling or 'uplighter' installation | 'Infinite' (extends to horizon) | 6 300 000 ($2\pi \times 10^6$) | 0.04 |

patterns. Extending our thoughts now to practical lighting situations, consider the following.

*What would be the effect of other light sources in the vicinity?* They would have the effect of increasing surface luminances without changing source image luminances, which would reduce the visual impact of highlights and the density of shadows. However, HLR is a metric for comparing the potential of alternative light sources to generate highlights, and is not a predictive measure of the luminance ratio that would be achieved in a particular situation. It may be noted that $L_{bl}$ is based on the reflectance of a dielectric material, but an electric conductive material may have much higher reflectance (Section 1.2). HLR indicates the potential of a source to create sharpness, but whatever visual effects are achieved will depend on the characteristics of the illuminated object and the surrounding light field.

*What would be the effect of moving the light source closer to the object?* The surface luminance will increase as $1/D^2$, but in the case of the highlight, it is the size of the source specular image, not its luminance, that will increase as $1/D^2$. This will have the effect of reducing the luminance contrast of highlights.

*If reducing source distance reduces highlight and shadow contrasts, can we increase these contrasts by increasing distance?* It takes some careful thought to understand the influence of source distance. Increasing source distance reduces the subtense solid angle as $1/D^2$, which reduces highlights in size but not luminance, and causes shadow edges to appear more sharply defined. If this is the only or principal source of illumination, surface luminances are reduced and appearance of sharpness is increased. However, if the purpose for installing the source was to provide a certain illuminance, then as we increase distance, we would have to increase luminous intensity to maintain illuminance. Raising the luminaire output increases highlight luminances as $D^2$, which again will have the effect of increasing the appearance of sharpness. This may seem counter-intuitive, but the theatre lighting people worked it out long ago. The follow-spotlights that pick out the star of the show are located as far from the stage as the theatre permits. I have heard Francis Reid, the English stage lighting designer, describe this as the 'eyes and teeth lighting', which is his graphic term for what I call 'sharpness'.

While HLR and the appearance of sharpness depend on the angular subtense of the source, rather than either the size of the luminaire or its distance, it is easier to visualize subtense in terms of two-dimensional angle (degrees) rather than solid angle (steradians). Nonetheless, it is solid angle that really holds the key to visualizing the sharpness of lighting, particularly when subtense is very small and HLR is high.

## *Sharpness and solid angle*

Consider a position below an expansive luminous ceiling, or a large uplighting installation, or an overcast sky; for all of these conditions, $\gamma \rightarrow 180°$; $\Omega \rightarrow 2\pi$ str; and HLR $\rightarrow 0.04$. This accords with the third 4 per cent rule, and there is a total lack of highlights. Veiling reflections pervade, even though CRF = 1.0, and these veiling reflections diminish detail contrast and colour saturation, and these effects cannot be avoided by head movements or other viewing adjustments. While these losses will be most evident on dark, glossy materials, they may pass unnoticed as appearance does not change with changing direction of view. The distinguishing characteristic of this type of lighting is that the light source is the dimmest source that can provide the illuminance. This condition may be seen as the ultimate in a quest for 'visual comfort'.

If we reduce the light source to the point where the luminance of the highlight equals the luminance of the white surface, then HLR = 1.0; $\Omega = 126,000 \mu$sr: and $\gamma = 23°$. This is still a fairly large source, and although highlights will appear subdued on a smooth white dielectric surface, they will be far more visible on dark coloured surfaces. We know that black cars polish up better than white cars, and we also know that all cars look dull on an overcast day.

Table 2.8 lists some familiar light sources with their maximum effective areas, and $\Omega$ values for a distance of 2 m. There is no need to strive for a high level of precision to compare an unlisted source with these values, as for example, the relative areas of the clear, pearl and soft white incandescent lamps are based on observation and estimation of the effective source size. It is quite simple to make comparative observations of the different potentials of these lamps to produce highlight patterns. Reflector lamps are included, but these data should be treated with some caution. It has been assumed for these compact sources that the reflectors appear to be fully flashed, but particularly for large reflectors or where the receiving surface is off beam centre, this may not be so. In such cases, the HLR will be underestimated.

The range of HLR values shown in Figure 2.39 is large, from HLR = 1 for the 126,000 μstr source, to HLR = 25,000 for a 5 µstr source, represented by a clear incandescent lamp at 2 m distance. This figure may be read in conjunction with Table 2.8, and it should be recognized that the purpose of HLR is not to predict what the ratio of highlights will be in a design situation, but to compare the potential of alternative light sources, keeping in mind that distance is another variable under the designer's control.

The study of three objects illustrated in Figure 2.22 shows that a single high HLR light source produces distinct highlight and shadow patterns where appropriate object characteristics are available conveying a clear sense of sharpness. The addition of other light sources or high reflectance surrounding surfaces may make these lighting patterns less distinct, particularly in the case of the shadow pattern which is weakened by ambient light. However, although these patterns may be reduced in strength, the sharpness due to high HLR sources is retained. The three objects can be used to observe these effects, but the author has also experimented with a single object designed to maximize the different appearances of the three lighting patterns. Figure 2.40 shows two views of the triple-pattern object, which comprises a matt white sphere surrounded by a clear sphere.

**Figure 2.40:** *The triple-pattern object shown (a) in the same location and lighting as for the three objects in Plate 5, and (b) without the spotlight*

The white sphere reveals the shading pattern and reflections on the clear sphere reveal the highlight pattern. The white discs on the clear sphere cast shadows on the white sphere revealing the sharpness of the shadow pattern. Figure 2.40(a) shows the triple-pattern object in the same location and lighting as for the three objects in Figure 2.21. The sensitivity of this object to lighting changes is indicated by the difference of appearance in Figure 2.40(b) where the only change is that the spotlight has been switched off. This object was made from items purchased from a craft shop.

It is interesting to note the similarities of those two familiar small light sources, the sun and the moon. As shown in Table 2.9, the angular subtense of the moon is just slightly smaller than that of the sun, as is evident at a solar eclipse, so despite the huge difference in the illuminances that they provide under optimal conditions, they are almost identical in their potential to provide highlights. Wait for a clear night with a full moon and test this by observation.

The purpose of this discussion has been to alert designers to the influence of light source size upon the appearance of illuminated objects. Lighting makes things visible by revealing contrasts, and source size influences all aspects of contrast. It affects the luminance contrast of detail and the saturation of surface colours, particularly for low contrasts or dark colours. It affects the highlights that reveal gloss and give the sensation of sparkle and glitter. It affects the formation of shadows, as revealed by the penumbra, being the zone between the full shadow (umbra) and no shadow. We could have examined any of these aspects of appearance to provide an objective scale relating to the impression of the sharpness of lighting. The highlight ratio is a convenient measure which identifies one aspect of the influence

Table 2.9 *Two distant light sources*

| Parameter | Sun | Moon |
|---|---|---|
| Diameter, m | $1.4 \times 10^9$ | $3.5 \times 10^6$ |
| Projected area $A$, m$^2$ | $1.5 \times 10^{18}$ | $9.5 \times 10^{12}$ |
| Distance $d$, m | $1.5 \times 10^{11}$ | $3.8 \times 10^8$ |
| Angular subtense $\alpha$, min | 32.1 | 31.7 |
| Solid angular subtense $\Omega$, $\mu$str | 67 | 64 |
| Highlight ratio, HLR | 1840 | 1890 |
| Luminance $L$, cd/m$^2$ | $1.5 \times 10^9$ | $2.5 \times 10^3$ |
| Luminous intensity $I$, cd | $2.25 \times 10^{27}$ | $2.3 \times 10^{16}$ |
| Illuminance $E$, lx | $1.0 \times 10^5$ | $1.6 \times 10^{-1}$ |

of source size, but which serves well as an indicator of the over-all sense of the sharpness of lighting.

Just because we have a measure that relates to the sharp-ness of lighting does not mean that our aim must be to maxi-mize sharpness or even to provide some level of sharpness. Lighting that is softly diffused – whether by fabric lamp shades, by reflection from a light-coloured ceiling, or by transmission through rice paper shoji screens – scores low on HLR, and it has its own aesthetic. It is lighting that minimizes differences of object characteristics, promoting a merging of forms and a modified sense of space. The important thing is to develop a feeling for when this aesthetic is to be the design objective, and then to achieve it with a clear sense of purpose rather than by default.

Worthey summed up his views with an anecdote:

> Suppose that the 'man in the street' is standing in front of a drugstore, diffusely lit by fluorescent lamps, looking in the plate glass windows. Suppose that it's a clear day, but the sun is fairly low in the western sky so that the mean luminance of the outdoor scene is equal to that inside the drugstore. What the man in the street will see, or what you and I will see, is that the scene in the drugstore looks washed out compared to the scene outdoors.
>
> …It looks washed out because it is washed out. Highlights are dim and large; blacks and saturated colours are covered by veiling reflections. This is in addition to the loss of colour contrast because of the inferior colour rendering of fluores-cent lights, the loss of black-white contrast because of the lack of shadows in the drugstore, and the enhancement of colour contrast outdoors due to the fact that the light from the west is reddish while that from the east is bluish.
>
> (Worthey, 1990)

Sharpness is the subjective dimension of lighting design that is determined by light source size and distance. This is because if we are to achieve a certain illuminance, the smaller we make the light source and the greater we make the distance, the greater must be the source luminance. Sharpness is not always wanted, but where it is a design objective, it needs to be pro-vided thoughtfully. According to user's attitude and sense of purpose, the overall effect may be perceived to have the spar-kle and stimulation of the fairground, or the intolerable glare (along with other forms of discomfort) associated with the den-tist's chair.

## 2.6  Luminous elements

Thus far we have examined visible characteristics of lighting in terms of how lighting interacts with and reveals the surfaces and the objects within the room. Inevitably, the luminaires have some impact on the appearance of the space. We can see many examples where the designers have sought to minimize that impact by concealing the lamps and building the luminaires into architectural details. These can take many forms: cornices to provide uplighting onto the ceiling; stepped ceiling perimeters to enable wallwashing; or low-brightness luminaires recessed flush with the ceiling. In all these cases the designers are expressing the wish to have illumination without luminaires.

### *Luminaires as design elements*

There are alternative design approaches. When the Sun King, Louis XIV, had the Hall of Mirrors at the Palace of Versailles illuminated with one thousand candles, this spectacular vision was celebrated by having the candles mounted on glittering crystal chandeliers. When gas engineers introduced the next wave of illumination technology, it was popular to illuminate the parlour with a gasolier, this being an elaborate multi-arm chandelier based on earlier cast metal candelabra. Derivative forms of decorative luminaires remain popular for domestic lighting, but also newer forms of 'architectural' luminaires are often used in commercial and recreational buildings. The renovated luminaires in the Philadelphia railway station shown in Figure 2.41 are switched on all day even though the daylight

Figure 2.41:   *The renovated luminaires in this Philadelphia railway station are switched on all day, even though the daylight streaming in through the windows provides perfectly adequate illumination*

streaming in through the windows provides perfectly adequate illumination. These are planned elements in the design concept which are intended to be seen, but this raises a potential conflict. We have seen how the phototropic effect draws attention to the brightest elements in the field of view, so is the aim to reveal the space and its contents, or to display the lighting equipment?

There is a conundrum that is familiar to lighting practitioners: 'One man's sparkle is another man's glare.' The foyer of the New York Central Railway Station is a busy place with continuous movement, and a recent refurbishment restored the night-time lighting which is now used all day, more to define the architectural space than to provide useful illumination, as shown in Figure 2.42(a). Turning one's view towards the railway platforms reveals huge, glittering chandeliers (Figure 2.42(b)), which must be a source of irritation and discomfort to the clerks who sit at the ticket counters, so why does the management not install comfortable, low-brightness luminaires instead? The answer is that 'the bright lights' impart an opulent atmosphere in this setting that sets the mood of the travellers and raises a sense of anticipation for the journey ahead. The travellers need to be able to read the details on their tickets, but this is not a sustained task and they can achieve this while they pass through the space without sensing discomfort. Their responses mean more to the management than those of the ticket clerks, who have to learn to cope or seek more comfortable occupations.

The reading hall of the Boston Library has a similarly opulent style, but here the luminaires have been chosen to make a quite different visual statement, shown in Figure 2.43. Despite the close proximity of the readers, this is a place for individual study and contemplation, and the luminaires define each reader's personal space in this large room.

The busy shopping centre in Kowloon, Hong Kong, shown in Figure 2.44 has a lively and vibrant atmosphere closer to NY Central Station, but the architectural style is entirely different. The brightness of the unshielded luminaires gains sparkle from a multitude of reflections from an elaborate stainless steel sculpture that hangs through almost the entire height of the atrium. At Harrods of London, the style of the retail premises is entirely different, and Figure 2.45 shows the extent to which that image is built up from carefully crafted and highly visible luminaires. Perhaps more so than beauty, glare is literally in the eye of the beholder.

**Figure 2.42:**  *The new
lighting that was part of a major
refurbishment of the main hall
at Central Station, New York,
concentrated on revealing the
architecture (a), but as travellers
move towards the platforms (b),
huge chandeliers dominate the
view*

Standards concerning the brightness of luminaires are largely
based on provision for workplaces, where the sort of factors
that might disturb the ticket clerks in New York Central Station
cannot be overlooked. Attention has focused onto the needs
of office workers, and in particular, on the avoidance of bright
reflected images of luminaires in computer screens. This con-
centration onto a single aspect has had unfortunate conse-
quences, and has led to many dismally unattractive workplaces
in which closely spaced, fully recessed luminaires concentrate
their light output vertically downwards. Such lighting undoubt-
edly avoids bright images reflected in the computer screens, in
fact the brightness of the luminaires can be so low that it may

*Figure 2.43:   The main reading room at Boston Library is an imposing and very public space (a), but the desk-mounted lamps mark out individual territories for the readers (b)*

(a)

(b)

be difficult to see whether they are switched on. Nonetheless, the harshness of the illumination attracts criticism. The vector/scalar ratio is high, and the appearance of strongly directional lighting streaming downwards from a dark ceiling has been described as the 'cave effect'. Perhaps the most surprising aspect of this form of lighting has been the vast number of office workers who have been subjected to its unpleasantness,

**Figure 2.44:** *This shopping centre in Kowloon, Hong Kong, has a lively and vibrant atmosphere. The brightness and sparkle of the unshielded luminaires is multiplied by reflections from an elaborate stainless steel sculpture that hangs through almost the entire height of the atrium*

as it has continued to be installed as the solution to the electronic office despite ample evidence to the contrary. At any rate, it has demonstrated that to design lighting with the single-minded aim of making the luminaires almost invisible can lead to very unsatisfactory results.

## Discomfort glare

In Section 2.2 we discussed disability glare, which occurs when the visibility of detail to be seen is reduced by scattered light within the eye from bright elements within the field of view, such as luminaires. There is another form of glare that is associated with the presence of bright luminaires in workplaces, and it is termed discomfort glare. There may be no noticeable loss of visibility, in fact, the effects of discomfort glare my not be apparent until after a prolonged period of exposure. It is for this

**Figure 2.45:** *Harrods of London employ large-scale and beautifully crafted luminaires to both make a statement of identity, and to distinguish individual spaces within the store (a to c)*

reason that it is particularly associated with workplaces in which workers have to maintain fixed viewing directions for long periods, and the symptoms are headaches, eyestrain, and fatigue. There are substantial interpersonal differences in susceptibility to discomfort glare.

Discomfort glare has been the subject of several research investigations. It has been found that subjective assessments of discomfort glare increase with the luminance of the glare source and its apparent size, and reduce with the ambient light level and the angle of separation between the glare source and the direction of view. Within certain limits, the effect of multiple glare sources is additive. There have been several attempts to devise discomfort glare rating systems, so that complete lighting installations can be assessed at the design stage, and a predicted value can be compared with a scale of limiting values related to various activities and viewing conditions. The Unified Glare Rating is probably the most widely used rating system, and while designers may encounter limiting UGR values being prescribed for some specific situations, this is more a way of users seeking to avoid exposing their workers to unsatisfactory lighting rather than a useful tool to enable a committed lighting designer to devise an installation that is well suited to the situation. It is important that a lighting designer is alert to the difficulties encountered by some people in coping with sustained and visually demanding work, but it is generally more productive to devise ways of avoiding the causes of discomfort rather than seeking to evaluate how much discomfort glare will be present. It may be added that studies comparing subjective assessments of actual lighting installations with calculated glare ratings generally show poor correlation.

## Luminaires and lighting design criteria

We have discussed the hierarchy of illuminances, for which the lighting designer makes decisions on how to employ local variations of illumination to attract attention and express differences of emphasis. In making these decisions, the appearance of luminaires may be given little attention and it is assumed that they will, as far as possible, be concealed. Even where a source of light is a focus of attention, such as an altar light or the Eternal Flame, this is unlikely to be a significant source of illumination and the lighting designer's concern is to ensure that the appearance of the surrounding surfaces does not detract. Bright or otherwise conspicuous luminaires would tend to upset the planned effect of the hierarchy of illuminances.

We have also examined what is meant by the sharpness of lighting, and how this relates to the angular size of the luminaire and the highlight ratio. Consider a retail display of glassware. We have already seen how the appearance of glassware has almost nothing to do with illumination (Figure 2.38), and the appropriate strategy for lighting involves the use of compact, high-luminance light sources mounted close to glassware. Should these sources be concealed? The highlights associated with the glassware are informative, revealing the forms, smoothness of surface, and the lustre of merchandise. The luminance of the lamps will inevitably be higher than the luminance of the highlights, and even though their brightness does not impart information about the glassware, it may add more sparkle to the scene and to the eye-catching qualities of the display. It is unavoidably a judgement call, and one that a lighting designer has to consider. After all, why does a formally laid-out dinner table appear so entrancing when the crockery, cutlery and glassware are illuminated by candlelight? And who would want to conceal the candle flames?

To quote J.M. Waldram again, 'If there's nothing worth looking at, there's nothing worth lighting.' Well, it sometimes happens that a lighting designer is confronted with a situation that needs lighting, and in which there is little or nothing worth looking at. To flood the space with light can do no more than reveal its blandness. This can be a situation in which the luminaires become the things worth looking at. Generally, this book has addressed situations where the designer's objective is to bring electric lighting to a space that has been designed by someone else, and the aim is to support the design objectives of the principal designer. A designer who steps beyond that role and undertakes to select or design luminous elements to be added to a space is moving into the realm of interior design, and there are many ways in which luminaires can become a vital part of the scene.

First it needs to be understood that an object does not need to be self-luminous. The space shown in Figure 2.46 is given a visual lift by the suspended luminous element, but closer inspection shows that it incorporates no light sources. The glittering highlights are due to remote spotlights, with high highlight ratios to achieve the necessary sharpness. Nor need the solution be complicated. Figure 2.47 shows the foyer of a small American hotel, in which a custom-made luminaire forms a central element in design composition. Figure 2.48 shows a

**Figure 2.46:**   *This eye-catching pendant (a) at the Hong Kong Cultural Centre appears to be a luminaire, but on close inspection (b) it is seen to be a specular metal sculpture lit by concealed spotlights*

**Figure 2.47:**   *The scale of the luminaire makes it a dominant element in this small hotel foyer*

**Figure 2.48:** *In this market café close to the waterfront in Stockholm, the luminaires express the nautical location; they add sharpness to the lighting; and they radiate a glowing sense of warmth*

**Figure 2.49:** *This simple arrangement of geometric luminaires in the waiting area of a New York architect's office make a design-conscious statement to every visitor*

market café close to the waterfront in Stockholm. The lumi-naires express the nautical location; they add sharpness to the lighting; and they radiate a glowing sense of warmth. Finally, the waiting area adjacent to the reception desk of this New York architect's office provides an opportunity for the firm to express their design skill (Figure 2.49), utilizing a pair of care-fully located and well-shielded standard lamps. There are aspects of applying luminous elements in lighting design that inevitably fall beyond the scope of this book.

# Measurable characteristics of lighting

3

There are many ways of measuring lighting. The ones that matter to a lighting designer are those that relate to the observation-based experience of lighting. It is for this reason that readers are encouraged to accompany observation with measurement.

The two sections in this chapter deal with illuminance-based and luminance-based measurements. In both cases, light is evaluated according to the photopic-adapted visual response (see Appendix A1) which ignores colour. It is possible to obtain a chroma-meter, which is an advanced type of illuminance meter that gives readings of illuminance, chromaticity and correlated colour temperature, but usually designers rely on colour data given by lamp manufacturers. There are no portable instruments that measure colour rendering.

## 3.1 Illuminance-based measurements

Illuminance is the measure of luminous flux density in lux, and it usually refers to either flux incident at a point on a surface, or the average value over a surface or a plane, such as a ceiling or the horizontal work plane. Illuminance meters are reasonably affordable, although they have to be purchased from a specialist supplier. The essential components of a photocell for measuring illuminance are shown in Figure 3.1. Quality is reflected by the precision of colour correction, which concerns how closely the spectral response of the instrument matches the photopic relative luminous efficiency function (see Appendix A1), and the precision of cosine correction, which is how closely the directional response of the instrument matches the cosine law of incidence. Cheaper instruments may be unreliable in both respects.

The most common use for illuminance meters is for checking whether lighting complies with various lighting recommendations or standards. These documents specify illuminance values for various activities, which may be justified on the basis that these are the light levels required to provide for a satisfactory level of visual performance, taking account of the category

*Facing page:  Federation Square, Melbourne, Victoria, Australia. Federation Square is the outcome of a 1996 architectural competition for a multi-purpose public development constructed over a dozen railway lines, and which connects the city of Melbourne to the Yarra River frontage. The design by Lab Architecture Studio includes this glazed concourse with an organic steel structure, which offers strikingly different daytime and night-time visual experiences*

**Figure 3.1:**  *Typical photocell of an illuminance meter, which may have a connecting lead to a separate measuring instrument or may be integrated into a single device. The photocell may be placed on an illuminated surface to measure the cosine-weighted incident flux from the entire hemisphere. Alternatively it may be used to measure eye illuminance as shown in Figure 2.3*

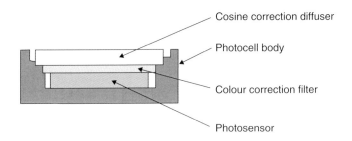

Cosine correction diffuser

Photocell body

Colour correction filter

Photosensor

of visual task associated with the activity. While this is always relevant wherever visually demanding activities occur, there is another way of using an illuminance meter that has more relevance to architectural lighting design.

It is a good habit for a lighting designer to carry an illuminance meter and to use it whenever lighting catches the attention, so that measurement becomes a part of the continual process of observation. Start with the overall sense of brightness. Some spaces appear dim; others appear bright; and some fall somewhere in between. We can measure mean room surface exitance by using the meter as shown in Figure 2.3, and as discussed in Section 2.1, we should aim to shield the meter from direct light from the luminaires.

To put this procedure into practice, you could start by finding a modern office that has uniform illumination provided by low-glare, recessed luminaires. If you measure the illuminance on the work surfaces, you are likely to find that it is between 500 and 750 lux. Now find another space that is well lit by indirect light, where ample illumination is provided by uplighters or wallwashers. If the space appears to be as well lit as a 500 lux office, you are likely to find that the work surface illuminance is only around 250 lux. Someone might want to tell you that this is a problem with indirect lighting, but no – it is a problem with the way that we measure direct lighting. If, rather than measuring illuminance on a notional horizontal work plane, you instead measure mean room surface exitance as shown in Figure 2.3, you might find that both situations give a reading between 150 and 200 lux. They look about the same, and this way, they measure about the same. Remember this appearance, and remember this value.

The experience can be even more dramatic if you can find a downlighting installation with low surface reflectances. Entrance halls and lift lobbies in prestigious office buildings quite often fit into this category. Here the ceiling receives no direct light, and the walls very little. Most of the luminous flux is directed, perhaps very efficiently, onto the floor where typically 80% of

**Figure 3.2:** *Measuring illuminances on the six faces of a cube*

it will be absorbed. If you measure the illuminance on the horizontal work plane, your meter may record a brilliant 750 lux, but what you are measuring is densely packed photons streaming through the void of space on their way to being virtually decimated beneath your feet. Mean room surface exitance, measured with direct light shielded, may be less than 100 lux, and this is the measurement that counts. The procedure may not seem very scientific, but it gives quantifiable aspects of lighting that relate to the appearances of illuminated spaces. The values given in Table 2.1 are simply an outline guide. Your task is to build onto this guide a scale of your own observation-based experience.

Lynes' procedure for recording perceived differences of illuminance is described in Section 2.3 and illustrated in Figure 2.19. When you notice that some distinct visual effect has been achieved by differences of illuminance, decide in your own mind where this effect fits in the range noticeable – distinct – strong – emphatic, and then measure the illuminance difference. You need to measure illuminance on the surfaces that are visually significant, and sometimes this is difficult to do without shielding the meter while you are taking the reading. It can be very advantageous to have a meter with a hold button that captures the reading. Another problem can be avoiding the attention of security staff while you are carrying out your investigations.

Illuminance meters are designed to measure light incident on a two-dimensional surface, while Chapter 2 pursued the concept of the three-dimensional distribution of illumination about a point in space. It is possible to measure spatial distributions of illuminance with a conventional illuminance meter, although rather tedious. Figure 3.2 shows illuminance being measured on one face of a supported cube, and five more measurements are needed to complete the cubic illumination measurements at this point. Figure 3.3 shows a custom-built six-sided photometer, and Figure 3.4 shows this device in use. One chair in the

**Figure 3.3:** *Six-sided cubic illumination meter developed at the Lighting Research Center*

**Figure 3.4:** *The cubic illumination meter in use in a small conference room where it is located at head height. It is controlled from the laptop computer*

small conference room has been removed, and the meter has been located to replace the head of one conference participant. The meter is connected to a laptop computer that scans the six photocells and generates real-time displays which can be set to give information relating to the shading pattern or to the distribution of eye illuminance at the point.

A less cumbersome form of cubic illuminance meter is shown in Figure 3.5. At first sight it appears quite unlike a cube, but think of a cube supported on one corner with its axis vertical, and three facets facing upwards and three downwards. The six cosine-corrected photocells measure six cubic illuminances, but not on the familiar *xyz* axes. If we refer to the measurement axes as *u*, *v*, and *w*, then the unit vector components (Section 6.4) on *xyz* axes can be determined from the following formulae (Cuttle, 2003):

$$\mathbf{e}_{(x)} = 0.707(\mathbf{e}_{(v)} - \mathbf{e}_{(w)})$$

$$\mathbf{e}_{(y)} = 0.816\,\mathbf{e}_{(u)} - 0.408(\mathbf{e}_{(v)} + \mathbf{e}_{(w)})$$

$$\mathbf{e}_{(z)} = 0.577(\mathbf{e}_{(u)} + \mathbf{e}_{(v)} + \mathbf{e}_{(w)})$$

This vertical-axis cubic illumination meter is shown mounted on a lightweight camera tripod in Figure 3.6, and the comparative

**Figure 3.5:** *Vertical axis cubic illumination meter. Six silicon photodiodes are aligned on the faces of a cube tilted so that one long axis is vertical. The axes of the opposing pairs of photodiodes are designated* u, v, *and* w

**Figure 3.6:** *The vertical axis cubic illumination meter is mounted on a tripod and controlled from a laptop computer, which scans the six photodiode outputs and computes vector and symmetric illuminances on the* x, y, *and* z *axes*

ease of use is evident. The meter is controlled from a laptop computer which gives readings for the familiar *xyz* axes.

## 3.2 Luminance-based measurements

The detector of a luminance meter is a colour-corrected photocell similar to that used in an illuminance meter, and the difference lies in the spatial distribution of light that is measured. Instead of receiving light from an entire hemisphere, a luminance meter has an optical system that restricts the field to a narrow cone, enabling the operator to focus the meter onto a selected target. The more narrow the receptive field, the more sensitive the detector and the more complex the optical system have to be. Currently available portable meters have receptive fields as small as one third of a degree, and such an instrument will typically provide through-the-lens aiming and read-out. The essential components of a luminance meter of this type is shown in Figure 3.7. Digital read-out to an external device may be an option. These instruments are expensive, and are more likely to be found in research laboratories than in design offices.

The foregoing text has placed emphasis on illuminance as a means of quantifying the illuminated scene, while in Section 2.1 the equivalence of eye illuminance in lux and adaptation level in candelas per square metre was explained (see Table 2.1). Both of these concepts relate to a large receptive field that is quite different from the restricted field of a luminance meter. If we restrict the field of a conventional illuminance meter by placing an internally blackened tube over the detector as shown in Figure 3.8, the meter will now respond to the average luminance of the field to which it is exposed. This will be a much wider field than that of a luminance meter, but that is not necessarily a disadvantage for lighting design work. The readings now given by the instrument have no absolute value, but can be used to make relative measurements of illuminated surfaces such as walls or work surfaces, although not of small fields such as bright elements of a luminaire reflector.

**Figure 3.7:**  *The essential components of a luminance meter. These components may be connected by a flexible lead to a measuring and recording instrument or may be integrated into a hand-held instrument that provides for through-the-lens viewing of the object being measured and the luminance reading*

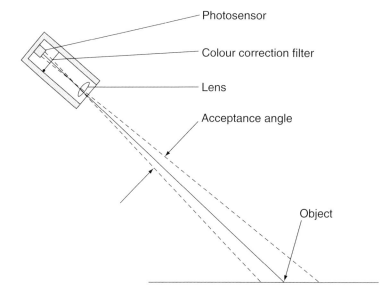

Photosensor

Colour correction filter

Lens

Acceptance angle

Object

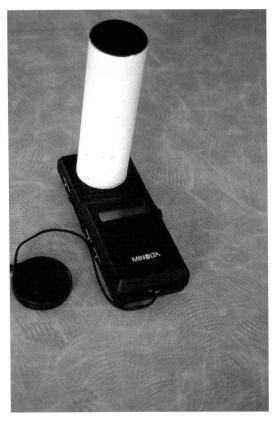

Figure 3.8:  *An illuminance meter adapted with a cardboard tube, internally sprayed matt black, for making relative luminance measurements*

Figure 3.9:  *A reading for the patterned worktop material is compared with a sheet of white paper to obtain an estimate of reflectance*

Measurements made in this way can be useful for checking illumination distributions of large matt surfaces (Section 2.3) or for making approximate measurements of room surface reflectances. For the latter, you need a white comparison surface. Calibrated white reference surfaces are available from specialist suppliers, but a sheet of high-quality white paper with a fully matt finish as shown in Figure 3.9 is sufficient to enable useful relative measurements, and the wide acceptance angle is an advantage when dealing with patterned surfaces. Care must be taken to avoid specular reflections when taking readings of the test surface.

# Part Two: Visualization

The creative skill of a lighting designer is the ability to visualize a design concept revealed by light. The more highly developed is the skill, the greater is the detail of the envisioned concept.

A lighting designer who aims to work in a particular field of design, such as architecture, interior design or landscape design, must develop an appreciative understanding of how designers in the chosen field conceptualize their work. From an understanding of the overall design concept, the lighting designer develops the vision of the design setting revealed by light. A hierarchy of things to be seen is determined and selection is made of object characteristics to be revealed. It is this selection that determines the characteristics of the lighting to be provided.

If daylight will be present for some of the time, its role in determining the perceived character of the space is likely to be crucial, and strategies for control of both daylight and electric lighting must be envisioned together. The aim is to devise a lighting distribution that is uniquely suited to the design situation, and which may be specified in terms that are capable of being realized.

# Envisioning the concept 4

Visualization is the process by which a designer develops a mental image of a design concept. The design situation is visualized in light, and several lighting concepts that can serve to guide this process are discussed in this chapter. The design concept is built up from observation-based experience, which involves both understanding how the attributes associated with elements in the field of view are perceived, and how these may be brought together to achieve a lighting design concept for an architectural space. The ability to visualize in this way is the defining skill of a lighting designer.

## 4.1 Seeing lighting clearly

Louis Erhardt has noted that 'Artists see things more clearly than other people.' The special attribute of lighting designers is that they see lighting clearly.

The basic purpose of visual perception is to enable recognition of object attributes. People frequently make critical visual assessments of objects that take into account a wide range of physical characteristics. Judgements of whether fruit is in a good state to eat, or whether a child is sick, are fine discriminations of a variety of object attributes. The lighting that we require in our everyday lives has to provide not only for discrimination of detail and colour, but also for distinguishing object characteristics such as rough from smooth, glossy from matt, wet from dry, translucent from opaque, flat from curved, and faceted from rounded. Providing for these needs may be described in terms of revealing the whole range of perceived attributes associated with object mode perceptions, but this does not necessarily describe people's conscious experiences.

In the perception of an object in an obvious illuminant such as sunlight or a lamp, variations in intensity caused by the shape of a surface are perceived directly as shape and not intensity changes. In fact this perception is usually so strong that it is almost impossible for the untrained observer to see the 'shading' of objects at all. Yet it is just this shading which the artist must see or the competent photographer must reproduce in

*Facing page: Festival Walk, Kowloon, Hong Kong. This busy shopping centre is adjacent to a major public transport interchange, and attracts a continual flow to its 200 shops, 27 restaurants, multi-screen cinema, and ice rink. The central themes of the design concept are light and space. These escalators are both reflectors and sources of light, and the appearance of the whole space changes dramatically with the changing phases of light, as illustrated in this pair of day and night photos*

consciousness if he is to produce the perception of the shape in the mind of the person observing his reproduction.

(Evans, 1948)

This is the basis of the frustration that upsets so many people who work with lighting. A friend tells a lighting designer of a delightful visit to an art gallery, or to an architectural icon, or to a new shopping mall. 'What did you think of the lighting?' the designer asks. 'What lighting?' is the reply. Of course, the visual experience would not have been delightful if the lighting had not made it so.

The point has been made that the mode of appearance in which a thing is perceived is not determined by the physical nature of the thing, but rather by the meaning that the viewer associates with the thing. For example, it is obvious that light scattered by diffusely reflecting matt surfaces is perceived differently from the specularly reflected highlights that are seen in glossy surfaces. Where such highlights occur randomly in the visual field, they comprise reflected glare or visual noise which detracts from the ability to recognize object attributes. Alternatively, highlights that appear to be associated with objects may serve to distinguish glossy from matt, or to provide the 'sparkle' of jewellery or crystal glass. The distinction between glare and sparkle is sometimes quoted as the great conundrum of lighting, but it is simply a matter of meaning. Where people perceive objects of fine, lustrous quality, it is because the lighting imparts sparkle. They may enjoy the appearance of the object, but it takes the trained eye of an artist, professional photographer, or an experienced lighting designer to 'see the lighting'. This is a necessary skill for them to 'reproduce in consciousness' a certain perception of object attributes. A lighting designer needs to have developed the skill to see lighting clearly.

The ability to select lighting that will enhance the appearance of certain object attributes is a skill that lighting people start to learn early in their careers. They have to learn what type of lighting will make jewellery sparkle, or make meat look fresh, or make furnishing fabrics look colourful. Acquiring these basic skills does not lead automatically to the ability to envision a design concept in light. That ability involves bringing observation-based experience into the mental construct that is the design concept. To explain what that means, we will follow in the footsteps of an artist.

Edgar Degas' parents were not pleased by his determination to become an artist, but they supported him nonetheless so that

**Figure 4.1:** *A daylit interior with a lateral flow of light. The Dance Class (Degas, 1875) La Classe de Danse, Degas Edgar, Gas Hilaire-Germain Edgar de (1834–1917), Copyright © Photo RMN/Hervé Lewandowski, Paris musée d'Orsay*

he never suffered the hardships encountered by some of the other young impressionist artists in late eighteenth century Paris. He grew up with a love of ballet, and he pursued this passion through his painting. Figure 4.1 shows a rehearsal area at the Paris Opera, and Degas' acute observational skills are evident. He contrasts the assertive stance of the ballet master with the taught, elegantly balanced poise of the dancer who is under his searching gaze. Around them are the slumped postures and tired limbs of the waiting dancers.

Also, the space is suffused with light. Obviously it is daylight. We cannot see the windows in this space, but in our minds we can not only locate the windows, but we can picture them in some detail. There are several clues that help us to form this perception. The glimpse through to the adjoining space is one. Another is the coherent lateral flow of light through the space, which is a familiar characteristic of rooms with side windows. Turn now to Figure 4.2. Here Degas shows us the same dance master with dancers doing similar things. Again there is a lateral flow of light, but in this case we instantly perceive artificial lighting. Actually, this is more likely to be gas lighting than electric lighting, but the question here is: what are the clues that the artist has presented to us so that we instantly perceive a different type of lighting?

Figure 4.2:   *A lateral flow of light, but not daylight. Hilaire-Germain-Edgar Degas, French (1834–1917). Rehearsal of the Ballet, ca. 1876. Gouache and pastel over monotype on paper, 21 3/4 × 26 3/4 inches (55.3 × 68.0 cm). The Nelson-Atkins Museum of Art, Kansas City, Missouri. Purchase: the Kenneth A. and Helen F. Spencer Foundation Acquisition Fund, F73-30. Photograph by E.G. Schempf*

Figure 4.3:   *A detailed study of interior lighting. Edgar Degas, The Dance Class, c. 1873, oil on canvas, 18¾ × 24½ inches. Corcoran Gallery of Art, Washington DC, William A. Clark Collection 26.74*

There are some differences in the setting, but surely the overriding difference is the sense of ambient illumination and flow of light. Even though this difference is instantly recognized, it is not easy to describe it. Degas had analysed it by observation and could reproduce it convincingly in fine detail.

Figure 4.3 is one of Degas' major compositions, and it represents a masterly study of lighting. We see one window facing us, and we infer another one round the corner illuminating the smaller space beyond. We know there are no windows behind us from the dimness of the illumination on the wall facing us and the silhouette of the staircase. This puts the dancers in a strong flow of light, imparting translucent glow to the tutus and strong modelling to the dancers. Note, however, that while the sense of flow of light is strong, there is a lack of sharpness. The shadow patterns cast by the legs of the dancer and the stool are softly defined. Without doubt, Degas saw lighting clearly.

How was this clarity of vision achieved? Was Degas such a gifted person that it required only a paintbrush to be put in his hand for the masterpieces to appear? There is ample evidence that he worked hard to develop his art.

When Degas died in 1917, his house in Paris, that was also his studio, was found to contain dozens of clay and wax figures. He only exhibited one sculpture – *The Little Dancer Aged Fourteen* – and in that sense these were not sculptures. There were figures of ballet dancers, thoroughbred horses, and women going about their ablutions. These were his fascinations and the recurring themes of his paintings and pastel studies, and he used the figures as tools to sharpen his observation. A friend has described a visit to Degas' house in which he slowly rotated a figure in the light of a candle so that they could watch the changing projection of the figure on a white wall. The figures are now very fragile, but several art museums have collections of castings made from the originals. The balanced poise of a ballet dancer (Figure 4.4), the frozen movement of a horse (Figure 4.5), and the relaxation of a woman taking a bath (Figure 4.6) can be seen captured in three-dimensional form. He studied these subjects meticulously. He actually had a bath installed in his studio for his models to climb in and out of. When a series of photographs by Eadweard Muybridge showing the exact movements of a horse in walking, trotting, cantering and galloping appeared in *La Nature* (Figure 4.7), Degas studied these pictures with care. He remarked to a friend that he had not previously understood how a horse moves, and the result of his observation entered his art. His earlier paintings had followed the convention of showing galloping horses as if flying, with legs stretched fore and aft, while later paintings captured a much more realistic sense of movement. It should be appreciated that this was in an age when everyone was familiar with the sight of horses and would instantly recognize the difference between a horse that was galloping or trotting. To recognize something is not the same thing as seeing it with the clarity needed to reproduce it.

Also found in Degas' house were many sketches and notebooks. These were his records of thousands of observations, and it was

Figure 4.4:   *Ballet dancer, first position (Degas)*

Figure 4.5:   *Horse figures (Degas)*

Figure 4.6:   *The tub (Degas, 1889)*

from these that he developed his figures, pastel sketches and
oil paintings. Figure 4.8 shows a rendering of the dance master
seen in Figures 4.1. and 4.2. This person is no figment of Degas'
imagination. This is Jules Perrot, who had been an international

Figure 4.7:    *Photographic study of horses in motion (Muybridge, c. 1887)*
(Source: *Dunlop, I.* Degas, *Thames and Hudson, 1979. Courtesy of Professor Aaron Scharf)*

Figure 4.8:    *Study for portrait of Jules Perrot (Degas, 1875) (courtesy of Philadelphia Museum of Art: The Henry P. McIlhenny Collection in memory of Frances P. McIlhenny)*

celebrity in his earlier years as a dancer at the Paris Opera, and later as a choreographer. Degas sketched the old man rehearsing dancers and then worked the image into several of his finished works. He could never have set up an easel to capture the intimacy and action of these busy and ever-changing situations. The three ballet scenes shown were produced by drawing on a variety of his rapidly recorded images. His numerous observations of dancers practising, resting, stretching, or standing in clusters, provided the range of forms and textures that he brought together in his composition. The uniting force of the composition is light, which flows through the space, interacting uniquely with every object it encounters. Notice how he has set M. Perrot into the two different light fields in Figures 4.1 and 4.2. Degas used every means at his disposal to study his chosen objects and their interactions with light, and it appears that he continued to study lighting throughout his working life.

Degas' financial stability enabled him to indulge in his fascinations: the ballet, horse racing, and women. Few of us are so fortunate. As lighting designers, we are likely to be working on a shopping mall this week, a church next week, and an airport terminal the week after. How can we be expected to develop a comparable ability to visualize lighting in a design concept? Whereas Degas studied specific objects, Section 2.3 discusses generic objects which generate highlight, shadow and shading patterns. While your experience of this exploration remains some paragraphs and photographs in a book, it is of limited practical value. When it becomes the memory of direct observation in a variety of lighting conditions, it can give rise to a vivid sense of how lighting can be understood in terms of its potential to generate lighting patterns. There is no evidence that Degas' analyses identified the three lighting patterns, but without doubt, for the restricted range of objects that he chose to observe, he developed deep understanding of lighting's potential to interact with those objects. The insight of the three lighting patterns, and the concepts of the sharpness and the flow of light, extend our scope to visualize lighting's interactions in different design situations. The three generic objects separate, as far as possible, the lighting patterns for observation. The art of drawing on one's own experience of these patterns and relating them to a design situation lies at the heart of visualizing a lighting concept.

## 4.2  Allusion and illusion

The basic purpose of visual perception is to enable recognition of object attributes. This presents the lighting designer with a choice of two options: either to support the process of visual perception by providing lighting that promotes confident recognition of object attributes, or to apply lighting in ways that mislead people about object attributes, even to the point of deliberately creating ambiguities or illusory experiences. As in the previous section, we will look at the work of an artist to explore this notion.

M.C. Escher was born in the Netherlands in 1898. His father had ambitions for his son and persuaded him to study architecture. However, one of Escher's tutors recognized his skill in graphic design and encouraged him instead to develop that

talent. Under the tutor's guidance, he developed high levels of skill in producing woodcuts, lithographs and mezzotints. He left his home country in 1922, and during the next fourteen years he developed a pleasant lifestyle. During the summers he would travel in Southern Italy, and also in other Mediterranean countries, and in the winters he would return to his studio in Rome and produce woodcuts from the many sketches he had made during his travels. Figure 4.9 is an example that shows his accomplished technique, and also his sense of the flow of light where he shows advancing surfaces catching the light as they squeeze the flow, leaving receding surfaces in the shade. Even so, there is as yet no sign of artistic genius.

In 1936 he visited the Moorish citadel of the Alhambra, which overlooks the city of Granada in Southern Spain. This magnificent group of buildings had been abandoned without a struggle following the defeat of the Moors by the Christian Spaniards, and is one of the world's outstanding examples of Moorish architecture. A feature of that culture is the manner in which art and architecture were integrated. While the attention of other tourists was no doubt directed towards the columns

Figure 4.10:   *Wall tiles at the Alhambra*

Figure 4.11:   *Sketch of wall tiles, Alhambra (Escher, 1936) (Copyright © 2008 The M.C. Escher Company-Holland. All rights reserved. www.mcescher.com)*

and pinnacles, Escher was fascinated by the intricate patterns of the tiles that cover much of the lower walls (Figure 4.10). He sketched them in meticulous detail, as shown in Figure 4.11.

In Section 1.1 we examined a few visual illusions, and Figure 4.12 shows another famous one. This is Rubin's figure, and it is an example of the figure–ground phenomenon. You may perceive two faces confronting each other, or you may perceive a black chalice. When one alternative becomes figure the other becomes ground. Once you have experienced the alternatives, it is virtually impossible to look at the figure without perceiving one or the other of them. Your perceptual process always seeks to attach meaning to the incoming flow of visual information. Also, it is virtually impossible to perceive both alternatives simultaneously. It would seem that figure needs ground to have meaning.

Returning to the Alhambra tiles, at a distance these surfaces appear as textures, but closer, the figure–ground phenomenon becomes apparent. The devices by which this effect is achieved are ingenious. The variety of sizes and shapes is far more limited

than would at first appear. In some cases, only one shape is used, and the figure–ground effect is achieved by colour contrast. The shapes share common boundaries, filling all of the available space. The more straightforward effects involve two colours, with more figure–ground options occurring where three or more colours are used.

The rise of fascism in Italy at this time was not to Escher's liking, and he left Rome for good and returned to the Netherlands by way of Switzerland and Belgium. No more did he travel to seek inspiration for his art. He set to work in whatever passed for a studio, and soon he was producing sketches of shapes with common boundaries that filled the space. Islam forbids images, but Escher took the artistic framework of the Alhambra tile makers and developed it with simple, familiar images from nature (Figure 4.13). From these sketches he produced the works that would eventually catch the imagination of the art world. Reputed to be his most popular work, 'Day and Night' shown in Figure 4.14, dates from 1938. The pattern of square fields flows skywards into a zone of ambiguity, where shapes could be fields or birds, and birds could be black or white. The birds fly outwards in rigid formations over night and day landscapes, each a mirror image of the other. This concept of filling two-dimensional space with figures that have shared boundaries and then developing them into the third dimension was pursued to produce extraordinary surreal cycles, as shown in Figure 4.15.

Escher now set about making analytical studies of visual illusions. Figure 4.16 shows a familiar illusion: the impossible triangle. Actually, it is not impossible. It can be constructed in solid form, but it has to be viewed through one eye from a fixed position to see the view shown in the figure. Escher examined this illusion

with care, and Figures 4.16 to 4.19 show the progression of his sketches in which he developed the illusion into architectural form, and produced his celebrated 'Waterfall' lithograph (Figure 4.20). The perspective of this work shows the water flowing over the waterfall, and running downhill through the zig-zag channel, to again drop over the waterfall. This play upon perspective clearly was a fascination for Escher at his time. 'Belvedere' (Figure 4.21), which he produced in 1958, is a spectacular example in which he shows us the visual illusion upon which it is based. At the bottom of the figure the sane man studies the impossible cube while the lunatic, restrained behind bars in this strange building, looks on uncomprehendingly.

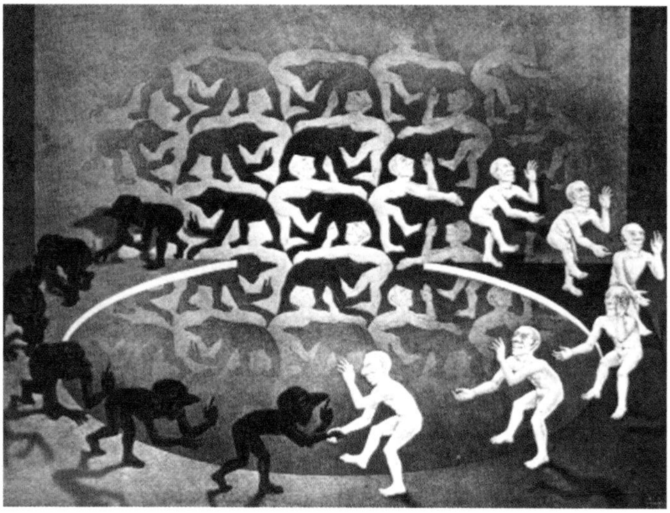

Figure 4.15: *Encounter (Escher, 1944) (Copyright © 2008 The M.C. Escher Company-Holland. All rights reserved. www.mcescher.com)*

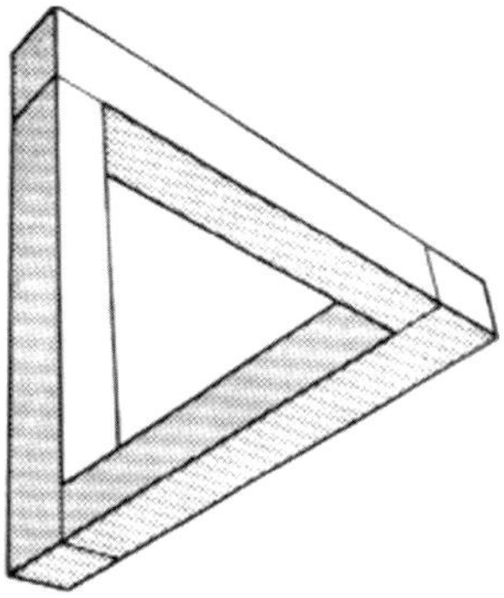

Figure 4.16: *The impossible triangle*

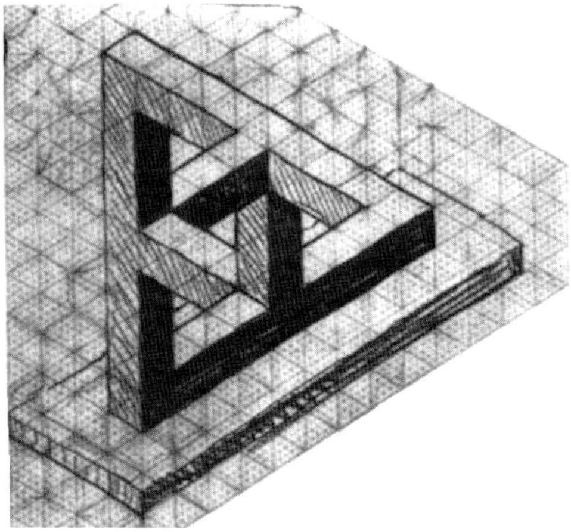

Figure 4.17: *Second development sketch for 'Waterfall' (Copyright © 2008 The M.C. Escher Company-Holland. All rights reserved. www.mcescher.com)*

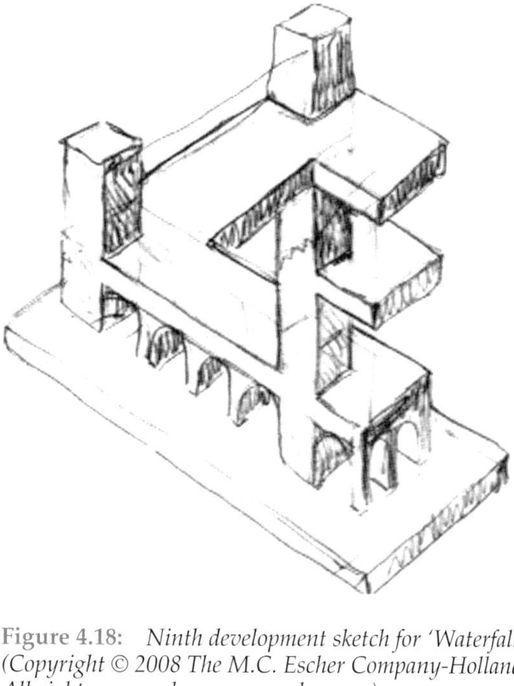

Figure 4.18: *Ninth development sketch for 'Waterfall' (Copyright © 2008 The M.C. Escher Company-Holland. All rights reserved. www.mcescher.com)*

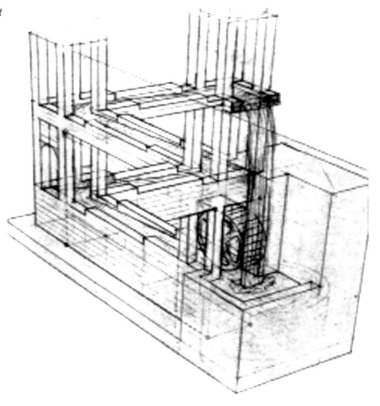

The relevance of Escher's work to this text is that he applied his acute powers of observation to understanding illusions, from which he developed his art works. There are many examples of illusory effects in architecture. From the temples of ancient Greece to the Gothic cathedrals of the middle ages, and through to the glass towers of the modern era, we can see examples of designers who have sought to challenge visual perception. They have worked with extended perspectives, forms that defy our sense of scale, and surfaces that lack substance. Subtle and restrained use of daylight has often been part of the effect. It follows that it is not necessarily the aim of lighting design to reveal clearly and accurately. While the visual perception process is working to recognize the worldly materials that surround us, designers may be seeking to put those materials together in ways that create appearances that are not simply the sum of their physical properties. It needs to be recognized that when a designer aims to create a visual experience that extends beyond revealing object attributes, what the designer is seeking to do is to mislead the perceptual process. For the examples given, Escher has worked from robust visual illusions that confuse the perceptual process under almost any lighting condition. His two-dimensional

**Figure 4.20:** *Waterfall (Escher, 1961) (Copyright © 2008 The M.C. Escher Company-Holland. All rights reserved. www.mcescher.com)*

**Figure 4.21:** *Belvedere (Escher, 1958) (Copyright © 2008 The M.C. Escher Company-Holland. All rights reserved. www.mcescher.com)*

representations are illusory in their fundamental nature, but they lack the opportunities to explore perceptual ambiguities created by interactions of light and form that are available to both artists and architects who work with three-dimensional forms.

We saw in Section 1.1 how the perceptual process tends to enhance contrasts at boundaries. It also works to reduce contrasts within boundaries, and this can be demonstrated by observing a plane surface, such as a wall or ceiling, through a visual reduction tube. A length of plastic or cardboard tubing about 2 cm diameter and 40 cm long will serve this purpose. What is perceived as a homogeneous material of more or less uniform appearance may be shown to vary substantially in brightness and colour. Why would the perceptual process be discounting luminous contrasts within boundaries while enhancing them at boundaries?

The basic purpose of visual perception is to enable recognition of object attributes. When a zone of a complex visual field is identified as representing an element such as a wall, it is perceived to have homogeneous properties. Gradual differences of brightness or colour are discounted unless they are perceived to indicate useful information such as curvature or texture. Differences that appear organized along a line are interpreted quite differently. If perceived as a boundary, this is important information, and the apparent difference is enhanced. It follows that whatever is the nature of the visual field that a designer chooses to present to a viewer, the viewer will mentally divide the field into elements. Within each element contrasts will appear diminished, and at boundaries contrasts will appear enhanced. If the designer's aim is to present a view for which perception will be quick, accurate and confident, the following principles should be observed:

• the number of visibly separate elements should be limited

• variation of colour and texture within each element should be minimized

• boundaries of elements should be clearly delineated.

The 'modern' architecture of the 1920s complies with these principles perfectly (Figure 4.22). When these buildings were new, their appearance was revolutionary. Now that they have become familiar objects, the clarity of their expression still catches our attention. They are pre-processed images that take a fast-track through the perceptual process.

Alternatively, a designer could opt for perceptual ambiguity by creating a visual field that acts against each of these principles. The obvious example is military camouflage, but architecture also offers scope for this approach as in Figure 4.23. In fact, these diametrically opposed design approaches can be applied to virtually any artefact, the difference being in the nature of the perception that is generated by the image of the object. In the former case, the designer presents visual clues that *allude* to the physical attributes of the object. In the latter case, the visual clues deliberately detract from those attributes to create a perception that is *illusory*. This is the basis for the distinction between allusion and illusion. There may be many reasons for taking this latter course. The aim may be to enhance the glossiness or the colourfulness of merchandise; it may be to stimulate a sense of excitement and unpredictability; or it may be to impart a sense of mystery and intrigue. Whatever the designer's intentions, the basic choice is a binary: to employ allusion or illusion.

It is not easy to provide sufficient illumination to satisfy basic needs for safe movement and to mislead perception. The visual illusions that have been referred to are notable because they can be relied upon to do so. However, in our daily lives we are

**Figure 4.22:** *A building that complies with the principles for quick, accurate, and confident perception. Maison Planeix, Paris, by Le Corbusier, 1924–28. (Source: Gans, D.,* The Le Corbusier Guide: Revised edition, *Princeton Architectural Press, 2000) (courtesy of Simon Glynn www. galinsky.com)*

**Figure 4.23:** *A building that does not comply with perceptual principles, but instead offers a play upon perceptual ambiguity. Casa Battló façade, Barcelona, by Antoni Gaudi, 1904–06. (Source: Futagawa, Y.,* Gaudi, *A.D.A. EDITA, Tokyo, 2003) (Copyright © Parth Patwari Great Buildings.com)*

Figure 4.24:   *Human scale, natural*
*and familiar materials, and a coherent*
*flow of light*

confronted with a constant flow of visual information, much of
it derived under deprived visual conditions. Gloom, distorted
colour appearance, and sun glare present gross challenges to
perception, and yet we seldom falter. For those of us with normal vision, the perceptual process generally manages to provide
a mental model of our surroundings that is sufficient for our
purpose. In the examples shown, Escher has sought to engage
our intellects by presenting images that cannot be resolved, and
we can enjoy the experience because we are conscious that we
are observing from a safe and stable situation. Architecture
forms the situation that encloses the viewer, and this changes
and intensifies the experience of perceptual ambiguity.

Figure 4.24 shows a domestic living room that could have been
designed with the intention of preserving visual constancy. The
scale is human and the materials are natural and familiar. Also,
the flow of light is coherent and the colour rendering is excellent.
The little boy in Figure 4.25 is in a similar setting, and he is comfortable and relaxed. The windows show that this room is set in
a lush, green environment, and they also provide a varied pattern of light and shade through the space. The boy has chosen
to set up his train set in a pool of light where the flow of light is
distinct. These are examples of what may be called *the architecture of reassurance.*

Figure 4.26 shows a residential dining room. There is no visual
contact with the outside, and what at first appears to be a connection to an adjoining space turns out to be a mirror. Perhaps
the most remarkable thing about this space is the fact that we
are able to understand it at all. Consider the table. The frame

Figure 4.25:   *The architecture of reassurance*

**Figure 4.26:**   *A perceptually challenging space (courtesy of Concord: Marlin)*

**Figure 4.27:**   *The architecture of arousal (courtesy of Concord: Marlin)*

comprises polished chromium tubes. This is a material that has no visible surface, and we infer the surface from the distorted reflected image of the surroundings. The table-top is clear glass, and here again, we infer a table-top from the appearance of objects supported in a plane where a table-top should be. We could go on picking our way through the items of this setting before concluding that virtually every aspect of the design presents a challenge to the perceptual process. This is an example of *the architecture of arousal*. Lighting has a special role here. Should anyone start to feel comfortable in this space, it can be instantly transformed to provide a new perceptual challenge as shown in Figure 4.27.

Perceptual reassurance occurs in architecture in many guises. The interior of Chartres cathedral (Figure 4.28) has subdued lighting in which the grey stone columns rise up to the gloom of the roof, but as you come around a corner you can be struck by the brilliance of the stained glass and play of light on the stone forms (Figure 4.29). The effect is arousing and illusory. Meanwhile the exterior of the cathedral is bathed in daylight which reveals every detail and shade of colour faithfully (Figure 4.30). There is no scope here for illusion until night falls, when the cathedral takes on an entirely different appearance. It loses its solidity; it seems to float above the ground; it appears to be luminous (Figure 4.31). On the turn of a switch it has been converted from allusion to illusion. Its appearance has changed from object surface mode to illuminant mode.

Visual constancy was reviewed in Section 1.1, and its relevance to allusion and illusion is obvious. While illusion depends upon

**Figure 4.28:**  *Chartres cathedral interior*                    **Figure 4.29:**  *A view inside the cathedral*

**Figure 4.30:** *Chartres cathedral exterior by day*

**Figure 4.31:** *Chartres cathedral exterior by night*

breaking down constancy, allusion is supported by preserving the visual constancies. This can be identified as a design philosophy that is associated with the architecture of reassurance. There are many good reasons for employing this approach. People waiting in an airport departure lounge, or in a dentist's waiting room, are not seeking perceptual stimulation from their environment. More generally, work locations and places where people are trying to find their way are spaces where it is sensible for designers to aim to preserve the visual constancies and provide for allusion. Generally, standards and recommendations for good lighting are guidance for constancy and allusion. Guidance for preserving visual constancy is discussed in Section 5.1.

Illusion is achieved by breaking the rules for visual constancy. This has to be done systematically to be effective, because perception is always seeking to make sense of the visual information flow and to provide a mental model that accurately and reliably represents the physical nature of the surrounding environment.

## 4.3 Lighting concepts

The design approach described in this book is based upon six lighting concepts:

- ambient illumination

- visual discrimination

- illumination hierarchy

- flow of light

- sharpness of lighting

- luminous elements.

These concepts have been discussed in Chapter 2 and are summarized below. In the next chapter we explore how these individual lighting concepts are developed into a total design concept for a specific situation. It is important to keep in mind that a lighting concept does not refer to something that is good or bad about lighting, but rather it identifies an aspect of lighting that influences the overall design concept. Design is not a linear process and the priority to be given to the concepts depends on the design objectives for the job in hand. The order in which they are listed is arbitrary. However, every one of lighting concepts is relevant to the overall design concept.

In the notes below, $\Delta+$ or $\Delta-$ indicate increasing/decreasing changes and $>$ or $<$ indicate greater/less than. Associated subjective scales are shown in italics, and note the difference between bipolar scales (e.g. *bright–dim*) and uni-polar scales (e.g. *brightness*).

## Ambient illumination

The aspect of illumination that relates to an overall subjective impression of the lighting within a space and to which the response of the visual system adjusts. It may be subject to temporal change, either as the lighting within a space varies over time or as the viewer moves from one space to another. See Section 2.1.

| | |
|---|---|
| *Mode of appearance:* | Non-located illumination. |
| *Design criteria:* | Overall impression of brightness: *bright–dim*. Overall illumination colour appearance: *warm–cool*. |
| *Related metrics:* | Mean room surface exitance, $M_{rs}$. Correlated colour temperature, CCT. |
| *Lighting objectives:* | $\Delta + M_{rs} \rightarrow$ Stimulation, fast-pace; Combine $M_{rs} > 200 \text{ lm/m}^2$ with CCT $> 5000 \text{ K}$ for sense of vitality, activity, efficiency, work ethic. |
| | $\Delta - M_{rs} \rightarrow$ Relaxation, slow-pace; Combine $M_{rs} < 100 \text{ lm/m}^2$ with CCT $< 3500 \text{ K}$ for sense of restfulness, cosiness. |

## Visual discrimination

Lighting for discrimination of detail and colour. See Section 2.2.

| | |
|---|---|
| *Mode of appearance:* | Located surface. |
| *Design criteria:* | Clarity of detail: *hazy–clear*. |
| | Visual performance. |
| | Clarity of colour: *colourfulness*. |
| *Related metrics:* | Task or object illuminance, $E_t$. |
| | Relative visual performance, RVP*. |
| | Colour rendering index CRI in conjunction with CCT. |
| *Lighting objectives:* | $\Delta + E_t$ for small detail and/or low task contrast. |
| | $E_t$ and C combination on the 'high RVP plateau'. |
| | Task-surround-background luminance gradient. Avoid disability glare and veiling reflections*. |
| | High CRI with CCT $> 4000$ K and $E > 1000$ lx to maximize colourfulness. |

*Disability glare and contrast rendering are discussed in the text but metrics are not given.
Sources listed in Further Reading offer some relevant measures.

## Illumination hierarchy

A distribution of illuminance and illumination colour appearance that reinforces an ordered sense of the visual significance of objects and room surfaces. See Section 2.3.

| | |
|---|---|
| *Mode of appearance:* | Located illumination. |
| *Design criteria:* | Emphasis, attraction of attention. |
| | Order, visual hierarchy of objects and room surfaces. |
| | Illumination colour appearance difference. |
| *Related metrics:* | Illuminance ratios, $E_{s1}/E_{s2}$. |
| | Reciprocal mega Kelvin difference, MK$^{-1}$. |
| *Lighting objectives:* | Illuminance ratios for 'perceived difference' of appearance. Visual task illuminance sets the anchor illuminance. |
| | Illumination colour appearance differences to enhance the visual effect of illuminance ratios, sunlight/skylight effect. |

## *Flow of light*

An impression of the directionality of lighting in terms of strength and direction, made evident by the shading patterns generated by three-dimensional objects which intercept the 'flow'. See Section 2.4.

| | |
|---|---|
| *Mode of appearance:* | May be perceived in located illumination mode (flow of light) or in object mode (form, texture). |
| *Design criteria:* | Strength of flow; *weak–strong, soft–harsh.* |
| | Direction of flow (e.g. lateral, downward). |
| | Shading patterns, revealing form and texture. |
| | Coherence of the flow of light: *coherence.* |
| *Related metrics:* | Vector/scalar ratio; $\lvert\mathbf{E}\rvert/E_{sr}$. |
| | Vector altitude angle $\alpha$ and vector azimuth angle $\beta$; alternatively the vector direction may be defined by the unit vector $\mathbf{e}$. |
| | Flow of light ratio, $\lvert\mathbf{E}_{ap}\rvert/E_{vhs}$. |
| *Lighting objectives:* | Refer to Table 2.7 to relate $\lvert\mathbf{E}\rvert/E_{sr}$ to apparent strength of flow. |
| | Relate direction of flow to features of illuminated objects. |
| | Coherence of the flow of light within the space. |
| | Distinction of daytime and night-time appearance. |

## *Sharpness of lighting*

An impression of lighting evidenced by sharply-defined highlight patterns on glossy surfaces and clean-cut boundaries of cast shadows. See Section 2.5.

| | |
|---|---|
| *Mode of appearance:* | May be perceived in object mode (gloss, lustre) or located illuminant mode (sparkle, glitter). |

| | |
|---|---|
| *Design criteria:* | Highlight patterns; *sharpness, brightness*. (Bright highlights may be recognized as glare or as sparkle according to context.) |
| | Shadow patterns; *soft–sharp, weak–strong*. (Strong shadows that have soft edges are likely to be recognized as shading patterns.) |
| *Related metrics:* | Highlight ratio, HLR. |
| | Source distance, $D$. |
| *Lighting objectives:* | High HLR for 'sharp' highlight and shadow patterns. Note the $D^2$ effect explained in the text. |
| | Low $M_{rs}$ for 'strong' shadow patterns. |
| | High contrasts in surrounding field for high contrasts in object appearance. |

(Note: The designer must consider both whether sharpness is an appropriate design objective and if the object properties are suitable for this attribute of lighting to be evident.)

## Luminous elements

Elements in the field of view that are perceived to be sources of light, which may include reflecting of trans-illuminated components of luminaires as well as direct views of lamps. See Section 2.6.

| | |
|---|---|
| *Mode of appearance:* | Located illuminant. |
| *Design criteria:* | Object brightness; *brightness, sparkling, glaring*[**]. |
| | Liveliness, a stimulating appearance. |
| *Related metrics:* | Source/background luminance ratio, $L_s/L_b$[***]. |
| *Lighting objectives:* | Brightness to provide for sparkle while avoiding glare. The sparkle may add to the overall impression of sharpness. |
| | 'Added element' decorations; 'something worth looking at'. |

[**]The appearance of a bright luminous element may be perceived as glare or as sparkle according to context and the meaning that is associated with it.

[***]Discomfort glare indices such as the Unified Glare Rating are sometimes quoted in this context.

# Concept development 5

The development of a lighting design concept involves applying the observation-based experience discussed in Part One to a design situation. Chapter 4 has shown different ways in which elements of experience and knowledge may be brought together to achieve a design concept or a work of art. In this chapter we look specifically at how a lighting designer brings together the elements of a lighting design concept.

## 5.1 Getting the picture

### A visual hierarchy

Howard Brandston was a colleague of mine for some years at the Lighting Research Center, and on several occasions I witnessed him sitting through a student presentation of a lighting design proposal where the student would give a detailed explanation of lamps, luminaires and controls. After a pause, Howard would ask, 'What is it that you wish me to see?' His aim was to stimulate the student to make a critical examination of the design intent, and this disarmingly simple question opens up the range of design issues. It implies that, in any situation, the lighting designer has options to cause some things to be noticed more than others. In order to direct people's attention purposefully, the designer establishes the concept of a visual hierarchy that is responsive to the overall design intent. For this to happen, the designer must be able to visualize the situation. The design concept has to develop as a clear and detailed image in the designer's mind. It should become a three-dimensional entity in which the designer is able to undergo the visual experience of the space, and above all, to see the lighting clearly.

### Unifying design concepts

As the design concept develops in the designer's mind into an increasingly detailed perception, there is a danger that the design intent will be killed by complexity. As each object is envisaged with its desirable attributes brilliantly revealed, so it becomes easy to lose sight of the overriding concepts that give

*Facing page: Reagan National Airport.*
*The New Terminal Complex designed by architect Cesar Pelli opened in 1997. In the daytime view the electric lighting has just been switched on, but it is completely dominated by the flood of daylight from the extensive glazed wall and the overhead skylights. As the daylight fades, the simple arrangements of reflector lamps within the branch-like steel structure (see inset) create a quite different aesthetic. Note: Top picture is daytime; Bottom picture is night time*

unity overall design concept. As we saw in Section 4.1, it was the notion of a coherent light field that brought Degas' dancers into a single composition. A distribution of light and shade that may be complex and varied in detail may become an instantly recognized and unified light field through having the characteristic of coherence. This occurs naturally in daylit interiors, and is the basis of the love affair that many architects express for the ever-changing flow of light that characterizes these spaces. However, it is not necessarily restricted to daylit spaces.

It is always instructive to envisage the daytime appearance of a space before starting to think about the electric lighting, which involves applying the observation-based experience described in Part One. Perhaps the daytime appearance needs the addition of electric lighting to reinforce a visual hierarchy, but is this to complement the daytime light field, or to overturn it? Is the daylight to retain its coherence with the electric lighting altering the balance of the lighting patterns on selected objects, or is the electric lighting to change the perceived flow of light within the space? How do these notions of lighting relate to the changes of appearance as daylight fades and electric lighting becomes the dominant force? The skill to envisage lighting three-dimensionally is crucial. Particularly in situations where the design intent would be supported by allusory references and preserving the visual constancies, the lighting concepts described in Section 4.3 become the guides by which lighting designers can express a clear sense of design purpose.

## User expectations

It is reasonable to assume that every person arriving at the design site has a reason for being there, and so each individual has certain expectations. There will be differences of expectations between those people for whom the space is familiar and those who are seeing it for the first time, and those who are coming to the space out of choice and those for whom it is a duty. These differing expectations are not of equal importance. It is more important that the customers like the ambience of a restaurant than that the waiters find their tasks easy to perform. Not all customers are of equal importance. Some restaurants seek to attract passing trade, while others depend upon maintaining a regular clientele. The former might place emphasis on the appearance of the restaurant seen from outside, while the latter may deliberately close off the view from outside.

The initial level of decision-making concerns: Whose responses matter? Why are they in the space? What are their expectations? The first stage of design development occurs when the mental concept develops from being perceived as a location to becoming a space that is seen through the eyes of a particular person. We will refer to this person as the viewer, and it is the expectations of this person that determine what are the relevant lighting criteria, and how these combine to form the design concept.

## Lighting design strategies

From the preceding two sections, the special skill of the lighting designer is the ability to envision the design situation in light, and this involves the ability to 'see the lighting clearly'. Is the experience to be allusory or illusory? Where the aim is perceptual reassurance, allusory clues will dominate and the visual constancies will be supported. Where the aim is to attract attention, illusory clues may be presented within an allusory setting, such as by merchandise cabinets within a hotel foyer. The lighting in the cabinets can be arranged to give emphasis to selected object characteristics, and the effect becomes illusory when the source of light is concealed. Where the aim is to achieve an enhanced appearance, the illusory clues must dominate to achieve visual constancy breakdowns. The perceptual process is very adept at making sense of ambiguous information. These initial decisions are major determinants of the overall strategy for the lighting.

Consider how these concepts relate to interior lighting design. Typically, most of the elements that comprise a room and its contents are perceived in surface mode and have many differences of attributes including differences of lightness. Materials such as glass or transparent plastic are perceptually more complex, as they may have some attributes that are perceived in surface mode and some which are perceived in volume mode. To provide for confident, unambiguous perceptions of surroundings these differences must be revealed, and for this purpose the lighting designer introduces luminaires which, generally, are perceived in illuminant mode and have the attribute of brightness. The illumination that they provide gives an overall impression of brightness, and also may impart patterns of light and shade that are perceived in illumination mode.

## The role of constancy

The situation described in the previous paragraph is one for which visual constancy holds. Lynes (1994) has identified the following precepts which act to maintain constancy:

- adequate light
- no disability glare

- high chroma, particularly on dimly lit surfaces

- a variety of colours

- small white surfaces ('separators')

- natural organic materials with characteristic colours and textures

- no large glossy areas

- sources of light should be obvious (but not necessarily visible)

- recognizable texture

- good colour rendering.

There are some good reasons why lighting designers should aim to maintain visual constancy. As explained in Section 1.1, the process of perception is a process of trying to make sense of an incessant flow of continually changing data, where usually the aim is to enable one to orientate and find one's way in a world of mostly stable objects. To this end, the process is attuned to filtering out effects of lighting patterns in order to construct a perception of spaces and objects whose physical characteristics are recognized and clearly identified, and which together comprise a perceived world of stable spatial relationships. The design of, for example, an airport departure lounge should support users' understandable wish to orientate, find their way, and to feel reassured of the stability of their environment.

However, a world of perfect visual constancy would be a plain vanilla world. There are times when people choose to challenge notions of a stable reality. Some ride roller coasters and some seek out nightclubs with strobe lights and other disorienting devices, but it is not necessary to go to such extremes to challenge visual constancy. When a designer determines a hierarchy of elements in the field of view and selects some of these to be enhanced, the implicit aim is to cause some loss of constancy. Constancy is not an all or nothing phenomenon, and whenever designers work to bring out the sheen of a material, or even to 'reveal its natural colour', they are modifying the perception of that material. To do this, they act against the precepts listed by Lynes. The light sources are concealed; sharp highlights and contrasts are provided; and often the selected object is separated from its surroundings by a frame or by low-reflectance materials. When a person can not judge illuminance, their assessment of lightness ceases to be related to reflectance. Such viewing conditions enable designers to make objects 'stand out' and to make colours 'glow'. These are situations in which illumination is being perceived in an object mode.

Returning to Brandston's question, what is it that you wish the viewer to see? Not anything is possible, but nonetheless, the lighting designer who learns to apply observation-based experience to visualizing the design concept can be said to have got the picture.

## 5.2  The Design Features Report

The Design Features Report (DFR) is the principal means by which the lighting designer communicates the concept to the client and other designers, notably the architect. Up to this point, the concept has been evolving as an image in the designer's brain. Now the designer has to share the concept so that it can be discussed, perhaps modified, and approved.

As the design concept is a unique combination of lighting concepts, so the descriptions and illustrations given in the DFR should reflect the priorities and emphasis of that combination. It is the client's approval that is being sought, and for this reason the DFR is addressed primarily to the client and secondarily to other designers. Much of the skill in preparing a DFR involves understanding the concerns of the client, and demonstrating how those concerns will be met.

Client's concerns differ vastly. Some are concerned with achieving a safe and productive workplace; others want to attract customers and sell merchandise; still others are anxious to achieve sustainability and utilization of renewable resources. All clients are concerned about cost. Very few are actually concerned with the quality of lighting. This is a recurring frustration that lighting designers have to learn to cope with. Whereas most people are willing to acknowledge that other people's perceptions of their surroundings are primarily derived from vision and that the visual process requires light in order to operate, it takes a special interest to appreciate how that perception may be influenced by the nature of the lighting. Very few clients want to hear about the unique combination of lighting concepts and their associated metrics. They want to know how the lighting will satisfy their concerns, and this is what the lighting designer must address in the DFR.

The DFR is, therefore, a crucial aspect of a designer's professional communication with the client. For a designer to be effective, communication with the client needs to reflect the designer's individual style and concern for the client's concerns. It is never easy to communicate the visual effects of lighting. It is highly instructive to supplement the exercises in observation described in Part One with sketching, because this directs the observer to identify the aspects of appearance that give rise to the visual effect. Generally, a good lighting concept would still look good in a black and white photograph. Try thinking through your concepts as black and white images. Try rendering them as sketches. Do not attempt to show light within the volume of the space, unless the appearance of high-intensity beams shining through a hazy or smoky atmosphere is part of your concept. Do not fall into the trap of showing luminaires belching out cones of grey or yellow fog. Show the patterns of light and shade on illuminated three-dimensional objects. Show the coherence of the flow of light. Capture the highlight patterns, and pick out the sparkle. While these terms may not mean much to the client, these are all recognizable aspects of appearance that distinguish lighting that has been designed for the situation from a standard lighting layout.

Every lighting designer has to develop a communication technique that suits their style and fulfils their needs. The technique favoured by the author is to start by sketching an outline perspective of the space onto medium-grey paper. Shading is then filled in using soft pencil or black crayon, and highlights are picked out using white crayon. This technique of separately rendering the light and the shade is more than an effective communication tool. It is useful in the design development stage as it focuses thinking onto how the illumination distribution and the arrangement of luminous elements support the design objectives.

It is inevitable that an increasing number of designers will choose to use computer rendering software to illustrate their design concepts. The attraction of this technology is obvious, but some caution is advisable. The use of three-dimensional computer graphical systems to generate the outline perspective so that it can be printed onto grey paper as described in the previous paragraph makes a lot of sense. To have the computer provide a full-colour rendering of the view raises some questions. The author's own research (Cuttle, 2001) has involved small groups of subjects undertaking subjective appraisals of several real situations with different lighting conditions, and also appraising the same views presented as computer-generated screen images and colour print-outs. The differences found included:

- Print-out images appeared darker (less bright) than either screen images of the real situation.

- For low-illuminance situations, both images were rated sub-stantially darker and with less ease of seeing than the real situation.

- Screen images were rated more pleasant and more attractive than print-out images.

- Both images appeared to have more shadow than the real situation.

- Print-out images received low ratings for colour appearance.

- Where glare or veiling reflections were noticed in the real situation, they were not apparent in the images.

It can, of course, be argued that different software or hardware would change the quality of the images, but at least this study warns against designers supposing that the output of one of these systems is assured to be a valid representation of the input. Nonetheless, computer-generated images are all around us, so what is their proper role in lighting design? In the author's opinion, to use these systems as design tools, whereby the designer thinks of an arrangement of luminaires and uses the computer to see how it would appear, is a recipe for disaster. There are too many aspects of appearance that matter in real life but which may be distorted or omitted by a computer image. However, the designer who develops the lighting concept as a mental image, and then uses the available controls to modify a computer image so that it represents the mental image, has an alternative means of communication.

# Part Three: Realization

The key to the lighting designer realizing the design concept is a technical specification document. It defines lamp watts and beam spreads; locations and aiming angles; fenestration and lighting circuit controls. It is offered with the promise, 'Install this equipment in accordance with these instructions and you will have the lighting that I have described to you.' This leap from the cerebral to the technical is the transformation that enables the lighting concept to be provided by a lighting installation. To rely on experience is to repeat what has been done before. To be innovative it is necessary for the designer to be technically competent.

Chapter 6 explains some procedures for predicting performance requirements of a lighting installation to achieve specific aspects of the lighting design concept. Chapter 7 gives guidance on documentation and procedures that the designer has to see through to ensure that the lighting design concept will be realized.

# Delivering the lumens

For stage and studio lighting, designers work 'hands on'. Commands can be called (or even shouted) to minions, and the effects of aiming, focusing, filtering and dimming luminaires are immediately visible and can be explored until the required effect is achieved. This is not possible for architectural lighting. The concept may be developed before the space has been built. Even when lighting is being proposed for an existing space, it usually is part of a larger scheme for renovation or renewal, so that the design situation will be different. The concept has to be developed in the mind, and then translated into a schedule of lamps and luminaires, locations and controls, which will then be negotiated, tendered, and installed. According to the type of installation, the designer may have some scope for on-site adjustments, but basically the success of the lighting design depends on the designer's skill in devising a technical specification that delivers the design concept. Technical competence is an essential skill for architectural lighting designers.

The process of developing a technical specification involves calculations. There are just two good reasons for a lighting designer to make calculations. One reason is that certain lighting performance parameters have been prescribed. Perhaps the client has stipulated that a certain illuminance is to be provided for a specific activity, or there may be a mandatory requirement for energy performance. Whatever the prescribed requirements, the designer must assume that those parameters will be checked, and must take due care to ensure that they will be provided. Illumination engineering procedures have been developed for this purpose, and useful texts are listed in the Bibliography.

The other reason is that the designer wants to ensure that the envisaged concept will be achieved. It is this second reason that is the concern of this chapter.

It often happens that an architectural lighting design concept includes some visually demanding activities for which specific light levels are required. A banking hall may have been designed

**Facing page:** *Prudential Center Mall, Boston, Massachusetts. The custom-designed pendant and wall-mounted luminaires by Christopher Ripman are an attractive feature by day, and at night time appear to be the principal sources of illumination. In fact, the night time lighting is provided primarily by metal halide downlighters which are barely visible at the apex of the glazed roof*

to impress clients who will spend only a few minutes in the space, but it must also meet the requirements of the tellers who work there all day. In situations of this sort, the light level to be provided for the tellers' locations can provide a key around which the designer constructs a scale of illuminances. Is the ambient light level to appear dim relative to tellers' worktops, or vice versa, or something in between? And how do these levels relate to the appearance of a featured artwork, or the bank's notice-board of current interest rates? The designer uses observation-based experience to develop the hierarchy of illuminance that is the essence of the design concept, but the purpose of this scale of illuminances is different from that of the prescribed values. No other person is going to check these illuminances. They are values that the designer uses to achieve the envisaged balance of illumination distribution, and the client and his architect judge the lighting designer's work on how well it achieves the lighting design concept that has been described to them. Staying with the banking hall example, it matters that the balance of illumination at tellers' locations and on objects selected for special attention is as conceived by the designer. That the designer used quantitative methods to achieve this is of concern only to himself or herself.

The purpose of the calculational procedures given in this chapter is to enable some of the lighting design concepts described in the previous chapters to be realized with a reasonable level of reliability. The lighting metrics employed are those that have been identified through observation as relating to aspects of how lighting may influence the appearance of an illuminated scene, and as such, differ from the metrics dealt with in illumination engineering texts.

The main function of these calculations is to enable appropriate lamp wattages to be selected. Most of the decisions concerning the lighting installation are made as the design concept develops. It is the lighting design concept that determines the luminaire light distributions and lamp colour characteristics that are needed. The architecture and the activities within the building exert a major influence over the choice of luminaire type. The geometry of the space and the module of the building elements effectively determine the luminaire layout. This leaves lamp wattage as the principal remaining factor to be decided, and this is where calculations come in. The preceding chapters have emphasized the importance of balance in achieving lighting design concepts, and this is where it becomes important that a lighting designer can relate lighting metrics to observation-based experience of lighting. Meeting code requirements and cost budgets will inevitably involve calculations, but the reason for

making calculations as part of the design process is quite different. It is to reduce one's level of uncertainty. We may start with a
guess, and refine that with an estimate, but to have confidence
that the intended effect will be achieved requires a calculation. It
goes without saying that the calculation will serve no useful purpose unless the designer understands how the predicted quantity
relates to the visual effect. For the designer to know how certain
lighting metrics relate to his or her observation-based experience
is essential for having confidence that the lighting specification
will achieve a truly novel and original visual effect.

While it is important that the lighting designer is able to make
quantitative assessments of the performance of a lighting installation, we should keep in mind the purpose of these assessments. Suppose it has been decided that general illumination
will be provided by a layout of ceiling-mounted luminaires with
metal halide lamps, and the available lamp wattages are 125,
250 and 400 watts. How precise do we need the calculation to
be? It is important that if we specify the 250 W lamp, we can
feel confident that 125 W would be too little and 400 W would
be too much. Lamps generally come in approximately 50%
wattage increments; this sets the level of precision required.
The procedures given in this chapter aim to enable designers to
pick the right lamp wattage, and users should not expect any
higher level of precision when they apply these procedures for
predicting lighting performance.

## 6.1 Indirect flux

In the foregoing text, we have seen how a lighting designer
may influence impressions of overall brightness by controlling
levels of mean room surface exitance $M_{rs}$, where $M_{rs}$ provides
the designer with a working estimate of eye illuminance. This
is achieved by ensuring that in each space the emitted luminous flux and its spatial distribution are appropriately matched
to the volume of the space and the distribution of room surface
reflectances. This section explains how this is done.

In Section 2.1, we derived an expression for mean room surface exitance:

$$M_{rs} = \frac{F_L \cdot \rho}{A(1 - \rho)} \text{ lm/m}^2$$

where $F_L$ = initial luminous flux emitted by the luminaires (lm);
$A$ = total room surface area (m$^2$); $\rho$ = room surface reflectance.

In this expression, the room surface reflectance is assumed to be uniform, which of course is not realistic. It was noted that the top line of the expression ($F_L \rho$) is the *first reflected flux* FRF, and that the bottom line is the *room absorption*, which may be indicated by the symbol $A\alpha$. For a room that comprises $n$ surfaces, these are determined by the following expressions:

$$FRF = \sum_{s=1}^{n} E_{s(d)} \cdot A_s \cdot \rho_s$$

$$A\alpha = \sum_{s=1}^{n} A_s \cdot (1 - \rho_s)$$

where $E_{s(d)}$ = direct illuminance of surface s (lux); $A_s$ = area of surface s (m$^2$); $\rho_s$ = reflectance of surface s.

From the foregoing, we can write the general expression for mean room surface exitance:

$$M_{rs} = FRF/A\alpha$$

To illustrate application of these expressions, we will take as an example a simple rectangular space which nonetheless involves all of the commonly occurring factors that need to be taken into account.

## Calculating the first reflected flux

A hotel lift lobby opens from the main foyer. It measures $10.4 \times 4.9 \times 3.2$ m high, and has four lift doors in each of the long walls as shown in Figure 6.1. It has only one short wall, as the other end of the lobby opens into the foyer. The walls are covered with a fawn-coloured material with a fabric finish that has a reflectance of 0.35. The lift doors are 1.7 m wide and 2.0 m high, and have a bright textured metal finish, reflectance 0.8. The ceiling is a pale cream colour ($\rho = 0.65$) and the floor is polished granite ($\rho = 0.15$).

How bright do we want the ambient illumination in this lobby to appear? We do not want its appearance to compete with the foyer, which is to be a moderately bright, welcoming space. We form the view that the lobby should appear noticeably less bright than the foyer, but obviously, we do not want it to appear dim. We measure the value of $M_{rs}$ in the foyer and find it to be 210 lux. A reader who has followed the observation exercises

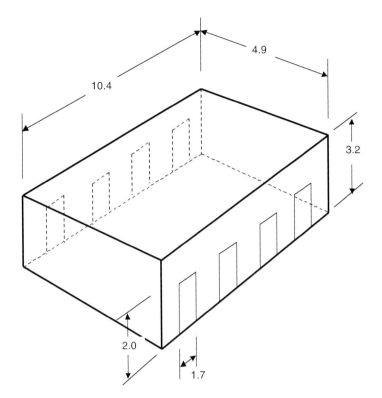

**Figure 6.1:** *Outline of lift lobby with four lift doors on each side*

described in Part One would be able to apply observation-based experience at this point, but for this example we will refer to the tabular guidance given in Part One. From Table 2.1 we see that an eye illuminance of 300 lux is likely to be assessed as a 'bright appearance' by a fully adapted observer, and 100 lux is likely to be assessed as 'acceptably bright'. As $M_{rs}$ provides our working estimate of eye illuminance, we can see that the measured value indicates a light level that accords with the design intent for the foyer. Turning to Table 2.6, we see that for a noticeable difference we need an illuminance ratio in the order of 1.5:1. This means that the $M_{rs}$ level for the lobby needs to be around two-thirds of the foyer level, so we set the target to provide a mean room surface exitance of 140 lux in the lobby. Referring back to Table 2.1, we note that this is well above the minimum for 'acceptably bright' appearance, and so should meet our objectives.

The next task is to calculate the room absorption $A\alpha$. The floor and ceiling are straightforward, but the walls require some thought. The two long walls are identical, so we will estimate the average reflectance of one of them. For the four lift doors

$\rho = 0.8$, and for the surrounding wall $\rho = 0.35$, so the average reflectance:

$$\rho_{wall} = \frac{(0.8 \cdot A_{doors}) + (0.35 \cdot (A_{wall} - A_{doors}))}{A_{wall}}$$

$$= \frac{(0.8 \cdot 13.6) + (0.35 \cdot (33.3 - 13.6))}{33.3}$$

$$= 0.53$$

We have only one end wall, so how do we deal with the opening to the foyer? If it opened to an unlit space, we would have to treat it as a heavily absorbing surface, as very few of the lumens incident on the plane of the opening will be reflected back. It would be like a black hole. However, in this case, it opens onto a space that has a higher light level, and this means that for every lumen that leaves the lobby, more than one lumen will come back into the lobby from the foyer. Instead of treating the opening as a light-absorbing surface, we should treat it as light-emitting surface.

Imagine a transparent membrane stretched across the opening. The area of the membrane is $4.9 \times 3.2 = 15.7\,m^2$, so that we will have $15.7 \times 140 = 2200$ diffusely reflected lumens incident on the lobby side of the membrane, and $15.7 \times 210 = 3300\,lm$ incident on the foyer side. The difference is $1100\,lm$, and this is a luminous flux gain to the lobby. It is approximately equal to the output of a 100 watt incandescent lamp, so it will not be of great consequence in this situation. For the moment, we will put this on one side.

To continue with calculating $A\alpha$, each surface absorption is the product of its area and its absorptance:

Surface absorption

| | |
|---|---|
| Ceiling | $10.4 \times 4.9 \times (1 - 0.65) = 17.8$ |
| 2 long walls | $2 \times 33.3 \times (1 - 0.53) = 31.3$ |
| Short wall | $4.9 \times 3.2 \times (1 - 0.35) = 10.2$ |
| Floor | $10.4 \times 4.9 \times (1 - 0.15) = 43.3$ |
| | Room absorption $A\alpha = \overline{102.6\,m^2}$ |

Then:

$$FRF = M_{rs}A\alpha$$

$$= 140 \times 102.6 = 14,400\,lm$$

But we have a gain of 1100 lm from the foyer, so that the first reflected flux to be provided by the lighting in the lobby is 14,400 − 1100 = 13,300 lm.

This is an important quantity. In order to achieve our objective of the ambient illumination in the lift lobby appearing to be just noticeably less bright than the ambient illumination in the foyer, while still appearing to be acceptably bright, this is the number of 'first-bounce' lumens that have to be put into the space. This first reflected flux is the source of the inter-reflected ambient illumination in the lift lobby.

## Providing the flux

The first reflected flux from surface s:

$$FRF_s = F_{s(d)} \, \rho_s$$

where $F_{s(d)}$ = the direct luminous flux onto surface s.

If we were to opt for an uplighting installation that put every lumen from the luminaires onto the ceiling, the total luminaire output would have to be 13,300/0.65 = 20,500 lm. Alternatively, if we were to install fully recessed luminaires in the ceiling that put every lumen onto the floor, the light output will have to be 13,300/0.15 = 88,700 lm. This huge difference makes the point that where the aim is to provide reflected flux within a space, it does not make sense to direct a large proportion of the light onto a surface that will absorb 85% of it. Illuminating the ceiling will be much more effective than lighting the floor, and the difference would be even greater if we had a sparkling white ceiling. However, before we rush ahead to specify an 'efficient' uplighting solution, let us think through how successful such an installation would be.

Imagine yourself inside the space. The luminaires direct their entire output onto the ceiling, making it the brightest visible surface and the effective source of illumination. The flow of light is vertically downwards, and although the light incident on a horizontal surface is softly diffused, very little light is reflected upwards from the dark floor. Consequently, a three-dimensional object in the space, such as person's head, shows a strong shading pattern. The techniques described in Section 6.3 could be employed to verify that the vector/scalar ratio will be high, and the effect of the vertical vector direction will be clearly evident in the form of shading of the eye sockets, and beneath the nose and chin. Although such shading patterns will be pronounced, there will be a lack of shadow and highlight patterns. The lift doors will be quite visible, but the bright textured metal finish will lack sparkle. For this to happen, we need not high illuminance, but sources that have high highlight ratio values.

At this point, a range of options opens up. For luminaires that distribute their luminous flux onto more than one surface we need to know the relative amount received by each surface. This problem has been addressed by the time-honoured 'lumen method', which has been used for average illuminance calculations since the 1930s. A room is treated as three cavities as shown in Figure 6.2, and for many years luminaire manufacturers have provided data sheets to enable users to calculate the average illuminance of the floor cavity plane, often referred to as the working plane. The relevant data are:

| | |
|---|---|
| *LOR* | The light output ratio, being the proportion of lamp lumens emitted by the luminaire. |
| *ULOR, DLOR* | The upward and downward light output ratios, being the components of *LOR* emitted above and below the ceiling cavity plane (e.g., for recessed luminaires, *ULOR* = 0 and *DLOR* = *LOR*). |
| *UF* | The utlilization factor, being the proportion of the lamp lumens incident on the floor cavity plane, both directly and by interreflection. |

**Figure 6.2:** *Section through a room showing how the space is divided into three cavities for average illuminance calculations*

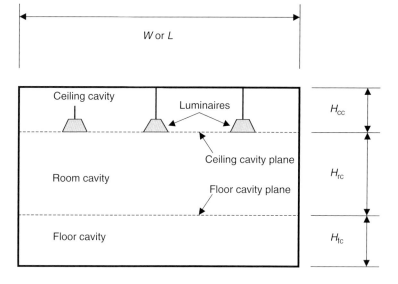

We can use these data to determine the distribution of direct flux onto the room surfaces. *UF* data is given in tables which take account of room proportions and surface reflectances, and quite often values are included for zero room surface reflectance, in which case $UF_0$ is the proportion of lamp lumens incident directly on the floor cavity plane. It follows that $(DLOR - UF_0)$ equals the proportion incident on the walls, and *ULOR* is the proportion emitted into the ceiling cavity. If *UF* data for zero reflectance are not given, use the lowest reflectance values listed, and take off a bit.

For mean room surface exitance calculations, we will usually make $H_{fc}$ (Figure 6.2) equal to zero, so that the floor cavity plane coincides with the floor, but when we use pendant luminaires, we have to allow for the effect of the ceiling cavity. We need to know the proportion of flux emitted into the cavity that will be reflected back into the space, and for this we determine the equivalent reflectance of the cavity plane, that is to say, we treat the ceiling cavity plane as being the ceiling, but having an equivalent reflectance $\rho_{eq}$ given by the expression:

$$\rho_{eq} = \frac{\rho_{av}\,(A_{cp}/A_{cs})}{1 - \rho_{av}\left[1 - (A_{cp}/A_{cs})\right]}$$

where $A_{cp}$ = area of the cavity plane; $A_{cs}$ = area of the cavity surfaces; $\rho_{av}$ = average reflectance of cavity surfaces.

By treating the ceiling cavity plane as the ceiling with reflectance $\rho_{clg} = \rho_{eq}$, we can determine the first reflected flux within the room cavity (Figure 6.2). While it might be acceptable to ignore the $\rho_{eq}$ calculation where the cavity is shallow, significant differences may occur where the cavity is deep, and particularly where the upper wall reflectance is different from that of the ceiling.

From the foregoing, it follows that first reflected flux:

$$FRF = F_{lamps}\,(ULOR \cdot \rho_{clg} + UF_0 \cdot \rho_{flr} + (DLOR - UF_0\rho_{walls})\,\text{lm}$$

which may be transposed to give the expression for the lamp lumens required for the installation:

$$F_{lamps} = \frac{FRF}{ULOR \cdot \rho_{clg} + UF_0 \cdot \rho_{flr} + (DLOR - UF_0)\rho_{walls}}\,\text{lm}$$

While this derivation from lumen method data serves to explain the process for planning a lighting installation to provide a given mean room surface exitance, it is becoming increasingly common for luminaire manufacturers to provide photometric data in the form of online plug-ins for use with lighting calculation software. Although these software programs are not designed to provide $M_{rs}$ data, we can, again with a little ingenuity, utilize them for this purpose.

In reality, the lighting for this space probably would comprise more than one system. It might combine ceiling lighting from a cove in the upper walls with ceiling-recessed wall-washers, and some luminous elements in the form of decorative glass wall fixtures or pendant luminaires. However, for this example we will opt for a simple installation. I have chosen a pendant luminaire comprising an open-top channel of perforated powder-coated steel, housing two linear fluorescent lamps giving a broad distribution of upward flux. This will give an even wash of light over the ceiling as well as lightening the upper walls. The relatively small amount of light emitted through the channel perforations will serve both to provide a direct lighting component within the space, and to overcome the silhouette appearance that is associated with suspended uplighters.

I have modelled the space in DIALux (available as a free download from www.dialux.com) and I have set the room surface reflectances as low as the program will permit, with the aim that the calculated illuminances will be due only to direct flux. Although I have opted for 'user specified' surfaces and have specified all surfaces as black, the program still allows for 5 per cent reflection, but this small error may be ignored. After some experimentation, I came up with a layout of six luminaires, each with $2 \times 28\,W$ lamps, shown in Figure 6.3. From the calculated values of average illuminance $E_{av}$ we can work out the total first reflected flux as shown in Table 6.1. The aim was to provide a *FRF* value of 13,300 lm, and the calculated value of 12,590 lm is acceptably close to this target. Nonetheless, it is hard to ignore the pitifully low values of workplane/floor illuminance shown in the chart, but of course this ignores interreflected flux. For reassurance, I have re-run the program with the actual surface reflectances, and Figure 6.4 confirms that the floor will be reasonably well lit.

Before we leave this example, we need to think about those metallic finish lift doors. The softly diffused light from this installation will not reveal their lustre, but a low-voltage spotlight recessed into the ceiling opposite each of the doors would

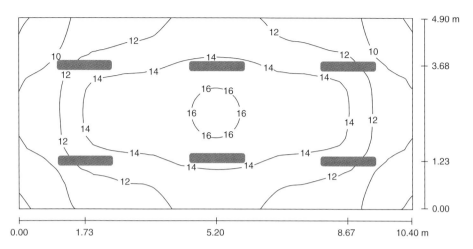

Height of Room: 3.200 m, Mounting Height: 2.700 m, Light loss factor: 0.67
Values in Lux, Scale 1:75

| Surface | $\rho$[%] | $E_{av}$[lx] | $E_{min}$[lx] | $E_{max}$[lx] | u0 |
|---|---|---|---|---|---|
| Workplane | / | 13 | 7.91 | 16 | 0.63 |
| Floor | 5 | 12 | 7.77 | 16 | 0.63 |
| Ceiling | 5 | 352 | 24 | 1677 | 0.07 |
| Walls (4) | 5 | 21 | 4.56 | 287 | / |

**Figure 6.3:** *Illuminance distribution for the lift lobby, calculated by the Dialux program. Room surface reflectances are the lowest values permitted by the software, so that mean surface illuminances enable estimates direct incident flux*

Table 6.1 *Determination of first reflected flux from average surface illuminances ($E_{av}$) calculated with assumed zero surface reflectances*

| Surface S | Area $A_s$ | Reflectance $\rho_s$ | $E_{av}$ (lux) | FRF (lm) |
|---|---|---|---|---|
| Ceiling | 51.0 | 0.65 | 352 | 11,670 |
| 2 × long walls | 66.6 | 0.53 | 21 | 741 |
| Short wall | 15.7 | 0.35 | 21 | 115 |
| Floor | 51.0 | 0.15 | 8 | 61 |
| | | | Total FRF | 12,590 lm |

provide the necessary sharpness. Choosing a combination of beam angle and distance out from the wall that gives coverage of each door with minimum spill light onto the wall is what matters: illuminance is not relevant. The choice of beam angles is limited, and a steep angle of incidence will provide an attractive highlight pattern. A 24° beam angle and a mounting position 750 mm out from the wall should work well. Whatever wattage is selected, the contribution to the general lighting will be quite small. Remember that the purpose of the spotlights is to provide localized sharpness, not general illumination.

Table 6.2 *Flux distribution (1)*

| Surface S | Area As (m²) | Reflectance ρs | Relative illuminance Es (rel) | Illuminance Es (lx) | Reflected flux (lm) | Direct illuminance (lx) | Direct flux Fs(d) (lm) | Lamp wattage (W) | Lamp watts per zone (W) |
|---|---|---|---|---|---|---|---|---|---|
| SANCTUARY | | | | | | | | | |
| altar front | 1 | 0.25 | 5 | 1000 | 250 | 939.2013129 | 939.2013129 | 218.41891 | |
| panelling | 8 | 0.7 | 3 | 600 | 3360 | 539.2013129 | 4313.610503 | 1003.165233 | |
| East wall | 20 | 0.6 | 1.5 | 300 | 3600 | 239.2013129 | 4784.026258 | 1112.564246 | |
| vault | 30 | 0.3 | 0.5 | 100 | 900 | 39.20131291 | 1176.039387 | 273.4975319 | |
| floor | 25 | 0.5 | 1.5 | 300 | 3750 | 239.2013129 | 5980.032823 | 1390.705308 | |
| N & S walls | 60 | 0.7 | 0.5 | 100 | 4200 | 39.20131291 | 2352.078775 | 546.9950639 | 4545.346293 |
| NAVE | | | | | 0 | -60.79868709 | 0 | 0 | |
| floor & chairs | 110 | 0.15 | 1 | 200 | 3300 | 139.2013129 | 15312.14442 | 3560.963819 | |
| chancel arch | 10 | 0.7 | 1 | 200 | 1400 | 139.2013129 | 1392.013129 | 323.7239835 | |
| N side of S arcade | 30 | 0.7 | 0.5 | 100 | 2100 | 39.20131291 | 1176.039387 | 273.4975319 | |
| S side of N arcade | 30 | 0.7 | 0.75 | 150 | 3150 | 89.20131291 | 2676.039387 | 622.3347412 | |
| S half of vault | 60 | 0.6 | 0.5 | 100 | 3600 | 39.20131291 | 2352.078775 | 546.9950639 | |
| N half of vault | 60 | 0.6 | 0.3 | 60 | 2160 | -0.79868709 | -47.92122538 | -11.14447102 | |
| W wall | 50 | 0.4 | 0.5 | 100 | 2000 | 39.20131291 | 1960.065646 | 455.8292199 | 5772.199888 |
| SOUTH AISLE | | | | | 0 | -60.79868709 | 0 | 0 | |
| East wall | 15 | 0.7 | 0.5 | 100 | 1050 | 39.20131291 | 588.0196937 | 136.748766 | |
| ceiling | 50 | 0.6 | 0.5 | 100 | 3000 | 39.20131291 | 1960.065646 | 455.8292199 | |
| S & W walls | 100 | 0.5 | 0.75 | 150 | 7500 | 89.20131291 | 8920.131291 | 2074.449137 | |
| floor and chairs | 45 | 0.15 | 1 | 200 | 1350 | 139.2013129 | 6264.059081 | 1456.757926 | 4123.785049 |
| NORTH AISLE | | | | | 0 | -60.79868709 | 0 | 0 | |
| East wall | 15 | 0.25 | 1 | 200 | 750 | 139.2013129 | 2088.019694 | 485.5859753 | |
| ceiling | 50 | 0.6 | 0.3 | 60 | 1800 | -0.79868709 | -39.93435449 | -9.287059183 | |
| N & W walls | 100 | 0.5 | 0.5 | 100 | 5000 | 39.20131291 | 3920.131291 | 911.6584398 | |
| floor and chairs | 45 | 0.15 | 1 | 200 | 1350 | 139.2013129 | 6264.059081 | 1456.757926 | 2844.715282 |
| Total surface area | 914 | | | Reflected flux | 55570 lm | | | Total Watts | 17286.04651 |

Indirect illuminance (E(i) or $M_{rs}$)
Anchor illuminance 200 lux

60.79868709 lux or lm/m^2
Beam efficacy (neta B) 4.3 lm/W

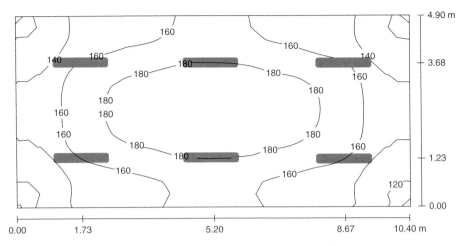

Height of Room: 3.200 m, Mounting Height: 2.700 m, Light loss factor: 0.67        Values in Lux, Scale 1.75

| Surface | ρ[%] | E_av[lx] | E_min[lx] | E_max[lx] | u0 |
|---------|------|----------|-----------|-----------|-----|
| Workplane | / | 161 | 112 | 195 | 0.70 |
| Floor | 10 | 158 | 107 | 190 | 0.68 |
| Ceiling | 70 | 396 | 79 | 1719 | 0.20 |
| Walls (4) | 50 | 124 | 71 | 440 | / |

**Figure 6.4:**  *The previously calculated floor illuminance is very low, so for reassurance, the program is run again for more realistic room surface reflectances*

Throughout all of this attention to detail, the important aim to keep in mind is that when the switch-on happens, the designer's envisioned concept, as well as the considerations discussed in Section 2.1, will be realized.

## 6.2 Flux distribution

As explained in Parts 1 and 2, the ability to visualize a design situation in terms of a hierarchy of illuminance is a fundamental design skill, and instead of devising a luminaire layout that will provide uniform illuminance, the objective is a layout that will give a prescribed diversity of illuminance. The example given is based on a proposal by J.A. Lynes (1987), who attributes the fundamentals of the procedure to J.M. Waldram's Designed Appearance Method (1954, 1978).

The stages of the procedure are indicated in Figure 6.5, and are described below:

1. The required illuminance for each surface $E_s$ is prescribed, and is multiplied by the surface area $A_s$ and the surface

Figure 6.5:   *Outline of the flux distribution procedure*

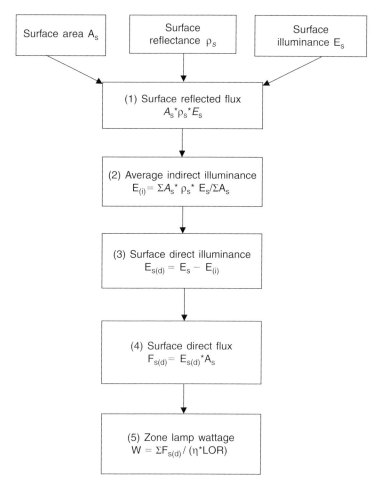

Figure 6.5:   *Outline of the flux distribution procedure*

reflectance $\rho_s$ to give the reflected flux (lumens) from that surface.

2.  The sum of reflected lumens from all surfaces is divided by the sum of surface areas to give the average indirect illuminance $E_{(i)}$. (It may be noted that this is our old friend, the mean room surface exitance $M_{rs}$, in another guise, as it represents the average value of indirect illuminance on all room surfaces, including an occupant's cornea.)

3.  The value of $E_{(i)}$ is subtracted from each surface illuminance $E_s$, and what is left is the required direct illuminance of that surface $E_{s(d)}$.

4.  Each value of $E_{s(d)}$ is multiplied by the surface area $A_s$ to give the direct flux required on the surface $F_{s(d)}$.

5.  The total lamp wattage required for each zone is estimated by dividing $F_{s(d)}$ by the luminous efficacy of the light source $\eta$ and an allowance for luminaire efficiency and other light

losses, and summing the values. This provides the information needed to devise a layout of lamps and luminaires to provide the prescribed surface illuminances.

It should be noted that stage 2 makes the only simplifying assumption that is incorporated into this procedure. It is assumed that the reflected flux is uniformly distributed. The likely errors involved by this assumption have been discussed in Section 2.3, and it is more a matter of common sense than photometry. The designer should ensure that he/she is aware of the types of situations where this assumption might incur unacceptable error.

The first step of the procedure is to prescribe the illuminance of every surface. You cannot prescribe only for the surfaces that interest you, as every surface that is visible is reflecting flux into the space, and is adding to $E_{(i)}$.

We start by identifying the visual tasks. These relate to the activities that involve being able to discriminate detail, and for which we are able to prescribe appropriate illuminances either by reference to Table 2.3 or to some other schedule of recommended or required illuminances. The visual tasks are not necessarily the things that we, as designers, identify as the most significant objects of the visual environment, but they concern visual functions that must be adequately provided for. As lighting providers, we must relate to the needs of the people who will use this space and what it is that they need to be able to see. A visual task might comprise anything from reading a prayer book to reading the roll of dice, but following from the discussion in Section 2.2, reasonable decisions can be made to prescribe an appropriate task illuminance. This value becomes the *anchor illuminance,* and every prescribed surface illuminance will be related to this value. If more than one task illuminance is prescribed, the lighting designer has to consider who is the viewer of principal concern, and what is illuminance to which they are adapted.

The workings of the procedure are best explained by following an example. Figure 6.6 shows a sketch of the interior of a small church. Obviously a uniform distribution of illumination would be inappropriate. The viewers of principal concern are the congregation in the nave, and for them, the sanctuary is the zone that should draw attention, and within the sanctuary, the altar is the natural object of focus. The aim is to devise a lighting design that will reinforce this hierarchy, and the illuminance ratios scale in Table 2.6 provides guidance on relating individual surface illuminances to the overall design concept. The contents of this table are reproduced below under column D heading.

Figure 6.6:   *Sketch of the interior of a small church*

Table 6.3 *Beam performance data for three types of integral reflector lamps*

| Lamp type | Beam type | Beam angle B | Beam intensity $I_B$ (cd) | Beam flux $F_B$ (lm) | Beam efficacy $\eta_B$ (lm/W) |
|---|---|---|---|---|---|
| Incandescent | SP | 12° | 5400 | 140 | 1.7 |
| PAR38 80 W | FL | 30° | 1800 | 290 | 3.6 |
| (LD = 1.0) | | | | | |
| Tungsten halogen | SP | 10° | 6500 | 120 | 1.6 |
| PAR30 75 W | FL | 30° | 2000 | 320 | 4.3 |
| (LD = 1.0) | | | | | |
| Metal halide | SP | 20° | 26,000 | 1300 | 18.6 |
| PAR38 70 W | FL | 35° | 12,000 | 1800 | 26.2 |
| (LD = 0.7) | WFL | 65° | 4500 | 2300 | 33.2 |

It is convenient to use a spreadsheet program for the flux distribution procedure. The instructions in the following text are for Excel software, and the resulting spreadsheet is Table 6.3. Bring up the Excel spreadsheet on your computer, and follow this example.

## Column A
List all the principal surfaces. It helps to arrange them in zones

## Column B
List the area $A_s$ of each surface. At the bottom of the column, sum the surface areas. To follow this example, click on B32, type in [=SUM(B7:B30)] (do not include the square brackets) and press ENTER.

## Column C
List the reflectance $\rho_s$ of each surface.

## Column D

Here we come to the creative bit. For each surface, designate an illuminance relative to the anchor illuminance. Start by identifying the visual tasks. The congregation needs to be able to read prayer books, so the illuminance of the nave and aisle seating areas must be sufficient for this. This will be the anchor illuminance, and in this column, each of these surfaces is given the value of one. Now move on to the other surfaces, and for this we make use, once again, of the illuminance ratios scale that was introduced in Section 2.3.

| Perceived difference | Illuminance ratio |
| --- | --- |
| Noticeable | 1.5:1 |
| Distinct | 3:1 |
| Strong | 10:1 |
| Emphatic | 40:1 |

Look down the fourth column (D) in Table 6.3 and note how this scale of ratios has been used to set each value of relative illuminance. This column is the designer's statement of how lighting will be employed to give balance, guide attention and provide selective emphasis. This is not a situation that calls for emphatic statements of difference. In this case, the designer has opted for a gradation of illuminance difference leading through the sanctuary to the altar, with a maximum ratio of 5:1. The designer is not restricted to the four values given in the table, and can interpolate al will. Some judgement has to be applied, as the gradient of change will affect the appearance. The confidence to do this is essentially a product of the extent to which observation-based experience has been developed.

This point marks the end of data input. From here on, Excel does all the work.

## Column E

The anchor illuminance has to be adequate for the task of reading hymn books and prayer books. However, this is not the type of sustained reading task that occurs in offices or libraries, and a lower illuminance would be permissible, and perhaps more appropriate. At this stage, we will opt for 200 lux of task illuminance, so this value becomes the anchor illuminance and is entered in D34.

Click on E7, and enter [=$D$34*D7]. (The $ signs indicate that the value in D34 is a constant.) The value 1000 appears, and this is the illuminance to be provided on the altar front. Click on this box and copy it by dragging it down the column to E30, and watch all the surface illuminances appear.

## Column F

The reflected flux from each surface is the product of the surface area $A_s$, the surface reflectance $\rho_s$, and the surface illuminance $E_s$. So, in F7 enter [=B7*C7*E7], and the value 250 pops up. Drag this box down the column, and watch all the other values of reflected flux appear. Obtain the total flux at the bottom of the column by entering [=SUM(F7:F30)] in F32, and calculate the average indirect illuminance $E_{(i)}$ by entering [=F32/B32] in F33.

## Column G

The direct illuminance $E_{s(d)}$ for each surface equals the total illuminance $E_s$ minus the indirect illuminance $E_{(i)}$. So in G7 enter [=E7-$F$33] and copy the formula down the column.

## Column H

The direct flux $F_{s(d)}$ for each surface is the direct illuminance $E_{s(d)}$ times the surface area $A_s$, so in H7 enter [=G7*B7] and copy down the column. This is the number of lumens that you must direct onto each surface to achieve the illuminance distribution prescribed in column D.

## Column I

We now estimate the lamp wattage that will deliver the required $F_{s(d)}$ onto each surface. This is obtained by dividing $F_{s(d)}$ by the beam luminous efficacy $\eta_B$, which is the same thing as luminous efficacy $\eta$ (lm/W) except that it takes account only of the lumens emitted within the beam. The difference between total light source lumens and beam lumens can be substantial.

For this example we will examine the use of aimable luminaires with integral reflector lamps mounted at the level of the eaves. The lamp manufacturers offer ranges of PAR (parabolic aluminized reflector) lamps for three types of light source: standard incandescent; tungsten halogen; and metal halide. For each source type, they offer various wattages and beam spreads, and we have to work out the beam lumens.

The lamp manufacturers specify the performance for reflector lamps by giving the luminous intensity (candelas) at the beam centre $I_{max}$, and the beam angle, which is the inclusive angle over which the intensity is not less than 50% of $I_{max}$. That is to say, for a reflector lamp for which $I_{max} = 1000\,cd$ and the beam angle is 30°, the intensity falls to 500 cd at 15° from the beam axis. In the following text, $B$ indicates the beam angle ($B = 30°$) and $b$ indicates the half-beam angle ($b = 15°$). We can now estimate the beam lumens:

$$F_B = \text{(average beam intensity)} \times \text{(beam solid angle)}$$
$$\qquad \times \text{(lumen depreciation factor)}$$
$$\quad = I_{av}\, 2\pi(1 - \cos b)LD$$
$$\quad = \tfrac{1}{2}\,(I_{max} + 0.5I_{max}) \times 2\pi(1 - \cos b)LD$$
$$\quad = 1.5\, I_{max}\,\pi(1 - \cos b)LD\,\text{lm}$$

Table 6.4 compares beam efficacies for three types of PAR lamps. We are accustomed to thinking of the luminous efficacies of incandescent, halogen and metal halide lamps being in the region of 12, 18 and 70 lm/W respectively, and it is quite sobering to realize how many of the lumens emitted by the source do not end up in the beam. This is particularly so for the SP (spotlight) lamps, and so we should make use of FL (floodlight) wherever practical. We will start by considering the tungsten halogen PAR30 FL, for which $\eta_B = 4.3$ lm/W. Enter this value in H34, and in I7 enter [=H7/$H$34], and copy down the column.

## Column J

It is convenient to sum the lamp wattages for zones. In J12, enter [=SUM(I7:I12)], and so on. For total lamp watts, enter [=SUM(I7:I30)] in J32.

The spreadsheet shown in Table 6.3 is now complete, but we certainly have not finished using it. The total lamp wattage is shown to be 17.3 kW, and as the lamp specification will certainly include some SP beam types, the actual load will be more than this. What would be the effect if, instead of tungsten halogen lamps, we used metal halide FL lamps giving 26.2 lm/W? Click on H34 and press Delete, and enter this value. Instantly columns I and J are revised, and the total watts reduce to 2.84 kW. This gives us power to spare, so why not look again at the overall illuminance? The indirect illuminance $E_{(i)}$ is 61 lux, and as this is equivalent to $M_{rs}$, we can use it as an estimate of eye illuminance. It can be seen from Table 2.1 that the overall appearance of the space is likely to be slightly dim. For some churches this appearance would be quite appropriate, but perhaps it is not what we want to achieve in this instance. We can

Table 6.4 *Flux distribution* (2)

| Surface S | Area As (m²) | Reflectance ρs | Relative illuminance Es (rel) | Illuminance Es (lx) | Reflected flux (lm) | Direct illuminance (lx) | Direct flux Fs(d) (lm) | Lamp wattage (W) | Lamp watts per zone (W) |
|---|---|---|---|---|---|---|---|---|---|
| SANCTUARY | | | | | | | | | |
| Altar front | 1 | 0.25 | 5 | 1750 | 437.5 | 1643.602298 | 1643.602298 | 62.73291212 | |
| panelling | 8 | 0.7 | 3 | 1050 | 5880 | 943.6022976 | 7548.818381 | 288.122839 | |
| East wall | 20 | 0.6 | 1.5 | 525 | 6300 | 418.6022976 | 8372.045952 | 319.5437386 | |
| vault | 30 | 0.3 | 0.5 | 175 | 1575 | 68.60229759 | 2058.068928 | 78.55224915 | |
| floor | 25 | 0.5 | 1.5 | 525 | 6562.5 | 418.6022976 | 10465.05744 | 399.4296733 | |
| N & S walls | 60 | 0.7 | 0.5 | 175 | 7350 | 68.60229759 | 4116.137856 | 157.1044983 | 1305.48591 |
| NAVE | | | | 0 | 0 | −106.3977024 | 0 | 0 | |
| floor & chairs | 110 | 0.15 | 1 | 350 | 5775 | 243.6022976 | 26796.25274 | 1022.757738 | |
| chancel arch | 10 | 0.7 | 1 | 350 | 2450 | 243.6022976 | 2436.022976 | 92.97797618 | |
| N side of S arcade | 30 | 0.7 | 0.5 | 175 | 3675 | 68.60229759 | 2058.068928 | 78.55224915 | |
| S side of N arcade | 30 | 0.7 | 0.75 | 262.5 | 5512.5 | 156.1022976 | 4683.068928 | 178.7430888 | |
| S half of vault | 60 | 0.6 | 0.5 | 175 | 6300 | 68.60229759 | 4116.137856 | 157.1044983 | |
| N half of vault | 60 | 0.6 | 0.3 | 105 | 3780 | −1.397702407 | −83.86214442 | −3.200845207 | |
| W wall | 50 | 0.4 | 0.5 | 175 | 3500 | 68.60229759 | 3430.11488 | 130.9204153 | 1657.855121 |
| SOUTH AISLE | | | | 0 | 0 | −106.3977024 | 0 | 0 | |
| East wall | 15 | 0.7 | 0.5 | 175 | 1837.5 | 68.60229759 | 1029.034464 | 39.27612458 | |
| ceiling | 50 | 0.6 | 0.5 | 175 | 5250 | 68.60229759 | 3430.11488 | 130.9204153 | |
| S & W walls | 100 | 0.5 | 0.75 | 262.5 | 13125 | 156.1022976 | 15610.22976 | 595.8102962 | |
| floor and chairs | 45 | 0.15 | 1 | 350 | 2362.5 | 243.6022976 | 10962.10339 | 418.4008928 | 1184.407729 |
| NORTH AISLE | | | | 0 | 0 | −106.3977024 | 0 | 0 | |
| East wall | 15 | 0.25 | 1 | 350 | 1312.5 | 243.6022976 | 3654.034464 | 139.4669643 | |
| ceiling | 50 | 0.6 | 0.3 | 105 | 3150 | −1.397702407 | −69.88512035 | −2.667371006 | |
| N & W walls | 100 | 0.5 | 0.5 | 175 | 8750 | 68.60229759 | 6860.229759 | 261.8408305 | |
| floor and chairs | 45 | 0.15 | 1 | 350 | 2362.5 | 243.6022976 | 10962.10339 | 418.4008928 | 817.0413166 |
| Total surface area 914 | | | | | Reflected flux | | | Total Watts | |
| | | | | | 97247.5 lm | 106.3977024 lux or lm/m^2 | | 4964.790076 | |

Indirect illuminance (E(i) or Mrs) 106.3977024 lux or lm/m^2
Anchor illuminance 350 lux    Beam efficacy (neta B) 26.2 lm/W

take a look at increasing the indirect illuminance to give a $M_{rs}$ value of 100 lm/m². Click on D34 and change the anchor illuminance to 350 lux. The indirect illuminance jumps up to 106 lux, and the total watts to 4.96 kW. This revised spreadsheet is shown as Table 6.5, and gives the entire distribution of surface illuminances and lamp wattages for an anchor illuminance of 350 lux provided by metal halide light sources. This version of the spreadsheet becomes our working document, and we can now apply the 'beam flux' method to plan an arrangement of light sources to provide this distribution.

## The 'beam flux' method

Circumstances will suggest a sensible order in which to proceed. To locate the luminaires at the eaves level, and just forward of roof arches, offers reasonable concealment, ease of installation, and not unduly difficult maintenance. The luminaires must be aimable so that light can be spread right across a wall or roof, or focused onto selected objects, such as the altar front.

We can now move on to select beam angles, using the data for the three 70 watt metal halide PAR38 lamps given in Table 6.4. We will start with the sanctuary. By applying some basic trigonometry we can see that lighting the roof vault and the upper walls from the eaves level calls for the WFL beam type to give even distributions of light across these surfaces from relatively short distance. The lower walls and floor can be lit from opposite sides, and the tighter FL beams are preferred to give glare control.

As we come on to smaller beam angles, we have to be more exact. Figure 6.7 shows what happens when the beam from a spotlight is directed at an angle onto a large flat surface. The beam shape is conical, but the beam pattern formed on the surface is an ellipse, which has minimum and maximum diameters

Table 6.5 *Selection of 70 W metal halide PAR38 lamps for lighting the sanctuary area*

| Surface s | Direct flux $F_{s(d)}$ (lm) | Beam type | Number of lamps |
|---|---|---|---|
| altar front | 1600 | NSP | see text |
| panelling | 7600 | SP | 6 |
| east wall | 8400 | WFL | 4 |
| vault | 2100 | WFL | 1 |
| floor | 10,400 | FL | 6 |
| N & S walls | 4200 | FL | 3 |
| | Total number of lamps | | 20 |

**Figure 6.7:** *The beam pattern cast by a spotlight directed obliquely onto a flat surface*

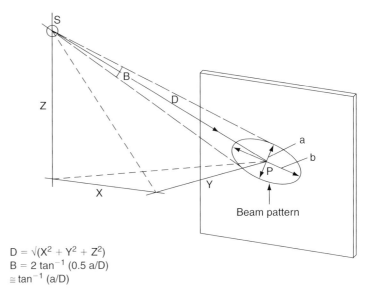

$$D = \sqrt{(X^2 + Y^2 + Z^2)}$$
$$B = 2 \tan^{-1} (0.5 \, a/D)$$
$$\cong \tan^{-1} (a/D)$$

*a* and *b* respectively. In order to spotlight an object such as the altar front with reasonable coverage, we want a beam angle *B* that matches *a* to the diagonal dimension of the altar. The location of the spotlight S is indicated by the dimensions *X*, *Y* and *Z*, and the distance from S to P:

$$D = \sqrt{(X^2 + Y^2 + Z^2)}$$

Then:

$$B = 2 \tan^{-1} (0.5a/D)$$
$$\cong \tan^{-1} (a/D)$$

If you are able to select a spotlight that has a beam angle which closely matches the calculated value of *B*, the illuminated surface will have good coverage but there will significant spill light, particularly if the light is incident at an oblique angle. This spill light might detract from the intended effect, and you will need a higher-intensity light source to get the required lumens onto the receiving surface. The usual situation is that the designer has to choose between beam angles that are either larger or smaller than the calculated value, and it can come down to a choice of whether to minimize spill or maximize coverage. There are, however, some alternative strategies to consider. Two or more narrow beam spotlights can be adjusted so that the edges of their beams overlap to give very good coverage with minimal spill light. Alternatively, a spreader lens can be fitted

Table 6.6 *Sum of cubic illuminance contributions due to direct light from three light sources plus indirect illumination*

| Source | Source location (X, Y, Z) | $I/D^3$ | Cubic illuminances (lux) | | | | | |
| --- | --- | --- | --- | --- | --- | --- | --- | --- |
| | | | $E_{(x)}$ | $E_{(-x)}$ | $E_{(y)}$ | $E_{(-y)}$ | $E_{(z)}$ | $E_{(-z)}$ |
| S1 | (−1.9, −2.7, 3.2) | 94.1 | | 179 | | 254 | 301 | |
| S2 | (−0.9, 2.8, 3.6) | 91.1 | | 82 | 255 | | 328 | |
| S3 | (2.7, −0.6, 1.8) | 254.6 | 687 | | | 152 | 458 | |
| Average indirect illuminance $E_{(i)}$ (equal to mean room surface exitance $M_{rs}$) | | | 260 | 260 | 260 | 260 | 260 | 260 |
| Total cubic illuminances | | | 947 | 521 | 515 | 666 | 1347 | 260 |

over the spotlight and rotated to the position where it increases the *a* dimension of the beam pattern without increasing the *b* dimension. Techniques such as these should only be used in situations where the lighting installation will be maintained by someone who can be relied upon to restore the settings after each lamp change.

Returning to the church lighting example, the altar and the panelling need to be lit from just behind the chancel arch to get light onto these vertical surfaces, and this means throws of around 8 m. At these distances, the subtended angles of the diagonals of the surfaces to be illuminated range from 8° for the altar front to 15° for the panelling. Table 6.6 shows a selection of lamp types for the sanctuary area. The SP beam type will work well for the panelling, but we need a different type of light source to get the 8° beam for the altar front. Mixing lamp types has to be done with care. The lamp manufacturer states the correlated colour temperature of the metal halide lamps to be 3200 K, and while this closely matches the CCT of a low-voltage halogen lamp, noticeable differences of colour rendering could be evident. While LV halogen can certainly deliver the required beam performance, it will be necessary to make a visual assessment of the lamp combination before specifying.

There are other factors to be considered. Although a single WFL lamp can deliver the beam lumens required for the roof vault, it may not give a satisfactory distribution of light. This could depend on how much light from the four WFL lamps illuminating the upper east wall will wash up into the vault. We have to think about how these lamps will be aimed. We must have enough lamps to be able to avoid harshness, and to be able to create the directional effects that we want. At the same time, we need to keep to a minimum the number of lamp types that we specify, and we must recognize that there will be more to the installation than just lamps. Luminaires with baffles or ring louvres are needed to control spill light onto surrounding surfaces and glare to the congregation and celebrants. We have noted that many of the lumens produced by the light source do not make it into the beam, and these are not wanted elsewhere. If the control devices significantly reduce the beam lumens, this must be allowed for. We can note that the 20 lamps selected in Table 6.6 have a combined wattage of 1400 W, and this is close to the value estimated in the spreadsheet.

When we are satisfied that we have all these factors in hand, we can get down to the serious business of planning the installation. The panelling behind the sanctuary table needs cast shadow to make it stand out from its flat background, but what balance of lighting do we need to provide such an effect? Refer again to the illuminance ratios scale. It takes an illuminance ratio of 1.5 to be noticeable, and a ratio of 3 to appear distinct. We can provide for a noticeable or a distinct light and shade effect by arranging more of the luminaires on one side, and for a coherent 'flow of light' we should maintain that balance throughout the church. The 'flow' could come from either side, but which?

There is no single right answer to this question, or to put it another way, there are two equally right answers. One proposition is that for a traditionally oriented church in the northern hemisphere, it is natural for the light to come predominantly from the south, and so that is the side for the dominant array of luminaires. The counter proposition is that the sun illuminates the church beautifully, but differently, as it tracks from east, through south, to west, and that the rightful role of electric lighting is expressed by having it fill in the remainder of the circuit. When the sun is not available to provide illumination, the light should flow from the north. Armed with both of these arguments, a lighting designer can justify whichever direction is judged to suit the job in hand. For a designer who, like the author, lives in the southern hemisphere, the arguments are interchanged.

From the sanctuary, we proceed through the building matching beam lumens to surface flux requirements. By the time we have worked our way through this church, we should have a good feeling about how it will appear. Also, we should have a sense of confidence that we can specify an installation which, when we have aimed the luminaires, will achieve our design intentions. Aiming the luminaires is a critical part of the process, and it pays to specify luminaires that can be relamped without losing their alignment. Of course we keep a copy of the spreadsheet on file, as this is the record of the design intentions. Equally important is the documentation to be prepared for whoever will maintain the installation, and this is referred to in Chapter 7.

## 6.3 Direct flux

The two previous sections have both led to points where the designer needs to be able to provide a controlled distribution of direct luminous flux over room surfaces and onto selected objects. The following three subsections address this need.

The $D^3$ *formula* is introduced, which enables the designer to select a lamp and luminaire combination that has the performance to provide a specific illuminance at a point on a surface. It is derived from the 'point-to-point' formula, so-called because it models the flow of luminous flux from a point source to a point on a surface. Mathematically, a point is defined as having no area, and obviously no real light source conforms to this, but providing the source is 'small', the error is likely to be acceptable. The *D/d correction* can be applied where the source is not small, and this greatly extends the usefulness of the $D^3$ formula and avoids the complications area source formulae. *Cubic illumination* takes these concepts into the third dimension, using six illuminance values to characterize the spatial distribution of illumination at a point in space. These procedures complement the *beam flux method* described in the previous section.

### The $D^3$ formula

The workhorse of illumination engineering is the time-honoured point-to-point formula, sometime referred to as the Inverse Square Cosine Formula (see Appendix A1). Referring to Figure 6.8:

$$E_q = I_p \cos \theta / D^2$$

where $E_q$ = illuminance at point P on plane q; $D$ = distance from point source S to point P; $I_p$ = luminous intensity of source S in direction of point P; $\theta$ = angle of incidence at P, which, as is shown in the figure, is *always* measured relative to the normal.

Note: Dimensions are indicated by upper case letters, whereas planes and axes are indicated by lower case letters.

**Figure 6.8:**   *Direct illuminance due to source S of point P on horizontal surface q*

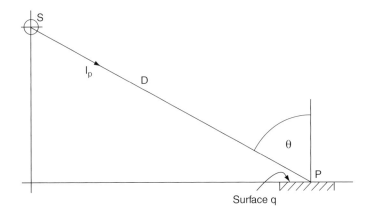

As has been mentioned, the formula is exact only for calculating illuminance due to a point source, but in practice, it is used for real sources which are small enough, relative to $D$, to be treated as point sources. This limitation will be discussed in the following subsection, and for now we will assume that our light sources are small enough to be treated as point sources.

There is a real difficulty in applying the inverse square cosine formula, and it is the problem of correctly determining the cosine of the angle of incidence. It is not difficult to do if we are dealing with a situation that can be represented as a two-dimensional diagram, provided that we remember that the angle of incidence is *always* measured relative to the normal to the surface of incidence. It is as we move into the third dimension that trouble erupts. It is not easy to envisage and correctly determine the angle of incidence onto a surface that is sloping and turned at an angle to the incident light. Fortunately, the difficulty can easily be avoided by transposing the inverse square cosine formula to give the $D^3$ formula, sometime referred to as the 'D to the 3' formula.

Figure 6.9 shows point P on plane q, where $\theta$ is the angle of incidence. It can be seen that $\cos \theta = Q/D$, where $Q$ is the orthogonal projection of $D$ onto the normal to plane q at P. Substituting for $\cos \theta$ in the inverse square cosine formula, we have the $D^3$ formula:

$$E_q = QI_p/D^3$$

The elimination of angles and cosines looks good, but how do we deal with the projection of $D$ onto the normal? This becomes

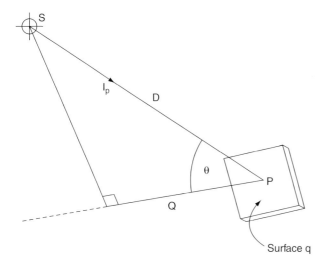

Figure 6.9: *Direct illuminance of point P on surface q where q may be of any orientation*

simple if we use a consistent system of dimensional coordinates. Follow this carefully, as we will use this system in the following sections.

Figure 6.10 shows the measurement point P at the intersection of three mutually perpendicular axes: *x*, *y*, and *z*. By convention, the *x* and *y* axes are horizontal and the *z* axis is vertical. The location of S relative to P is specified in terms of *X*, *Y*, and *Z* dimensional coordinates on *x*, *y* and *z* axes. Note again; use capitals for dimensions, and lower case for axes and planes.

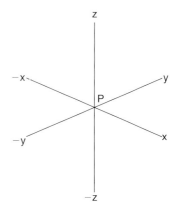

Figure 6.10: *The mutually perpendicular x, y and z axes may be used to define a point in space, or to define any direction at that point*

### A two-dimensional example

Now let's consider a simple application of the $D^3$ formula. Figure 6.11 shows a point P on a horizontal plane illuminated by a source S, where S has a symmetrical intensity distribution as shown. The dimensions are $X = 0$, $Y = 2.2\,\text{m}$, $Z = 1.5\,\text{m}$. In this case, we can see that the angle at S from the nadir (downward vertical) is equal to $\theta$. In practice, we cannot eliminate angles entirely, as we must find $\theta$ in order to read off the intensity. So:

$$\theta = \tan^{-1}[(X^2 + Y^2)^{0.5}/Z]$$

$$= \tan^{-1}(2.2/1.5)$$

$$= 56°$$

We refer to the luminaire polar curve, and let us suppose that we read $I(\theta)$ to have a value of 2520 cd.

**Figure 6.11:** *Point P on a horizontal plane illuminated by source S, where the symmetrical luminous intensity distribution of S is indicated by the curve shown*

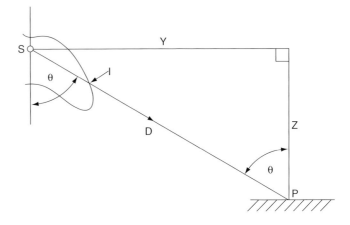

Next calculate '*D* to the 3':

$$D^3 = (X^2 + Y^2 + Z^2)^{1.5}$$
$$= (4.84 + 2.25)^{1.5}$$
$$= 18.9 \text{ m}^3$$

Where does the projection of *D* appear? The normal to the incident surface is coincident with the *z* axis, and the projection of *D* is simply the height of the source above the illuminated plane: in this example, 1.5 m. So, the illuminance at P:

$$E = Z \times I(\theta)/D^3$$
$$= 1.5 \times 2520/18.9$$
$$= 200 \text{ lux}$$

As stated at the outset, this is a simple case, and it would be reasonable to point out that it would have been no more difficult to have used the inverse square cosine formula. The advantages of the $D^3$ formula do not emerge until we consider a three-dimensional problem.

## A three-dimensional example

You propose to light a wall 4.8 m long × 3.0 m high with wall-washers. Your difficulty is that the manufacturer's tabular data shows the performance for the luminaire at 1.8 m spacing and mounted 900 mm out from the wall. While this seems reasonable for 600 mm square ceiling tiles, as often happens in practice, the edge row of tiles has been cut so that if the luminaires are centred in the tiles, they will be 1125 mm out from the wall.

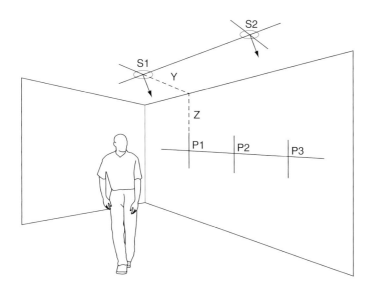

**Figure 6.12:** *Two wallwashers illuminating a wall. The distance out from the wall is Y and the height above the measurement points is Z. For S1, the X dimension for P1 is zero*

Of course this will reduce the wall illuminance, but also you are wondering whether the illuminance will be sufficiently uniform if you were to use only two wallwashers at 2.4 m spacing. The situation is illustrated in Figure 6.12.

To investigate the situation, you need to have photometric data for the luminaire that gives the distribution of luminous intensity. Some manufacturers give this information in their catalogue, but generally they can provide the data on request. Luminous intensity in candelas may be shown as a table or a chart for vertical angles $\alpha$ and horizontal angles $\beta$.

You start by determining your criteria. Between the two luminaires, you want the direct illuminance at eye level to be not less than 150 lx, and the variation to be not more than 1.5:1. Your procedure will be to calculate the illuminances at points P1, P2 and P3 due to source S1 only. Point P2 will be equally illuminated by sources S1 and S2, so the final illuminance at P2 will be twice the calculated value. Similarly, the final illuminance at P1 will be the sum of the calculated values for points P1 and P3, so that the average direct illuminance,

$$E_{av} = 2(E_{P1} + E_{P2} + E_{P3})/3$$

and

$$E_{max}/E_{min} = (E_{P1} + E_{P3})/(2 \times E_{P2})$$

The next step is to locate the three measurement points; P1, P2 and P3; relative to source S1, in terms of dimensional coordinates on the $x$, $y$ and $z$ axes. The dimensions are:

|    | $X$ | $Y$ | $Z$ |
|----|-----|-------|-----|
| P1 | 0   | 1.125 | 1.5 |
| P2 | 1.2 | 1.125 | 1.5 |
| P3 | 2.4 | 1.125 | 1.5 |

For each point, calculate:

$$D^3 = (X^2 + Y^2 + Z^2)^{1.5}$$

Calculate the luminaire coordinate angles:

$$\alpha = \tan^{-1} ((X^2 + Y^2)^{0.5}/Z)$$
$$\beta = \tan^{-1} (X/Y)$$

Look up the values of $I(\alpha,\beta)$ on the luminous intensity distribution table or chart for the luminaire.

This gives us all the data we need:

|    | $\alpha$ (degrees) | $\beta$ (degrees) | $I(\alpha,\beta)$ | $D^3$ (m$^3$) |
|----|--------------------|-------------------|-------------------|---------------|
| P1 | 37                 | 0                 | 1170              | 6.6           |
| P2 | 48                 | 47                | 760               | 11.0          |
| P3 | 60                 | 65                | 560               | 28.2          |

In every case, the normal to the wall plane lies in the $Y$ dimension, so the $D^3$ formula takes the form:

$$E = Y \times I(\alpha,\beta)/D^3$$

Then,

$$E_{p1} = 1.125 \times 1170/6.6 = 200 \, \text{lx}$$

and similarly,

$$E_{p2} = 77 \, \text{lx}$$
$$E_{p3} = 22 \, \text{lx}$$

Then

$$E_{av} = 2(200 + 77 + 22)/3 = 199 \, \text{lx}$$

and

$$E_{max}/E_{min} = (200 + 22)/(2 \times 77) = 1.44$$

So, both of the criteria have been satisfied, and you can go ahead and specify.

We clearly have a useful tool in the '*D* to the 3' formula, but as it is only a restated form of the point-to-point formula, it shares its limitation: it assumes a point source. We can overcome that limitation, and that gives us a truly flexible formula.

## The *D/d* correction

The point-to-point formula assumes light from a point source illuminating a point on a surface. A point source is a theoretical concept, for which all rays emerge from a common point and diffuse outwards into space, and this is the underlying concept of the inverse square law of illumination. Real sources always differ from point sources on the first of these counts, and may also differ on the second. Either of these differences can cause errors in applying the law.

Real sources have finite size, so that rays leave from different points, and travel different distances to a point where they arrive with different angles of incidence. Also, the rays may not diffuse. The illuminance due to a laser beam does not vary with distance, or more precisely, it is attenuated only by atmospheric absorption and scattering, so it does not obey the inverse square law. Fortunately, we can assume spatial diffusion for the commonly used light sources, but that still leaves the size aspect to worry about.

The time-honoured treatment is to apply the five-times rule. If the maximum source dimension is $d$ (Figure 6.13), then the minimum distance $D$ for application of the inverse square law is five times $d$. The rule is $D > 5d$ 'for an error of less than one-half to one per cent' (Levin, 1982).

Consider a $1200 \times 600\,$mm recessed fluorescent luminaire in a ceiling that is 2.5 m above floor level. The maximum luminaire dimension, $d = (1.2^2 + 0.6^2)^{0.5} = 1.3\,$m, so that the minimum distance for applying the law is $5 \times 1.3 = 6.5\,$m. If we want to calculate the illuminance on a 700 mm high working plane beneath the luminaire, the distance is a mere 1.8 m. The maximum permitted luminaire dimension at this distance

Figure 6.13:  *Luminaire distance*
*D and maximum dimension d*

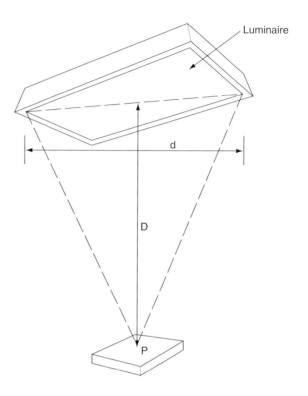

is 1.8/5 = 360 mm, which means that, for calculation purposes, we must divide the luminaire into eight 300 × 300 mm elements. This is called discretization. Each discrete element is assumed to have the same photometric distribution as the whole luminaire, but only one eighth of the intensity. So, instead of calculating for one source, we calculate for eight sources and sum the results. As the room is likely to have more than one source, we quite quickly reach the point where manual calculations become impractical. It is not always convenient to use a computer program, so we will take a closer look at the five-times rule ('the Rule').

The rationale for the Rule was propounded by Dr J.W.T. Walsh in 1958. Figure 6.14 shows a point P illuminated alternatively by a point source S1, and a diffusing disc source S2 of radius *r*. The distance from P to either S1, or to the centre of S2, is *D*.

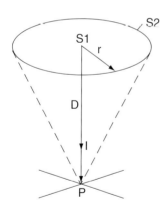

Figure 6.14:  *The point P may be*
*illuminated alternatively by point*
*source S1 or the disc source S2*

For S1, the illuminance at P is given exactly by the inverse square law:

$$E_{S1} = I_{S1}/D^2$$

where $I_{S1}$ is the luminous intensity of the source in the direction of P.

For the disc source, Dr Walsh derived the illuminance from fundamental principles, but we will take a short cut. Reference to an illumination engineering textbook (for example, Simons and Bean, 2001) gives the disc source formula, which may be expressed as:

$$E_{S2} = M_{S2}r^2/(D^2 + r^2)$$

where $M_{S2}$ is the exitance of source S2.

For a diffuse source, the luminous intensity normal to the surface equals the luminous flux output divided by $\pi$, so that:

$$I_{S2} = M_{S2}\pi r^2/\pi = M_{s2}r^2$$

so

$$E_{S2} = I_{S2}/(D^2 + r^2)$$

Then, if we let $I_{S1} = I_{S2}$, the error involved in applying the $E_{S1}$ expression instead of the $E_{S2}$ expression is:

$$\text{Error} = (E_{S2} - E_{S1})/E_{S2} = 1 - (D^2 + r^2)/D^2$$

As the maximum dimension of the disc luminaire $d = 2r$, then if $D/d = 5$, the error is 0.01, or 1 per cent. Dr Walsh also gives error values for a diffusing linear source, which are approximately two thirds of the disc source values. In this way, Dr Levin's quotation is confirmed, and the disc source can be seen as a worst case.

It is reasonable that the scientists who work in photometric laboratories should work to the highest practical standards to provide users with reliable performance data. The demands of users vary with application, and as has been explained, the procedures offered in this book aim to enable designers to make appropriate lamp wattage selections, where the available wattage range typically is based on 50% increments. In other words, we want procedures with an expected accuracy of $\pm25\%$. This accuracy (or inaccuracy) would be the product of all of the uncertainties incorporated in the procedures, but even so, it may be asked why we should go to inordinate lengths to ensure that the potential error of the calculation that is central to the procedure will be less than 1.0%?

Figure 6.15 shows the error for a diffuse disc source as a function of $D/d$. We could ask: how much error would be acceptable? But this is not the right question. What we see here is not random error, like tolerance. This is a predictable departure from a calculated value. Always, if we treat an area or linear diffusing source as if it were a point source, we will overestimate the illuminance. This effect can be allowed for by applying an appropriate correction, which can be done by reference to Figure 6.15, or by calculating the $D/d$ correction factor from the expression:

$$C_{(D/d)} = \frac{(D/d)^2 - 0.25}{(D/d)^2}$$

This is a 'worst case' correction factor, and applies to circular and rectangular diffuse sources. For linear and narrow strip sources, the constant can be increased from −0.25 to −0.17.

Let's look again at our $1200 \times 600$ mm recessed fluorescent luminaire 1.8 m above the work plane. The value of $D/d$ is $1.8/1.3 = 1.38$, so;

$$C_{(D/d)} = ((1.38)^2 - 0.25)/(1.38)^2$$

**Figure 6.15:** *The error due to applying the point-to-point formula to an area source is always negative. The maximum error occurs for a disc source and depends on D/d as shown in the chart*

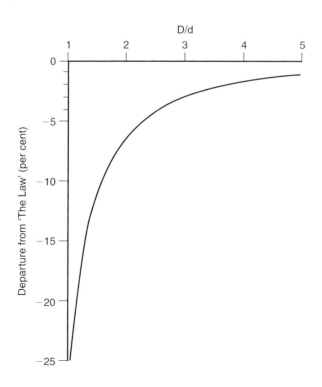

If we treat the luminaire as a point source, and then multiply the calculated illuminance by 0.87, we should be on track, at least within the overall level of accuracy that we can expect. Instead of having to calculate for eight discrete sources, we have only to calculate for one. For a luminaire that is more linear than circular, the value of the constant increases from $-0.25$ towards $-0.17$, causing $C_{(D/d)}$ to have a value closer to one.

This does not mean that the five-times rule becomes irrelevant. Photometrists should continue to use the Rule, as they do not know for what applications their data will be used, and they should aim to provide data that avoids error from all sources as far as that is practical. Computer programmers should be guided by the same considerations. However, a designer who is cognizant of the application and the level of accuracy expected has an alternative to the tedium of discretization. The $(D/d)$ correction makes the $D^3$ formula become a wonderfully versatile calculation tool.

## Cubic illumination

Illuminance is essentially a two-dimensional concept insofar as it is concerned with the distribution of luminous flux at a point on a surface. To extend into the third dimension, so that we can consider the distribution of illumination at a point in space, imagine the small cube shown in Figure 6.16 centred at the point. The surfaces of the cube are aligned parallel to the $x$, $y$ and $z$ axes, and the six surface illuminances are specified $E_x$, $E_{-x}$, $E_y$, $E_{-y}$, $E_z$ and $E_{-z}$, so that $E_z$ is the familiar horizontal illuminance. It can be seen that the cubic illuminances are opposed pairs on three mutually perpendicular planes.

Six illuminances at a point seems like a lot of trouble, but the $D^3$ formula makes short work of the cubic illuminance calculations. In Figure 6.17, consider a 50 watt halogen reflector lamp, such as the MR16 EXT, located at S1 and aimed so that its peak beam candlepower, $I = 9150$ candelas, is directed towards P. The location of S1 relative to P is defined by dimensions on the $x$, $y$ and $z$ axes. For this example $X = -1.9$ m (the sign indicates the direction of this dimension on the $x$ axis), $Y = -2.7$ m, and $Z = 3.2$ m. Then:

$$D^3 = ((-1.9)^2 + (-2.7)^2 + (3.2)^2)^{1.5} = 97.2 \text{ m}^3$$

and

$$I/D^3 = 9150/97.2 = 94.1$$

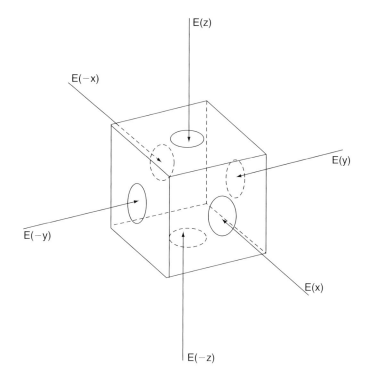

Figure 6.16:    *The cubic
illumination at a point in space is
defined by six illuminances on the
faces of a small cube centred at the
point. It is convenient for the faces
of the cube to be aligned normal to
the x, y and z axes*

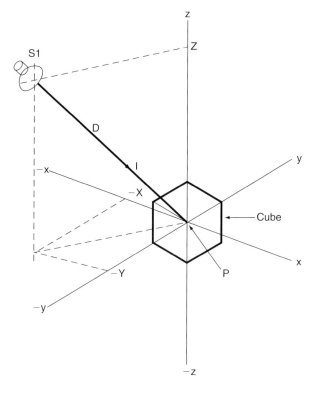

Figure 6.17:    *The spotlight
located at S1 is aimed so that its
peak beam intensity is directed
towards P*

As can be seen from Figure 6.17, the projection of $D$ onto the normal to each of the illuminated surfaces is given by the dimensions that define the location of S, so that:

$$E_{(x)} = -1.9 \times 94.1 = -179 \text{ lux}$$

$$E_{(y)} = -2.7 \times 94.1 = -254 \text{ lux}$$

$$E_{(z)} = 3.2 \times 94.1 = 301 \text{ lux}$$

Yes, it really is as simple as that: no angles, no cosines, and three illuminances for the price of one. However, we do have to keep an eye on those signs. Note that $E_{(x)} = -179$ lux, which is simply another way of writing $E_{(-x)} = 179$ lux. All of the cubic illuminance values are positive, and as we add the contributions from different sources on each surface of the cube, we find separately the sums of $E_{(x)}$ values and $E_{(-x)}$ values, as they are the illuminances on opposite sides of the cube. Table 6.7 shows two more sources of the same type added at S2 and S3. Check through the calculations to show yourself how simple it is.

We can sum the columns to give the direct illuminances on surfaces of the cube, and for an outdoor application that would be sufficient. However, for indoor lighting we have to make allowance for indirect light. A precise evaluation of the indirect illuminance onto each face of the cube would be a tedious calculation, and instead we are going to take a short cut and assume that indirect light is uniformly distributed. In other words, we assume that each surface receives the same indirect illuminance $E_{(i)}$, which is equal to the mean room surface exitance $M_{rs}$. Table 6.7 includes an allowance for $E_{(i)}$, which could be calculated by either of the procedures given in Sections 6.1 and 6.2, and this is added in to give the six cubic illuminances. The assumption that the contribution of indirect light to the cubic illuminances is uniform is not unreasonable. In an indoor space where the proportion of indirect illumination is low, it will have little visible effect and so it would be a waste of time to

**Table 6.7** *Vector analysis of the six cubic illuminances from Table 6.6. All values are in lux*

| Cubic illuminances | | Vector components | Symmetric components |
|---|---|---|---|
| $E_{(x)}$ 947 | $E_{(-x)}$ 521 | $\mathbf{E}_{(x)}$ 426 | $\sim E_{(x)}$ 521 |
| $E_{(y)}$ 515 | $E_{(-y)}$ 666 | $\mathbf{E}_{(y)}$ −151 | $\sim E_{(y)}$ 515 |
| $E_{(z)}$ 1347 | $E_{(-z)}$ 260 | $\mathbf{E}_{(z)}$ 1087 | $\sim E_{(z)}$ 260 |
| | | $|\mathbf{E}|$ 1177 | $\sim E$ 432 |

Table 6.8 *Analysis of the illumination solid at a point. All values are in lux*

| Cubic illuminances | | Vector components | Symmetric components |
|---|---|---|---|
| $E_{(x)}$ 380 | $E_{(-x)}$ 290 | $\mathbf{E}_{(x)}$ 90 | $\sim E_{(x)}$ 290 |
| $E_{(y)}$ 270 | $E_{(-y)}$ 480 | $\mathbf{E}_{(y)}$ −210 | $\sim E_{(y)}$ 270 |
| $E_{(z)}$ 570 | $E_{(-z)}$ 220 | $\mathbf{E}_{(z)}$ 350 | $\sim E_{(z)}$ 220 |
| | | $|\mathbf{E}|$ 420 | $\sim E$ 260 |

evaluate its spatial distribution. Where the proportion of indirect light is high, it is likely to be diffused so that its contribution to the visible effect will be to soften the directional effect of the direct light rather than to impart a distinct directional effect. While this assumption is recommended for general practice, the user should be alert for situations where indirect light could be both dominant and directional. For a more rigorous treatment of indirect illuminance, see Simons and Bean (2001).

The reason for working out the cubic illuminances is to enable vector analysis of the illumination solid. In Table 6.8 the cubic illuminances from the foregoing example are analysed. For the *x*, *y* and *z* axes, the vector and symmetric components are determined. For the vector component on the *x* axis:

$$\mathbf{E}_{(x)} = E_{(x)} - E_{(-x)}$$
$$= 947 - 521 = 426 \text{ lux}$$

The other two axes are dealt with similarly. Note that $\mathbf{E}_{(y)}$ has a negative value. The cubic illuminances are always positive as the illuminance contributions of each face of the cube are summed, but opposite vector components are subtracted and the sign of the resultant indicates the direction in which it acts. The magnitude of the illumination vector:

$$|\mathbf{E}| = (\mathbf{E}_{(x)}{}^2 + \mathbf{E}_{(y)}{}^2 + \mathbf{E}_{(z)}{}^2)^{0.5}$$
$$= [(426)^2 + (-151)^2 + (1087)^2]^{0.5} = 1177 \text{ lux}$$

The symmetric component on each axis is what is left when the vector component is taken away:

$$\sim E_{(x)} = (E_{(x)} + E_{(-x)} - |\mathbf{E}_{(x)}|)/2$$
$$= (947 + 521 - 426)/2 = 521 \text{ lux}$$

$\sim E_{(y)}$ and $\sim E_{(z)}$ are determined similarly. The average value of the symmetric component:

$$\sim E = (\sim E_{(x)} + \sim E_{(y)} + \sim E_{(z)})/3$$
$$= (521 + 515 + 260)/3 = 432 \text{ lux}$$

The illumination vector contributes one quarter of its value to the scalar illuminance, so that:

$$E_{sr} = |\mathbf{E}|/4 + \sim E$$
$$= (0.25 \times 1177) + 432 = 726 \text{ lux}$$

Then the vector/scalar ratio:

$$|\mathbf{E}|/E_{sr} = 1177/726 = 1.62$$

And the vector altitude:

$$\alpha = \tan^{-1} [\mathbf{E}_{(z)}/(\mathbf{E}_{(x)}^2 + \mathbf{E}_{(y)}^2)^{0.5}]$$
$$= \tan^{-1} [1087/((426)^2 + (-151)^2)^{0.5}] = 67°$$

This analysis tells us that although three spotlights are proposed, and a fairly high scalar illuminance will be achieved, the effect will be a moderately weak flow of light predominantly from above. The spotlights are located so that all vertical surfaces of the cube receive direct illumination, but as all of the spotlights contribute to the upper horizontal surface and none to the lower surface, the overall effect is high vector altitude and a flow of light that is more downwards than sideways, even though all of the direct light is coming in from the sides. Although the indirect illuminance appears to be small compared with the direct illuminances, it plays an important role in keeping down the value of the vector/scalar ratio.

## 6.4 The light field

In the previous section it was shown that the cubic illumination concept can be used to perform vector analysis of the illumination solid using nothing more advanced than school-level trigonometry. However, we can work far more effectively with vector illumination concepts by using vector algebra. The advantage is that this form of mathematics provides a framework for lighting calculations that deals concisely and consistently with both dimensions and illuminances, and this opens up opportunities to really explore illumination as a three-dimensional concept. In fact, the only disadvantage is that rather too many designers are unfamiliar with vector algebra, and so at the risk of irritating some readers, we will take this section at a gentle pace.

Before starting, it should be pointed out that vector algebra is made far more simple if you have a calculator that can handle vector functions. In the following text, expressions are given for the vector functions so that they can be worked through on a standard scientific calculator or entered into a programmable calculator, but it is much more convenient to use a calculator that operates vector functions on single keystrokes.

Figure 6.18 shows a rectangular room that contains one light source S, and a measurement point P. Their positions can be defined by position vectors, which are specified in terms of $(x, y, z)$ coordinates, where the origin $(0, 0, 0)$ has been chosen so that all points within the room are defined by positive $x, y, z$ values. If S is 1.2 m across on the $x$ axis, 4.8 m along on the $y$ axis, and 2.7 m up on the $z$ axis, then $\mathbf{S} = (1.2, 4.8, 2.7)$. This system of plotting points in three-dimensional space in terms of $x, y, z$ coordinates is fairly self-evident, but why is S suddenly shown as $\mathbf{S}$? It is because S is a point, and $\mathbf{S}$ is a vector. More exactly, it is a position vector that defines the position of S. $\mathbf{S}$ starts at the origin and has its head at S, and both its magnitude and its direction are totally defined by the coordinates $(1.2, 4.8, 2.7)$. These coordinates are the components of the vector on the $x, y$ and $z$ axes, so that $\mathbf{S} = (\mathbf{S}_{(x)}, \mathbf{S}_{(y)}, \mathbf{S}_{(z)})$.

**Figure 6.18:** *The locations of position P and light source S are defined by position vectors defined by dimensions on the x, y and z axes*

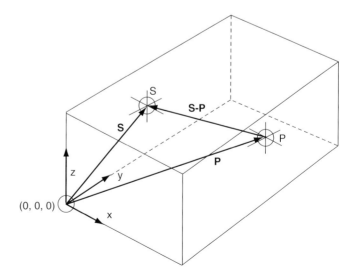

We could define the positions of all of the light sources in the room as **S**1, **S**2…**S**N vectors, and we could similarly define a grid of measurement positions. In this case we consider just one position P, which is defined by **P**(2.1, 1.5, 0.7). In print, we signify a vector by bold type.

In the previous subsection we added vectors by completing the parallelogram and this is shown in Figure 6.19, where **C** = **A** + **B**. Instead of this graphical approach, we can simply add the vectors. As the vectors shown are two-dimensional, they can be defined in terms of $x$ and $y$ components, so that $(\mathbf{C}_{(x)}, \mathbf{C}_{(y)}) = ((\mathbf{A}_{(x)} + \mathbf{B}_{(x)}), (\mathbf{A}_{(y)} + \mathbf{B}_{(y)}))$. We can also subtract vectors, and this is very useful. Referring to the same figure, **B** = **C** − **A**, and this can be achieved by subtracting the components: $(\mathbf{B}_{(x)}, \mathbf{B}_{(y)}) = ((\mathbf{C}_{(x)} - \mathbf{A}_{(x)}), (\mathbf{C}_{(y)} - \mathbf{A}_{(y)}))$. **B** is the difference between **C** and **A**, and is the vector defining the position of point C relative to point A.

Now return to Figure 6.18. The point P is illuminated by source S, and if we subtract **P** from **S**, we have the vector that defines the location of S relative to P. If we call this vector **Q**, then $\mathbf{Q} = \mathbf{S} - \mathbf{P} = ((\mathbf{S}_{(x)} - \mathbf{P}_{(x)}), (\mathbf{S}_{(y)} - \mathbf{P}_{(y)}), (\mathbf{S}_{(z)} - \mathbf{P}_{(z)}))$. While some calculators will perform this function on a single keystroke, you can work it through the expression to get the answer:

**S** − **P** = **Q**(−0.9, 3.3, 2.0)

So, from the point P, the position of source S is defined by **Q**, and this enables both the distance and the direction of S to be easily obtained. The magnitude of a vector is its absolute value, which is given by the expression, $|\mathbf{Q}| = (\mathbf{Q}_{(x)}^2 + \mathbf{Q}_{(y)}^2 + \mathbf{Q}_{(z)}^2)^{0.5}$. In this case, $|\mathbf{Q}| = 3.96\,\text{m}$, and this is the distance of S from P. For the direction of S from P, we employ a simplification of three-dimensional geometry: the unit vector. This is a vector that has a length of one unit, and as we are dealing

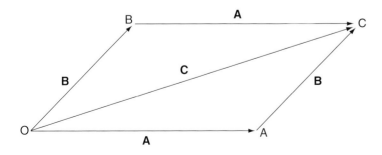

Figure 6.19: *Vector addition and subtraction (see text)*

with position vectors, this is one metre. Its $(x,y,z)$ coordinates are the projections of the one metre vector onto the $x$, $y$ and $z$ axes, and it is obtained by dividing the vector by its own magnitude. We will use lower case to distinguish the unit vector, so that $\mathbf{q}_{(x)} = \mathbf{Q}_{(x)}/|\mathbf{Q}|$, and so on for $\mathbf{q}_{(y)}$ and $\mathbf{q}_{(z)}$. The unit vector defining the direction of S from P is $\mathbf{q}(-0.227, 0.833, 0.505)$. Actually, the values of this triplet are the cosines of the angles between $\mathbf{Q}$ and each of the $x$, $y$ and $z$ axes.

Now we move on from position vectors to the illumination vector. Cosines keep popping up in illumination calculations. Consider the point-to-point formula introduced in the previous subsection:

$$E_q = I_p \cos \theta/D^2$$

where $E_q$ = illuminance at point P on plane q, which may be of any orientation with regard to source S; $D$ = distance from point source S to point P; $I_p$ = luminous intensity of source S in direction of point P; $\theta$ = angle of incidence at P, which as is shown in the figure, is *always* measured relative to the normal.

As explained, this formula is the workhorse for illumination calculations. From the foregoing we have the value of $D$, but we lack the value of $\cos\theta$. Not only can we subtract and divide three-dimensional vectors, but we can multiply them: in fact, we have more than one way of doing so, but for the moment we are going to look at just one of these – *the dot product*. When we take the dot product of two unit vectors, which is just a particular way of multiplying them together, the result is the cosine of the angle between them. Look at Figure 6.20. The angle of incidence $\theta$ is between $\mathbf{Q}$ and the normal to the surface. We have $\mathbf{q}$ and we need $\mathbf{n}$, which is the unit vector for the normal to the horizontal surface. What would be the coordinates of a one metre long, vertical vector at P? The answer is $(0,0,1)$. The dot product of $\mathbf{q}$ and $\mathbf{n}$, indicated $\mathbf{q} \cdot \mathbf{n}$, can be calculated by $\mathbf{q} \cdot \mathbf{n} = ((\mathbf{q}_{(x)} * \mathbf{n}_{(x)}) + (\mathbf{q}_{(y)} * \mathbf{n}_{(y)}) + (\mathbf{q}_{(z)} * \mathbf{n}_{(z)}))$. For the example we are considering, $\mathbf{n}_{(z)} = 1$, so that $\mathbf{q} \cdot \mathbf{n} = 0.505$, which as has been mentioned, is the cosine of the angle between $\mathbf{Q}$ and the z axis. It is important to grasp this point.

It is an immense advantage to have a coordinated system for dealing with both dimensions and luminous flux, and we can extend it to include also luminous intensity. If the light source is a spotlight that will be aimed at P, then $I_p$ will be the peak beam intensity of the spotlight, which we can read from a

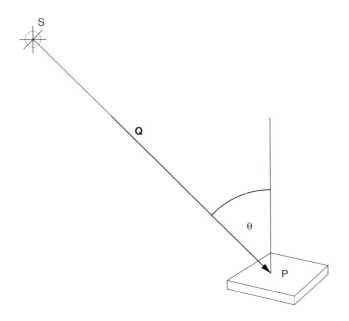

Figure 6.20: *The illumination vector **Q** at point P due to source S*

photometric data sheet. If the luminaire is not aimed at P, we have to read the luminous intensity in the direction of P from the polar curve. To do this, we have to know the altitude and azimuth angles of the direction of P from S. We have seen how the direction of S from P is defined by **q**(−0.227, 0.833, 0.505), and we can reverse the sense of this unit vector by reversing the signs to give −**q**(0.227, −0.833, −0.505). If we take the arccos (or cos⁻¹) for each value of the triplet, we have the angles in degrees which define the direction of P from S. We can use these to read off the luminous intensity of the light source in the direction of P from the polar curve of the luminaire. Let us suppose that the value is 4650 candelas. We now have everything to complete the point-to-point calculation.

The regular formula:

$$E_q = \frac{I_p \cdot \cos \theta}{D^2}$$

can be rewritten:

$$E_q = \mathbf{q} \cdot \mathbf{n} \times \frac{I_p}{|\mathbf{S} - \mathbf{P}|^2}$$

$$= 0.505 \times \frac{4650}{(3.96)^2} = 150 \text{ lux}$$

We have found that the direct illuminance due to S on a horizontal plane at P is 150 lux, and in fact, we are well on the way to obtaining the cubic illuminances. Think back to the point where we entered the coordinates of the normal unit vector, **n**, as (0, 0, 1). What would have happened if we had entered (0, 0, −1)? The answer is that the result would have been −150 lux, showing that if we define the direction of measurement at P as vertically downwards, rather than upwards, the sign changes, indicating the direction of incidence on the measurement plane. To obtain the cubic illuminances at P due to S, successively enter **n** as (1, 0, 0), (0, 1, 0), and (0, 0, 1), to give $E_{(x)} = -67$ lux, $E_{(y)} = 297$ lux, and $E_{(z)} = 150$ lux.

Table 6.7 shows how illuminance contributions from surrounding sources can be added to give the cubic illuminance values, and this approach provides an alternative way of obtaining the cubic illuminances. However, it does far more than that. It enables us to explore viewpoint-dependent illumination metrics.

While the vector/scalar ratio and the vector direction together provide an indication of the potential of an illumination distribution to form a shading pattern on the surface of an opaque three-dimensional object, as we have seen in Section 2.4, the appearance of the shading pattern varies with the observer's direction of view. Of course, the object's form determines the configuration of the shading pattern, but if we simplify the object to a matt white sphere we have the opportunity to observe the potential of the lighting to impart a shading pattern onto an object. We also have the opportunity to observe how that potential varies with changing direction of view.

We can define a viewpoint V with a position vector, as we did for P and S, and then determine the direction of view for similarly defined object locations by vector subtraction. Alternatively, when we are concerned about a particular object of regard, it is convenient to define the viewpoint relative to that point. Suppose yourself to be seated in the congregation of the church that formed the example in Section 6.2, and you are looking at the preacher in his pulpit. The pulpit is on the north side of the sanctuary, and you are near the middle or the nave. Figure 6.21 shows the x, y and z axes intersecting at the preacher's head. This point is the origin of the view vector, and your head is its termination. If the view vector is **V**(4, −12, −2), then |**V**| = 12.8 m, and the unit vector defining your direction of view is **v**(0.31, −0.94, −0.16).

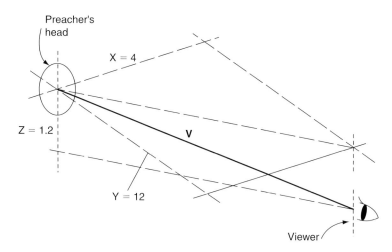

Preacher's head

X = 4

Z = 1.2

V

Y = 12

Viewer

**Figure 6.21:** *Referring back to the example of lighting a small church in Section 6.2, the view vector for a member of the congregation who is looking towards the preacher's head is defined by dimensions on the x, y and z axes*

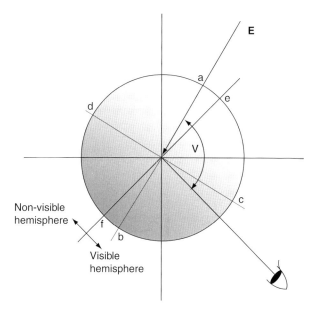

E

a

d

e

V

c

Non-visible hemisphere

f

b

Visible hemisphere

**Figure 6.22:** *The normal to the view vector divides the sphere into visible and non-visible hemispheres. The average illuminance of the visible hemisphere reduces as the view angle V increases. The illuminance difference between points a and b is the greatest to occur between any pair of opposite points on the surface of the sphere. The illuminances at points c and d are equal. The maximum illuminance difference that the viewer sees at opposite points on the perimeter of the visible hemisphere occurs at e and f, and this difference equals the value of the apparent illumination vector*

If the vector/scalar ratio is sufficient to impart a distinct shading pattern, the appearance of the visible hemisphere will vary as the angle between the view vector and the illumination vector changes. A readily observed change is that as we change our direction of view, the illuminance of the sphere appears to change. As shown in Figure 6.22, our view vector defines the visible hemisphere, and as the angle between the view and illumination vectors reduces, so the average illuminance of the visible hemisphere increases. The average illuminance of the visible hemisphere is given by:

$$E_{vhs} = [|\mathbf{E}|(1 + \mathbf{e} \cdot \mathbf{v})/4] + \sim E$$

For this expression, we again employ the principle that the illuminance of a plane or a three-dimensional solid is equal to the sum of illuminances due to the two components of the illumination solid. When the view vector is coincident with the illumination vector, the contribution of **E** to $E_{vhs}$ is half its value, declining to zero when the vectors are mutually opposed. As the illuminance due to the symmetric component on a hemisphere of any orientation must be equal to that on the opposite hemisphere, it follows that the contribution of $\sim E$ is equal to its own value irrespective of orientation.

Another observable change is that when the angle between the view direction and the vector direction is a right angle, the two points of maximum illuminance difference are visible at opposite points on the perimeter of the visible hemisphere. The illuminance difference is equal to the vector magnitude |**E**|, and for other view directions, the maximum observable difference varies as the apparent vector:

$$|\mathbf{E}_{ap}| = |\mathbf{E}|(1 - \mathbf{e} \cdot \mathbf{v}^2)^{0.5}$$

This expression shows that when the illumination vector and the view vectors are coincident, the apparent vector reduces to zero. This does not mean that the illuminance of the visible hemisphere is uniform, but rather that the illuminance at any point on the perimeter of the visible hemisphere equals the illuminance at the opposite point. For this direction of view, $E_{vhs}$ has its maximum value, while for the opposite direction of view, $\mathbf{E}_{ap}$ is again zero and $E_{vhs}$ has its minimum value.

These two metrics can be combined to give the apparent vector/ visible hemisphere ratio $|\mathbf{E}_{ap}|/E_{vhs}$. This is the ratio of the maximum observable illuminance difference to the average illuminance of the visible hemisphere. It has been termed the flow of light ratio (FoLR) and proposed as an indicator of the perceived directional strength of lighting as it might affect the appearance of a shading pattern seen from a specific direction of view (Cuttle, 1997). As shown in Figure 6.23, when the direction of view is at 90° to the illumination vector direction, the FoLR

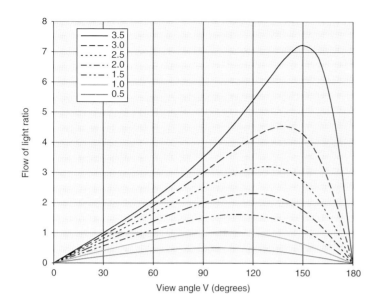

equals the vector/scalar ratio. However the strongest impression of flow of light occurs when this angle exceeds 90°, and this is particularly so for high values of $|\mathbf{E}|/E_{sr}$ due to the decline of $E_{vhs}$ as the view angle approaches 180°.

## Example: the flow of light

Table 6.9 shows the analysis of the distribution illuminance about a point, where the six cubic illuminances may have been obtained either by calculation or by measurement. As has been explained, the vector components are the illuminance differences given by $\mathbf{E}_{(x)} = E_{(x)} - E_{(-x)}$, and the symmetric components are the remainders where, $\sim E_{(x)}$ equals the lesser of $E_{(x)}$ and $E_{(-x)}$. Then $|\mathbf{E}| = (\mathbf{E}_{(x)}^2 + \mathbf{E}_{(y)}^2 + \mathbf{E}_{(z)}^2)^{0.5} = 420$ lux, and $\mathbf{e} = \mathbf{E}/|\mathbf{E}|$, so that $\mathbf{e} = (0.215, -0.502, 0.837)$. This table of data enables us to derive a wealth of information about how the light field surrounding the point will interact with a three-dimensional object that is placed at the point.

The average illuminance over the whole surface of the sphere is the scalar illuminance. The vector component contributes one quarter of its value to the scalar illuminance, while the symmetric component contributes its whole value, so that:

$$E_{sr} = 0.25 * |\mathbf{E}| + \sim E$$
$$= 0.25 * 420 + 260 = 365 \text{ lux}$$

And the vector/scalar ratio:

$$|E|/E_{sr} = 420/365 = 1.15$$

These two metrics relate to the illumination distribution at the point. If a three-dimensional object is located at the point, and the location of the point is defined by the position vector, **P**(5, 7, 4), how will the illumination distribution affect the appearance of the object when it is viewed from (8, 2, 5)?

The view vector at P:

$$V = (8, 2, 5) - (5, 7, 4) = (3, -5, 1)$$

The absolute value of **V**, which is the distance from P to the viewing position,

$$|V| = ((3)^2 + (-5)^2 + 1)^{0.5} = 5.9$$

and the view unit vector,

$$\mathbf{v} = \mathbf{V}/|V| = (0.507, -0.845, 0.169)$$

Then:

$$E_{vhs} = |E| * (1 + (\mathbf{e} \cdot \mathbf{v}))/4 + {\sim}E$$

$$= 420 * (1 + 0.675)/4 + 260 = 440 \text{ lux}$$

$$|\mathbf{E}_{ap}| = |E| * (1 - (\mathbf{e} \cdot \mathbf{v})^2)^{0.5}$$

$$= 420 * (1 - 0.456)^{0.5} = 310 \text{ lux}$$

And the flow of light ratio:

$$|\mathbf{E}_{ap}|/E_{vhs} = 310/440 = 0.71$$

From the viewing position, the object will appear to be 'catching the light' to some extent, as the average illuminance of the visible hemisphere is 440 lux compared with a scalar illuminance of 365 lux. The vector/scalar ratio of 1.15 corresponds to a moderately weak flow of light, and from the viewing position, the directional effect on the object will become weak, as the ratio of the apparent vector to the average illuminance of the visible hemisphere is 0.71.

## Example: planar illuminance

To calculate the illuminance on a horizontal or vertical plane by conventional procedures is fairly straightforward, but life becomes quite complicated when faced with planes of other orientations. Consider, for example, a blackboard supported on an easel, or an inclined drafting table. Once we have the cubic illumination specification, we can obtain a good estimate of the illuminance of a plane of any orientation passing through the point.

We will stay with the illumination distribution given in Table 6.9, and we will consider the surface passing through the point P shown in Figure 6.24(a). The plane of incidence is specified by the normal unit vector **n**, and it becomes easy to visualize the situation if we suppose the surface to be a 2 m square, so that both the width vector **w** and the height vector **h** are unit vectors as they are one metre long. The plane is vertical, so that **h** is coincident with the $z$ axis at P, and the horizontal rotation of the plane is such that **w** forms an angle of 60° with the $x$ axis. For this case, defining **h** in terms of $(x,y,z)$ is easy; **h** = (0,0,1). For **w**, you will have to look a little more carefully to work out that **w** = [(cos 60°), (sin 60°),0] = (0.5, 0.866, 0). It is a useful check to remember that for a unit vector, $X^2 + Y^2 + Z^2 = 1$.

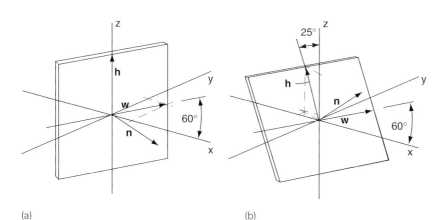

(a)                                               (b)

**Figure 6.24:** *(a) A vertical surface at 60° to the x axis. (b) The surface is tilted back 25° from the z axis*

This defines **h** and **w**, but where is **n**? Here we make use of the other way of multiplying vectors, known as the *cross product*. The cross product of two vectors is a vector that is normal to both, and if the two vectors that you start with are unit vectors, the outcome will also be a unit vector. To work this out manually is a bit tedious; $\mathbf{A} \times \mathbf{B} = (A_{(y)} B_{(z)} - A_{(z)} B_{(y)}, A_{(z)} B_{(x)} - A_{(x)} B_{(z)}, A_{(x)} B_{(y)} - A_{(y)} B_{(x)})$; but if you enter vectors **h** and **w** onto a suitable calculator and enter the CROSS command you get **n**(0.866, −0.5, 0). Remember that if you are working with the actual vectors, you must divide the vector by its absolute value to get the unit vector.

We could go ahead and calculate the planar illuminance, but now that we have the principle in mind, let's take the example a step further. In Figure 6.24(b), we move the problem into the third dimension by holding the surface steady on its horizontal axis, and tilting it back through 25°. What have we changed? **w** = (0.5, 0.866, 0), just as it did before, but now we have a different **h**. The z component, $h_{(z)}$, is easy to see; it is equal to cos 25°. The projection of **h** onto the horizontal plane is sin 25°, and from this we can determine the x and y components as previously, bearing in mind that the projection of **h** is normal to **w**, and that $h_{(x)}$ will be negative. In this way, **h** = ((sin 25° × −cos 30°), (sin 25° × sin 30°), cos 25°) = (−0.366, 0.211, 0.906). The cross product **w** × **h** gives us the normal unit vector of the surface, **n** = (0.785, −0.453, 0.423).

Now we can proceed to calculate the planar illuminance due to the vector component:

$$\mathbf{E}_{pr} = |\mathbf{E}| \times (\mathbf{e} \cdot \mathbf{n})$$

$$= 420 \times 0.75 = 320 \text{ lux}$$

For the planar illuminance due to the symmetric component we could simply add the mean value, *E*, but we can obtain a better estimate of the symmetric illuminance normal to the surface by using the expression:

$$\sim\!E_{pr} = (\sim\!E_{(x)}\, n_{(x)}{}^2) + (\sim\!E_{(y)}\, n_{(y)}{}^2) + (\sim\!E_{(z)}\, n_{(z)}{}^2)$$

$$= 290(0.785)^2 + 270(-0.453)^2 + 220(0.423)^2$$

$$= 270 \text{ lux}$$

We may note that this value is slightly different from $\sim E$. Now, the total planar illuminance at P for this inclined surface:

$$E_{pr} = \mathbf{E}_{pr} + \sim E_{pr}$$

$$= 320 + 270 = 590 \text{ lux}$$

If this treatment seems to you to be a little daunting, just try working out the total illuminance of this surface by trigonometry.

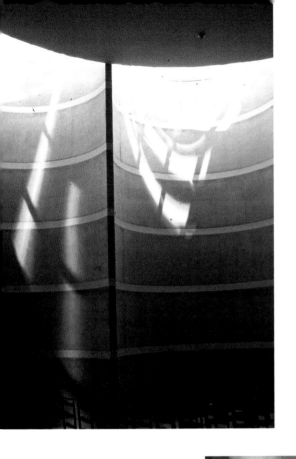

# Getting the lighting you want  7

Table A3.1 provides a summary of the lighting design concepts discussed in Section 4.3. This combination of concepts is the vehicle for the designer's visualization of the design situation in light. It forms the basis for the design features report and the designer's discussions with the client and other designers working on the project, and when the client gives approval for the design proposal, the understanding is that the designer will deliver the lighting that has been described. This requires a quite different type of communication.

## 7.1 Lighting specification

Specification is not simply a document: it is a process. The designer moves on from developing the design concept and defining lighting design objectives to meeting the client's expectations for:

- providing lighting that meets the agreed design objectives

- meeting installation performance requirements, which includes aspects such as ensuring compliance with regulations and standards, meeting energy performance targets and sustainability objectives, and making provision for maintenance and effective lighting controls

- achieving all of the above within budget.

These objectives require that the lighting designer not only prepares a sound specification document, but also follows its implementation throughout the construction process. The International Association of Lighting Designers has produced 'Guidelines for Specification Integrity' (www.iald.org), and while this document is in some respects specific to North American practice, it provides a useful framework that can be modified to suit practitioners virtually anywhere. Specification integrity concerns ensuring that the client gets the quality of

*Facing page: The Class of 1959 Chapel, Harvard Business School, Cambridge, Massachusetts. The austere interior of this non-denominational chapel, designed by Moshe Safdie in 1992, may be enlivened by shafts of chromatically dispersed sunlight. The building's cylindrical form incorporates a perimeter skylight containing long, liquid-filled acrylic prisms which are rotated by a computerized control to refract sunlight into the chapel interior*

lighting installation that has been agreed with the designer, and it needs to be recognized that there are numerous pitfalls for unwary or inexperienced lighting designers which can cause them to lose control over what is actually installed.

It is essential that the lighting designer is conversant with the range of products available from the lighting industry, including luminaires and their accessories, lamps and controls. To be able to choose the most appropriate lighting equipment for each project, the designer must be informed on:

• photometric performance options and optical accessories
• luminaire construction, finishes, quality options and cost implications
• luminaire mounting options and requirements for particular applications
• electrical characteristics, energy performance and control options
• availability, delivery options and ongoing service.

To maintain a current database on equipment, the designer will have to establish good working relationships with the lighting industry. It is not sufficient to rely on catalogues and websites for information. The designer must get to know the people who can give reliable answers to technical questions, who can arrange delivery of sample luminaires at short notice, and can discuss 'specials'. Any luminaire that is not defined by a catalogue number is a special, and the difference can be anything from a standard luminaire with a custom finish or a different lamp socket, to a unique design. The lighting designer must know where to go to and whom to contact for specials.

Lighting designers like 'single name' specifications, whereby the manufacturer's name and the model reference for every item of equipment is stated, but not all clients permit this. Some clients require multiple names, so that the lighting designer may have to specify three alternative sources for each item of equipment. Others require performance criteria specifications, requiring the designer to specify a range of performance criteria that will ensure that any compliant equipment will satisfy the design objective. These procedures enable the client to compare alternative bids for the installation, but it becomes more difficult for the designer to ensure that the envisaged concept will be achieved.

There is no recognized format for the lighting specification, although established firms invariably have a house style. The essential features are:

• a schedule of equipment grouped according to application, with details of costs (if appropriate) and power loads

• layout drawings of luminaire locations cross-referenced to the schedule, indicating electrical circuits and locations of controls

• detail drawings of special mountings and any associated construction work

• detail drawings and schedule of materials for any special luminaires or other unique designs.

The lighting specification may be incorporated into the project construction documentation, and is expected to be the basis of bids for the construction work. The designer needs to maintain involvement, as there are opportunities for the lighting speci-fication to be compromised at every stage from bidding to completion of the installation. A recurring threat for which the designer must be always vigilant is substitution. This involves 'equivalent' equipment being substituted for the specified equipment. It happens quite often that projects have cost over-runs in the early stages, and in the later stages project manag-ers are looking for opportunities to cut costs. Lighting occurs in the later stages, and tends to be an easy target. The light-ing designer should ensure that the agreement (see Section 7.2) makes it clear that substitutions can be accepted only with the designer's approval. It can also be worthwhile to add that the designer's appraisal of substitutions proposed by others will incur an additional fee.

The final inspection invariably finds the contractors stressed and desperately trying to achieve a completion deadline. This is a time when the lighting designer has to be firm and stand ground. It is the last chance to ensure that the installed equip-ment matches the specification, and equipment that could not be checked earlier during construction may now be difficult to access. This may be the time to adjust aimable luminaires, and the specification should make it clear that the contractor has to provide ladders, platforms or whatever access facilities are needed. The designer must insist that adjustments are made under his or her observation, and must not allow the process to be rushed. It may be necessary to delay final aiming and focus-ing until furniture or artwork has been installed. Meanwhile, opportunities for close examination of luminaires are useful for checking the quality of the installation work. Damaged ceiling tiles or fingermarks on reflectors must not be allowed to pass.

Some practices develop a 'punch list' for checking off equipment and identifying faults to be rectified by the contractor. This is an aspect of the job for which there really is no substitute for experience, and young designers should actively seek opportunities to accompany experienced colleagues on site inspections. All the attention to detail that has been put into the design phase can be lost if the designer fails to get the contractor to complete the installation to a matching standard.

## 7.2 Contractual agreements

Before any work proceeds, an agreement between the lighting designer and the client, who is usually the owner, should be drawn up and signed. The agreement should define the scope of the work and the designer's services, the designer's and the client's responsibilities, and the basis for payment.

The International Association of Lighting Designers IALD (www.iald.org) and the Professional Lighting Designer's Association PLDA (www.pld-a.org) have prepared standard forms of agreement for use by their own members. As an agreement is intended to be legally enforceable, the advice of a lawyer is recommended to adapt the 'boilerplate' agreement to suit national or state legal requirements.

# Appendix A1
# Technical concepts, terms and symbols

The science of photometry and the practice of illumination engineering have together developed the technology that defines and quantifies lighting.

**Luminous flux** is radiant flux evaluated according to the CIE (International Commission on Illumination) Relative Photopic Response, sometimes referred to as the $V(\lambda)$ function, where $V$ is the relative human sensation of brightness according to the wavelength of radiant flux $\lambda$ (lambda). It refers to the light-adapted visual response, which usually applies for architectural lighting. Other functions may be appropriate for lower adaptation levels.

The luminous flux emitted by a lamp is measured in lumens. The **luminous efficacy** of a lamp is the measure of the lamp's performance in converting electrical power into luminous flux, and is measured in lumens per watt.

**Illuminance E** is the density of luminous flux *incident* at a point on a surface. One lux equals one lumen per square metre.

If the illuminance at P is 100 lux, this means that the density of *incident* luminous flux is 100 lumens per square metre. This can be written $E_p = 100\,lx$. If the **reflectance** $\rho$ of the surface is 0.6, then 60% of the incident flux is reflected from the surface. The **exitance** $M$ at P is 60 lumens per square metre, meaning that the density of *emerging* luminous flux $M_p = 60\,lm/m^2$.

Table A1.1 *The essential terminology of lighting*

| Lighting quantity | Symbol | Unit | Abbreviation |
|---|---|---|---|
| Luminous flux | $F$ | lumen | lm |
| Luminous efficacy | $\eta$ | lumen per watt | lm/W |
| Illuminance | $E$ | lux | lx |
| Exitance | $M$ | lumen per square metre | lm/m² |
| Luminous intensity | $I$ | candela | cd |
| Luminance | $L$ | candela per square metre | cd/m² |

*Facing page: Grand Central Terminal, New York. This façade floodlighting should cause any lighting designer to stop and observe. Too often 'floodlighting' is taken literally, and the façade is flooded with light. In this case, a restrained approach has exploited the low ambient illumination condition to reveal selected architectural features, sometimes by luminaires mounted on the façade and sometimes by spotlights mounted on buildings across the street, to achieve a striking Gestalt. Although we seldom have such low ambient illumination inside our buildings, opportunities for a similar approach to interior architectural lighting should not be overlooked*

Figure A1.1:   *The CIE relative photopic response (V(λ) function)*

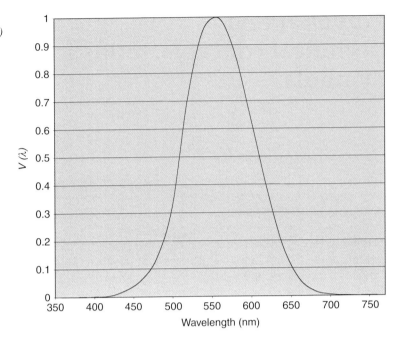

Figure A1.2:   *(a) Illuminance is the density of incident luminous flux at P. (b) Exitance is the density of emerging luminous flux at P*

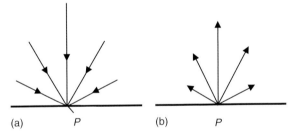

(a)      *P*              (b)      *P*

It follows that:

$$\rho = M/E$$

and

$$M = E\rho \ \text{lm/m}^2$$

If several measurements are taken of the illuminance due to a single, small light source, all in the same direction but at different distances $D$, it will be found that the ratio $E/D^2$ has a constant value. The reason for this is quite easy to understand, as shown in Figure A1.3.

The value of $E/D^2$ provides the measure of the illuminating power of a light source. It is given the term **luminous intensity**, and is specified in candelas, where, by definition, *one candela*

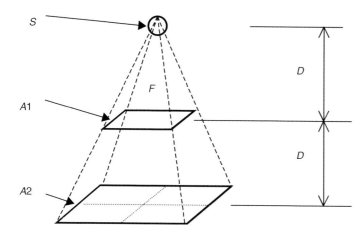

**Figure A1.3:** *Light source S projects F lumens onto area A1 at distance D, producing illuminance E1 = F/A1 lux. At distance 2D, the same luminous flux would be spread over area A2, where A2 = 4 A1, so that E2 = ¼E1; or generally, E is proportional to 1/D²*

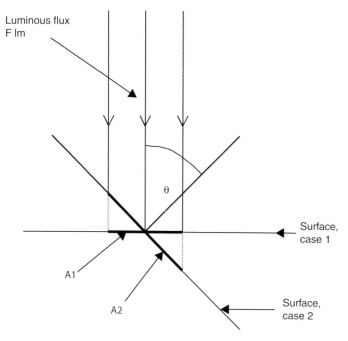

**Figure A1.4:** *In case 1, luminous flux F lm is at normal incidence onto a surface where the illuminated area is A1, and E1 = F/A1 lx. In case 2, the surface has been tilted away from the source, so that the angle of incidence is θ. The illuminated area A2 = A1/cos θ, and so E2 = E1 cos θ*

*gives one lux at one metre.* The distribution of luminous intensity of luminaires, or of directional light sources such as reflector lamps, is specified in candelas, so that $E = I/D^2$. This is an expression of the *inverse square law of illumination,* and it can be used to calculate illuminance at any distance, providing the size of the source is small in relation to the distance, and the illuminated surface is normal to the direction of the source.

If the surface is tilted away from the direction of the source, illuminance reduces in accordance with the *cosine law of illumination* as shown in Figure A1.4.

The inverse square law and the cosine law are combined to give the **point-to-point formula**:

$$E = I \cos \theta / D^2 \, \text{lx}$$

This very useful formula is used to calculate illuminance from a point source to a point on a surface. Note carefully: $\theta$ is *always* measured between the incident ray and the normal to the surface.

**Luminance** is the measure of the stimulus that produces the sensation of brightness. Figure A1.5 shows a light source S in an observer's field of view. The luminous intensity is $I$ cd in the direction of the observer, and $A$ is the area of the source projected in the observer's direction of view, so for this direct view of the source, $L = I/A$ cd/m$^2$.

Consider now the appearance of the illuminated surface. If the surface is perfectly matt, the reflected light will be completely diffused. Most architectural surfaces can be assumed to be diffusing reflectors, even if they are not perfectly matt. This enables their relative appearances to be described in terms of exitance, which is a simple concept. However, if the surface is glossy, the observer will see the reflected image of the source, which will impart a highlight to the appearance of the surface. The reflected light is no longer diffused, and the appearance of the surface changes with direction of view.

**Figure A1.5:** *An observer has both a direct view and a reflected view of a light source*

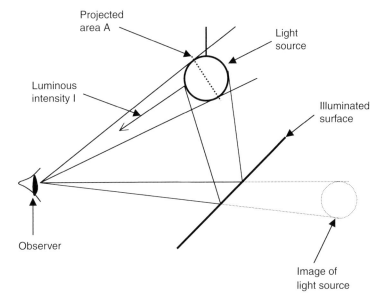

For a mirror or polished metal surface seen from a specific view-point, the luminance of every element seen in the reflected view will be equal to the luminance of the element in the direction of the reflecting surface, less a reflection loss. For a semi-gloss surface, the situation becomes even more complicated, as the reflected image appears indistinct and spread, and its luminance is due to a combination of specularly and diffusely reflected light.

For a perfectly matt surface,

$$L = E\rho/\pi \text{ cd/m}^2$$

The photometric data provided by luminaire manufacturers often gives luminance distributions, and, like luminous intensity, luminance does not vary with distance. The luminance of a luminaire image reflected by a *specular reflector* is the product of the luminaire luminance in the direction of the reflecting surface and the reflectance of the surface for the angle of incidence at the surface. As illustrated in Figure A1.5, this applies to a specific direction of view. It can readily be appreciated that prediction of luminance values for anything other than matt surfaces in real interiors is extremely tedious, and where this is necessary, the only practical solution is to employ computer software. Meanwhile, architectural lighting calculations usually assume that all surfaces are perfect diffusers.

## Summary of expressions

These expressions indicate the relationships between the terms used in lighting.

1. Reflectance (for matt surfaces), exitance and illuminance:

$$\rho = M/E$$

and

$$M = E\rho \text{ lm/m}^2$$

2. The point-to-point formula:

$$E = I\cos\theta/D^2 \text{ lx}$$

3. Luminance (for matt surfaces):

$$L = E\rho/\pi \text{ cd/m}^2$$

# Appendix A2
# Terms and symbols used in the text

Table A2.1

| Symbols | Terms | Units |
|---|---|---|
| $A_s$; $A_{rs}$ | Area of surface s; total room surface area | $m^2$ |
| $B$; $b$ | Beam angle, half beam angle | degrees |
| $E_P$ | Surface illuminance at point P | lx |
| $E_s$; $E_{rs}$ | Mean illuminance of surface s; mean room surface illuminance | lx |
| $E_{sr}$ | Scalar illuminance | lx |
| $E_{(d)}$; $E_{(i)}$ | Direct illuminance; indirect illuminance | lx |
| $E_{(x)}$, $E_{(-x)}$ | Opposed cubic illuminances on x axis | lx |
| $\sim E_{(x)}$; $\sim E$ | Symmetric illuminance on x axis; mean symmetric illuminance | lx |
| $\mathbf{E}$; $|\mathbf{E}|$ | Illumination vector; illumination vector magnitude | lx |
| $F$; $F_L$ | Total luminous flux; flux emitted by luminaire(s) | lm |
| $I$ | Luminous intensity | cd |
| $L_s$ | Luminance of surface s | $cd/m^2$ |
| $M_s$; $M_{rs}$ | Exitance of surface s; mean room surface exitance | $lm/m^2$ |
| $\rho_s$ | Reflectance of surface s | |
| $\alpha_s$ | Absorptance of surface s | |
| $A\alpha_s$; $A\alpha_{rs}$ | Absorption of surface s; total room surface absorption | $m^2$ |
| $\Omega$ | Solid angle subtense | Steradians |
| $\gamma$; $\gamma/2$ | Subtense angle, half subtense angle | Degrees |

# Appendix A3
# Summary of lighting concepts, design criteria, and associated metrics

Table A3.1

| Lighting concepts | Design criteria | Associated metrics |
|---|---|---|
| Ambient illumination (Section 2.1) | Overall brightness illumination colour appearance | Mean room surface exitance $M_{rs}$ Correlated colour temperature $CCT$ |
| Visual discrimination (Section 2.2) | Clarity of vision visual performance Colourfulness | Task or object illuminance $E_t$ Colour rendering index $CRI$ in conjunction with $E$ and $CCT$ |
| Illumination hierarchy (Section 2.3) | Emphasis, attention order, visual hierarchy colour appearance difference | Illuminance ratios, $E_{s1}/E_{s2}$ $MK^{-1}$ difference |
| Flow of light (Section 2.4) | Strength and direction of flow Shading patterns; form and texture; coherence of flow | Vector/scalar ratio $|\mathbf{E}|/E_{sr}$ Vector direction Flow of light ratio $FLR$ |
| Sharpness (Section 2.5) | Highlight patterns, sparkle shadow patterns maximizing contrasts | Highlight ratio $HLR$ Source–object distance $D$ |
| Luminous elements (Section 2.6) | Brightness, sparkle, liveliness glare avoidance 'Something worth looking at' | |

# Appendix A4
# Summary of calculations

## A4.1 Mean room surface exitance

For uniform room surface reflectance $\rho$:

$$M_{rs} = \frac{F_L \cdot \rho}{A(1-\rho)} \ \text{lm/m}^2$$

where
$F_L$ = initial luminous flux emitted by the luminaires (lm)
$A$ = total room surface area (m$^2$).

The upper line of the expression, $F_L\,\rho$, is the first reflected flux:

$$FRF = \sum_{s=1}^{n} E_{s(d)} \cdot A_s \cdot \rho_s$$

The lower line of the expression, $A(1-\rho)$, is the room absorption:

$$A\alpha = \sum_{s=1}^{n} A_s(1-\rho_s)$$

where
$E_{s(d)}$ = direct illuminance of surface s (lux)
$A_s$ = area of surface s (m$^2$)
$\rho_s$ = reflectance of surface s.

The general expression for mean room surface exitance:

$$M_{rs} = FRF/A\alpha$$

Total lamp lumens required to provide $FRF$:

$$F_{lamps} = \frac{FRF}{ULOR \cdot \rho_{clg} + UF_0 \cdot \rho_{flr} + (DLOR - UF_0)\rho_{walls}} \ \text{lm}$$

where
$ULOR$ = upward light output ratio
$DLOR$ = downward light output ratio
$UF_0$ = utilization factor for zero room surface reflectance.

The equivalent reflectance of a cavity plane (See Figure 6.2):

$$\rho_{eq} = \frac{\rho_{av}\left(A_{cp}/A_{cs}\right)}{1 - \rho_{av}\left[1 - \left(A_{cp}/A_{cs}\right)\right]}$$

where
$A_{cp}$ = area of the cavity plane
$A_{cs}$ = area of the cavity surfaces
$\rho_{av}$ = average reflectance of cavity surfaces

## A4.2 Flux distribution

Refer to Figure 6.5 for outline of the flux distribution procedure.

Beam lumens:

$$F_B = 1.5 I_{max}\,\pi(1 - \cos b)LD$$

where
$I_{max}$ = maximum beam luminous intensity (cd)
$b$ = half beam angle
$LD$ = lumen depreciation factor.

## A4.3 Direct flux

The $D^3$ formula for illuminance at point P on plane q (See Figure 6.9):

$$E_q = Q\,\frac{I_p}{D^3}\,\text{lux}$$

where
$I_p$ = luminous intensity in direction of P
$D$ = distance of source S from P
$Q$ = orthogonal projection of $D$ onto the normal to the plane Q at P.

Note that for $x, y, z$ axes:

$$D^3 = (X^2 + Y^2 + Z^2)^{1.5}$$

For 'large' source, apply the $D/d$ correction factor:

$$C_{(D/d)} = \frac{(D/d)^2 - 0.25}{(D/d)^2}$$

where $d$ = maximum diameter of luminaire.

The $-0.25$ constant applies for a worst-case disc or spherical source. For a linear or narrow strip source the constant rises to $-0.17$.

For cubic illumination calculations (See Figure 6.16) the illumination vector component on the $x$ axis:

$$\mathbf{E}_{(x)} = E_{(x)} - E_{(-x)}$$

The magnitude of the illumination vector:

$$|\mathbf{E}| = (\mathbf{E}_{(x)}^2 + \mathbf{E}_{(y)}^2 + \mathbf{E}_{(z)}^2)^{0.5}$$

The symmetric illuminance value on the x axis:

$$\sim E_{(x)} = (E_{(x)} + E_{(-x)} - \mathbf{E}_{(x)})/2$$

The average symmetric illuminance:

$$\sim E \cong (\sim E_{(x)} + \sim E_{(y)} + \sim E_{(z)})/3$$

The scalar illuminance:

$$E_{sr} = |\mathbf{E}|/4 + \sim E$$

And the vector altitude:

$$\alpha = \tan^{-1}[\mathbf{E}_{(z)}/(\mathbf{E}_{(x)}^2 + \mathbf{E}_{(y)}^2)^{0.5}]$$

## A4.4 The light field

Planar illuminance at point P due to source S (See Figure 6.18):

$$E = \mathbf{q} \cdot \mathbf{n} \frac{I_P}{|\mathbf{S} - \mathbf{P}|^2} \, \text{lx}$$

where
$\mathbf{q}$ = unit vector at P in the direction of source S
$\mathbf{n}$ = unit vector at P normal to incident plane
$\mathbf{S} - \mathbf{P}$ = position vector of S relative to P.

For cubic illuminances, successively enter $\mathbf{n}$ as (1,0,0), (0,1,0) and (0,0,1) to give values of $E_{(x)}$, $E_{(y)}$ and $E_{(z)}$.

The average illuminance of the visible hemisphere (See Figure 6.22):

$$E_{vhs} = |\mathbf{E}|(1 + \mathbf{e} \cdot \mathbf{v})/4 + \sim E$$

where
$\mathbf{e}$ = illumination unit vector
$\mathbf{v}$ = view unit vector.

The apparent illumination vector:

$$\left|\mathbf{E}_{ap}\right| = |\mathbf{E}|(\mathbf{1} - \mathbf{e} \cdot \mathbf{v}^2)^{0.5}$$

The flow of light ratio:

$$\text{FoLR} = |\mathbf{E}_{ap}|/E_{vhs}$$

# References

Bodmann, H.W. (1967). Quality of Interior Lighting based on Luminance. *Trans. Illum. Eng. Soc. (London)*, **32**(1), 22–40.

Boyce, P.R. and Cuttle, C. (1990). Effect of Correlated Colour Temperature on the Perception of Interiors and Colour Discrimination Performance. *Lighting Res. Technol.*, **22**(1), 19–36.

Boyce, P.R. and Rea, M.S. (1987). Plateau and Escarpment: The shape of visual performance. *Proc. 21st. CIE Session, Venice*.

CIBSE (1994). *Code for Interior Lighting*. Chartered Institution of Building Services Engineers, London.

Cuttle, C., Valentine, W.B., Lynes, J.A. and Burt, W. (1967). Beyond the Working Plane. *Proc. 16th. CIE Session, Washington DC, P67–12, 12pp.*

Cuttle, C. (1971). Lighting Patterns and the Flow of Light. *Lighting Res. Technol.*, **3**(3), 171–189.

Cuttle, C. (1991). On Sumpner's Principle. *Lighting Res. Technol.*, **23**(2), 99–106.

Cuttle, C. (1997). Cubic Illumination. *Lighting Res. Technol.*, **29**(1), 1–14.

Cuttle, C. (1999). Modes of Appearance and Perceived Attributes in Architectural Lighting Design. *Proc. 24th. CIE Session, Warsaw.* **1**, 116–118.

Cuttle, C. (2001). An Investigative Assessment of Visualisation. *Proc. 35th. Annual Conference of the Australian and New Zealand Architectural Science Association, Wellington, New Zealand (CD ROM).*

Cuttle, C. (2003). An Integrated System of Photometry, Predictive Calculation and Visualisation of the Shading Patterns Generated by Three-Dimensional Objects in a Light Field. *Proc. 25th CIE Session, San Diego*, **D2**, 34–37.

Cuttle, C. (2004). Brightness, Lightness, and Providing 'A Preconceived Appearance to the Interior'. *Lighting Res. Technol.*, **36**(3), 201–216.

Davis, R.G. and Ginthner, D.N. (1990). Correlated Color Temperature, Illuminance Level, and the Kruithof Curve. *J. Illum. Eng. Soc. (New York)*, **19**(1), 27–38.

Dillon, R.F., Pasini, I.C. and Rea, M.S. (1987). Survey of Visual Contrast in Office Forms. *Proc. 21st. CIE Session, Venice*.

Evans, R.M. (1948). *An Introduction to Color*. Wiley.

Gershun, A.A. (1939). The Light Field. Translation by Moon, P. and Timoshenko, *G. J. Maths and Physics*, **18**, 51–151.

Hebbelynck, H. (1987). Reflections on Reflection. *Proc. 21st. CIE Session, Venice*.

IESNA (2000). *Lighting Handbook, 9th edition*, Illuminating Engineering Society of North America, New York.

Jay, P.A. (1967). Scales of Luminance and Apparent Brightness. *Light & Lighting*, **60**(2), 42–45.

Jay, P.A. (1971). Lighting and Visual Perception. *Lighting Res. Technol.*, **3**(1), 133–146.

Jay, P.A. (1973). The Theory of Practice in Lighting Engineering. *Light & Lighting*, **66**(10), 303–306.

Jay, P.A. (2002). Subjective Criteria for Lighting Design. *Lighting Res. Technol.*, **34**(2), 87–99.

Katz, D. (1935). *The World of Colour*. Kegan Paul, Trench, Trubner & Co.

Kruithof, A.A. (1941). Tubular Luminescence Lamps for General Illumination. *Philips Technical Review*, **6**(2), 65–73.

Levin, R. (1982). The Photometric Connection – Part 2. *Lighting Design + Application, Oct 1982*.

Loe, D., Mansfield, K. and Rowlands, E. (2000). A Step in Quantifying the Appearance of a Lit Scene. *Lighting Res. Technol.*, **32**(4), 213–222.

Lynes, J.A. (1987). Patterns of Light and Shade. *Lighting in Australia*, **7**(4), 16–20.

Lynes, J.A. (1994). Daylight and the Appearance of Indoor Surfaces. *Proc. CIBSE National Lighting Conference, Cambridge, England*, pp. 98–110.

Lynes, J.A., Burt, W., Jackson, G.K. and Cuttle, C. (1966). The Flow of Light into Buildings. *Trans. Illum. Eng. Soc. (London)*, **31**(3), 65–91.

McCandless, S.R. (1958). *A Method of Lighting for the Stage, 4th. edition*. Theatre Art Books, New York.

Marsden, A.M. (1970). Brightness–luminance relationships in an interior. *Lighting Res. Technol.*, **2**(1), 10–16.

Rea, M.S. (1986). Towards a Model of Visual Performance: Foundations and data. *J. Illum. Eng. Soc. (New York)*, **15**(2), 41 57.

Rea, M.S. and Ouellette, M.J. (1991). Relative Visual Performance: A basis for application. *Lighting Res. Technol.*, **23**(3), 135–144.

Simons, R.H. and Bean, A.R. (2001). *Lighting Engineering: Applied Calculations*. Architectural Press.

Van Kemanade, J.T.C. and van der Burgt, P.J.M. (1988). Light sources and colour rendering: Additional information to the $R_a$ index. *Proc. CIBSE National Lighting Conference, Cambridge, UK*. pp. 133–143.

Waldram, J.M. (1954). Studies in Interior Lighting. *Trans. Illum. Eng. Soc. (London)*, **19**, 95–133.

Waldram, J.M. (1976). The Principles of Designed Appearance. *Commonwealth Association of Architects, London*, (Slide-tape lecture).

Waldram, J.M. (1978). Designed Appearance Lighting. Chapter 5 in *Developments in Lighting – 1* (J.A. Lynes, ed.), pp. 113–138, Applied Science.

Walsh, J.W.T. (1958). *Photometry, 3rd. edn*. Constable, pp. 141–145.

Weale, R.A. (1963). *The Ageing Eye*. H.K. Lewis.

Worthey, J.A. (1989a). Geometry and Amplitude of Veiling Reflections. *J. Illum. Eng. Soc. (New York)*, **18**(1), 49–62.

Worthey, J.A. (1989b). Effect of Veiling Reflections on Vision of Colored Objects. *J. Illum. Eng. Soc. (New York)*, **18**(2), 10–15.

Worthey, J.A. (1990). Lighting Quality and Light Source Size. *J. Illum. Eng. Soc. (New York)*, **19**(2), 142–148.

# Further reading

Professional lighting designers have to access information from many sources. They must be able to ensure that the regulations and standards that they refer to are current and that they are fully informed on the latest developments in lamp, luminaire and controls technology. Design software is an ever-changing field, but at the time of writing there are no computer programs available that make use of the lighting concepts described in this book. Even so, computer programs can be employed to greatly facilitate the calculation procedures, as is explained in Chapter 6.

Lighting guides on general and specific applications are available from the Society of Light and Lighting, London (www.cibse.org) and the Illuminating Engineering Society of North America, New York (www.iesna.org).

In addition to all of the web-based and CD-ROM material, the author firmly believes that every design office should include an old-fashioned bookcase containing the designer's personal library. In addition to this book, the following titles are recommended as a basis for such a collection.

## Reference sources

Boyce, P.R. (2003). *Human Factors in Lighting, 2nd edition*. Taylor and Francis.

CIBSE (2006). *SLL Code for Lighting*. Chartered Institution of Building Services Engineers, London.

Coaton, J.R. and Marsden, A.M. (eds.) (1997). *Lamps and Lighting, 4th edition*. Arnold.

Fairchild, M.D. (2005). *Color Appearance Models, 2nd edition*. Wiley.

Illuminating Engineering Society of North America (2000). *Lighting Handbook, 9th Edition*. IESNA.

Purves, D. and Lotto, R.B. (2003). *Why we see what we do: An empirical theory of vision*. Sinauer.

Simons, R.H. and Bean, A.R. (2001). *Lighting Engineering: Applied Calculations*. Architectural Press.

## Lighting design

Cuttle, C. (2007). *Light for Art's Sake: Lighting for Artworks and Museum Displays*. Butterworth-Heinemann.

Gordon, G. (2003). *Interior Lighting for Designers, 4th edition*. Wiley.

Hyatt, P. (ed.) (2007). Masters of Light: Designing the Luminous House. Images Publishing.

Kahn, L.I. (1975). *Light is the Theme*. Kimbell Art Foundation.

Lam, W.M.C. (1977). *Perception and Lighting as Formgivers for Architecture*. McGraw-Hill.

Major, M., Spiers, J. and Tischhauser, A. (2005). *Made of Light: The Art of Light and Architecture*. Birkhäuser.

Meyers, V. (2006). *Designing with Light*. Abbeville Press.

Michel, I. (1996). *Light: The Shape of Space*. Van Nostrand Reinhold.

Millet, M. (1996). *Light Revealing Architecture*. Van Nostrand Reinhold.

Phillips, D.R.H. (1999). *Lighting Modern Buildings*. Architectural Press.

Steffy, G.R. (2002). *Architectural Lighting Design, 2nd edition*. Wiley.

Tregenza, P. and Loe, D. (1998). *The Design of Lighting*. Spon.

## Daylighting

Ander, G.D. (1995). *Daylighting Performance and Design*. Van Nostrand Reinhold.

Bell, J. and Burt, W. (1995). *Designing Buildings for Daylight*. Construction Research Communications, London.

Evans, B.H. (1981). *Daylight in Architecture*. Architectural Record Books.

Fontoynont, M. (ed.) (1999). *Daylight Performance of Buildings*. James & James.

Guzowski, M. (2000). *Daylighting for Sustainable Design*. McGraw-Hill.

Lam, W.M.C. (1986). *Sunlighting as Formgiver for Architecture*. Van Nostrand Reinhold.

Loe, D. (1998). *Daylighting Design in Architecture: Making the Most of a Natural Resource*. BRECSU, Building Research Establishment, UK.

Robbins, C.L. (1986). *Daylighting: Design and Analysis*. Van Nostrand Reinhold.

# Index